Pa

This stud
analysis t
literary)
knowledg

The autho
the recurr
of imagin;
pass both
(including
Potter and
as popular

User frien

- Clear
  discour
- Numero
  reading
- An ansv

Patterns in
theory or
language, Linguistics, and English literature, as well as for non-native
speakers of English studying English as a foreign language.

Joanna Thornborrow teaches English Language and Linguistics at
Roehampton Institute London. **Shân Wareing**, also at Roehampton
Institute, is Assistant Director of Educational Development.

The INTERFACE Series

> A linguist deaf to the poetic function of language and a literary scholar indifferent to linguistic problems and unconversant with linguistic methods, are equally flagrant anachronisms – Roman Jakobson.

This statement, made over twenty-five years ago, is no less relevant today, and 'flagrant anachronisms' still abound. The aim of the INTERFACE series is to examine topics at the 'interface' of language studies and literary criticism and in doing so to build bridges between these traditionally divided disciplines.

Already published in the series:

The Discourse of Advertising
Guy Cook

Language, Literature and Critical Practice
Ways of analysing text
David Birch

Literature, Language and Change
Ruth Waterhouse and John Stephens

Literary Studies in Action
Alan Durant and Nigel Fabb

Language in Popular Fiction
Walter Nash

Language, Text and Context
Essays in stylistics
Edited by Michael J. Toolan

The Language of Jokes
Analysing verbal play
Delia Chiaro

Language, Ideology and Point of View
Paul Simpson

A Linguistic History of English Poetry
Richard Bradford

Literature about Language
Valerie Shepherd

Twentieth-century Poetry
From text to context
Edited by Peter Verdonk

Textual Intervention
Critical and creative strategies for literary studies
Rob Pope

Feminist Stylistics
Sara Mills

Twentieth-century Fiction
From text to context
Peter Verdonk and Jean Jacques Weber

Variety in Written English
Texts in society: societies in text
Tony Bex

English in Speech and Writing
Investigating language and literature
Rebecca Hughes

Language Through Literature
An introduction
Paul Simpson

The Series Editor
Ronald Carter is Professor of Modern English Language at the University of Nottingham and was National Coordinator of the 'Language in the National Curriculum' Project (LINC) from 1989 to 1992.

Patterns in Language

An introduction to language and literary style

Joanna Thornborrow and
Shân Wareing

LONDON AND NEW YORK

First published 1998
by Routledge
11 New Fetter Lane, London EC4P 4EE

Simultaneously published in the USA
and Canada
by Routledge
29 West 35th Street, New York,
NY 10001

Typeset in Times and Futura by
Keystroke, Jacaranda Lodge,
Wolverhampton

Printed and bound in Great Britain by
Biddles Ltd, Guildford and King's Lynn

*British Library Cataloguing in
Publication Data*
A catalogue record for this book is
available from the British Library

*Library of Congress Cataloguing in
Publication Data*
Thornborrow, Joanna, 1957–
    Patterns in language : an
introduction to language and literary
style / Joanna Thornborrow and Shân
Wareing.
        p.   cm. — (Interface)
    Includes bibliographical references
and index
    1. Language and languages–Style.
2. Style, Literary. I. Wareing, Shân,
1966— . II. Title. III. Series:
Interface (London, England)
P301. T49   1998
809—dc21   97-23795
CIP

ISBN 0–415–14063–3 (hbk)
ISBN 0–415–14064–1 (pbk)

We would like to dedicate this book to our friends, Ruth Heaton and Gillian Porter Ladousse

Contents

Acknowledgements

Many people have contributed, directly and indirectly, to the genesis of this book.

Our interest in stylistics began in the mid-1980s when we were graduate students in the Programme of Literary Linguistics, at the University of Strathclyde. Alan Durant, Nigel Fabb, Martin Montgomery and Sara Mills were all people who at that time influenced our thinking and writing in very many ways.

Within the programme in English Language & Linguistics at Roehampton Institute London, we have been able to put our ideas into practice through being given the opportunity to teach an introductory course in the language of literary texts, and an honours level course in stylistics. The students who have taken these courses over the years have been a considerable source of inspiration and have provided us with invaluable feedback about what undergraduate students in modular systems tend to know, and tend not to know, about the structure of English.

We have discussed ideas and tried out analyses with many of our colleagues in the English Department at Roehampton and with students at Kingston University, and some of the texts we use in the book have been their suggestions.

Thanks are due to the editors at Routledge, who have been supportive, helpful and patient, and to Ron Carter, for his encouragement.

We would particularly like to thank Joanna Armitage,

Martin Chorley, John Corbett, Mary Dumble, Keith Green, Kieran O'Halloran and Linda Thomas, for taking the time to read and comment on various parts of the text; also some of our students, Karen Eatock, Andrea Lutz and Sabina Middleton, for letting us use their data; and our partners, Martin Chorley and Ian Hutchby, for their advice and support. Finally, thanks to Alice and Nico, for their constant reminders that there is life outside the text!

We have tried wherever possible to take into account all their suggestions, criticisms and comments, but any of the book's remaining inaccuracies or defects are of course our own responsibility.

The authors and publishers would like to thank the following for permission to reproduce copyright material:
'Immigrant' reprinted from Fleur Adock's *Selected Poems* (1983) by permission of Oxford University Press. The extract from *London Fields* by Martin Amis is reprinted by permission of Jonathan Cape. The extract from *Wise Children* by Angela Carter is reproduced by permission of the Estate of Angela Carter c/o Rogers, Coleridge & White Ltd., 20 Powis Mews, London W11 1JN. Copyright © Angela Carter 1991. Mitsubishi Space Wagon advert, reproduced with permission. Cookelectric advert reproduced by permission of Seeboard. Excerpts from 'The Lovesong of J. Alfred Prufrock' and 'Ash Wednesday' by T. S. Eliot are reprinted by permission of Faber & Faber and Harcourt Brace & Company. Copyright © T. S. Eliot 1964, 1963. Thanks to Faber & Faber Ltd and Grove/Atlantic, Inc. for permission to reprint the extract from *Professional Foul* by Tom Stoppard. The extracts from *Finnegan's Wake* by James Joyce are reproduced by permission of the Estate of James Joyce, c/o Faber & Faber. Copyright © the Estate of James Joyce. Pablo Picasso's *Les Demoiselles d'Avignon* and James Rosenquist's *Marilyn Monroe I* reproduced by permission of the Museum of Modern Art, New York. Extract from *Sunlight on the Garden* by Louis MacNeice, reprinted by permission of David Higham Associates Ltd. John Constable's *The Hay Wain* reproduced by permission of The National Gallery. The extract from *The Enchanter's Endgame* by David Eddings is reproduced by permission of Transworld Publishers Ltd. 'Wind' by Ted Hughes and 'You're' by Sylvia Plath are reproduced by permission of Faber & Faber Ltd and HarperCollins Publishers Inc.. 'Glasgow Sonnets' taken from *Selected Poems* by Edwin Morgan is reprinted by permission of Carcanet Press Ltd. Poems 76, 249 and 1172 are reprinted by permission of the publishers and the Trustees of

Amherst College from *The Poems of Emily Dickinson*, Thomas H. Johnson, ed., Cambridge, Mass., The Bellknap Press of Harvard University Press. Copyright © 1951, 1955, 1979, 1983 by the President and Fellows of Harvard College. The extract from *Sexing the Cherry* by Jeanette Winterson is reprinted with permission. Copyright © Jeanette Winterson 1989. Nissan New Terano II advert reproduced with permission. The extract from *Praxis* by Fay Weldon is reprinted by permission of Curtis Brown Group Ltd. The lines from 'love is more thicker than forget' are reprinted from *Complete Poems 1904–1962*, by E. E. Cummings, edited by George J. Firmage, by permission of W. W. Norton & Company Ltd. Copyright © 1991 by the Trustees for the E. E. Cummings Trust and George James Firmage. The extract from 'Not waving but drowning' from *Me Again Collected Poems* by Stevie Smith and published by Virago Press, is reprinted by permission of Little Brown & Co.. The short story by Toni Rodgers is reprinted by permission of *Just 17*. The list of phonetic symbols for transcribing English from *Practical Phonetics* by Wells and Colson is reprinted by permission of Pitman Publishing. The extract from *Lolita* by Vladimir Naboko is reprinted by permission of Weidenfeld and Nicolson. The extract from *Arms and the Man* by Bernard Shaw is reprinted by permission of The Society of Authors on behalf of the Bernard Shaw Estate. The extract from *Horses Make A Landscape More Beautiful* by Alice Walker and published by The Women's Press is reprinted by permission of David Higham Associates Ltd. The extracts from *The Black Tower* by P.D. James are reproduced by permission of Greene & Heaton Ltd. Copyright © 1975 P.D. James, published by Faber & Faber Ltd. The extract from *Top Girls* bt Caryl Churchill is reprinted by permission of Methuen. The extract from *Small World* by David Lodge is reprinted by permission of Martin Secker & Warburg and Curtis Brown Group Ltd. The lines from 'The Rhinoceros' by Ogden Nash are reprinted by permission of Andre Deutsch Ltd and Curtis Brown Group Ltd. The extract from 'A Night Out' by Harold Pinter is reproduced by permission of Grove/Atlantic Inc. and Faber & Faber Ltd.

While the authors and the publishers have made every effort to contact copyright holders of the material used in this volume, they would be happy to hear from anyone they were unable to contact.

Joanna Thornborrow

Shân Wareing

May 1997

Chapter 1

Introduction

1.1 About You . . .

This book is about how you can use knowledge about language to explore the language choices made in texts. We have tried to tailor it to the needs of different readers. For example, you may be interested primarily in literature, with no previous knowledge of linguistics; on the other hand, you may know more about language than literature, and be interested in the application of linguistics to texts. You may already be studying stylistics, and want a book that covers both the linguistic principles and some literary applications. English may or may not be your first language, and that will have consequences for how confident you feel in analysing the grammar of English – someone who has learnt a language 'formally' (i.e. has had formal grammar teaching) often has more explicit knowledge of its grammar than someone who has learnt it through use. A person who has grown up speaking a language however, will probably find it easier to judge the significance of the differences between one style and another.

The purpose of this book is to provide you with some of the analytic tools with which to approach the analysis of a wide range of texts, from both literary and non-literary sources. We have not assumed that you have any explicit knowledge of the sound structures or grammatical structures of English. If you learnt English formally (either because you are not a native speaker, or because you have been taught grammar), you may find that the contents of some parts of the book are already familiar. Skip any parts which deal with aspects of language you feel confident about, but you might like to use the suggested follow-up reading to extend your knowledge. In case you have not encountered some of the terms and concepts of language analysis such as verbs and phonemes (or in case you would like to be reminded!), we have also included definitions and exercises to start you off.

We enjoy using stylistics to analyse texts. We have aimed to include enough appropriate information in this book to enable you to tackle stylistic analyses. We also hope we have done it in such a way as to share our own enjoyment of the processes with you.

1.2 What is stylistics?

You may very well be asking this question. Here are two definitions from different sources:

STYLISTICS

A branch of linguistics which studies the characteristics of situationally-distinctive uses of language, with particular reference to literary language, and tries to establish principles capable of accounting for the particular choices made by individuals and social groups in their use of language.

(The Fontana Dictionary of Modern Thought, 1977,
2nd edn 1988)

STYLISTICS

The study of style; . . . just as style can be viewed in several ways, so there are several different stylistic approaches. This variety in stylistics is due to the main influences of linguistics and literary criticism. . . .

By far the most common kind of material studied is literary; and attention is largely text-centred. . . . The goal of most stylistics is not simply to describe the formal features of texts for their own sake, but in order to show their functional significance for the interpretation of the text; or in order to relate literary effects to linguistic 'causes' where these are felt to be relevant. . . . Stylisticians want to avoid vague and impressionistic judgements about the way that formal features are manipulated. As a result, stylistics draws on the models and terminology provided by whatever aspects of linguistics are felt to be relevant.

(Wales, 1989: A Dictionary of Stylistics)

From these definitions, you can see that stylistics is concerned with the idea of 'style', with the analysis of literary texts, and with the use of linguistics. 'Style' is usually understood within this area of study as *the selection of certain linguistic forms or features over other possible ones*. For example, what makes the writing of Jane Austen or E. M.

Forster distinctive, and some would say, great, is not only the ideas expressed, but the choices they made from the language available to them. A stylistic analysis of the styles of these writers could include their words, phrases, sentence order, and even the organization of their plots.

The writers whose 'styles' have in the past tended to most interest stylisticians (people who practise stylistics) have usually been the so-called 'canonical' texts – those found on traditional under-graduate English degree reading lists. The methods used to analyse 'style' have been drawn from linguistics, the study of language.

We can say that some key aspects of stylistics are:

- the use of **linguistics** (the study of language) to approach **literary texts**
- the discussion of texts according to **objective criteria** rather than according purely to subjective and impressionistic values
- emphasis on the **aesthetic** properties of language (for example, the way rhyme can give pleasure)

To complicate matters, however, we need to qualify this definition slightly. For example, the first point made above states that stylistics is the study of *literary* texts through linguistics. However, the definition of what is 'literary' is contentious. It is often treated as a self-evident category, but in fact our assumptions about what is 'literary' fre-quently depend on the judgements of the academics who select the texts on university degrees, and on the major publishing houses like Faber and Faber. The plays and poems of Shakespeare and the novels of Dickens are generally agreed to be literary, while adverts and newspaper reports are usually agreed not to be literature. How-ever, reports and adverts may share linguistic structures and functions with texts written by Shakespeare or Dickens. Defining 'literariness' is in fact a very grey and ambiguous area; consequently, the kind of texts which we will be looking at, using the methods of stylistics, often exceed the boundaries of what is commonly taken to be 'literary'.

Now let us examine the second part of the definition further. Is it true that stylistics is objective (i.e. scientific and not influenced by the opinions or personality of the analyst) rather than subjective and impressionistic (depending on 'gut feelings' or reflecting the emotions and culture of the analyst)?

The scholars who developed the process of stylistic analysis originally claimed it to be objective in order to emphasize the contrast between stylistics and its precursor, literary criticism. Literary criticism was, and still is, the practice (usually conducted at universities) of reading an extract from a text closely, and selecting features from it to comment on and analyse – perhaps to show how the passage or poem was typical or atypical of a specific writer's work, or of a period or genre (i.e. a particular kind of writing), and importantly, to assess how *good* or *bad* a piece of literature it was. Thus literary criticism involved explicit value judgements, but on criteria which individual literary critics could select for themselves. Another critic might select quite different criteria, and thus reach a quite different judgement about how 'good' or 'bad' the text was.

This method of analysis has been popular on university degree courses in English Literature for most of this century. The process of stylistics was developed to provide a less intuitive, less personal method of analysis – one which would depend instead on the observable facts, the language of the text, and a 'scientific'[1] discipline to interpret them: linguistics. By concentrating on the language of the text, and accepted linguistic methods of categorizing and interpreting, it was argued that stylistics did not reflect the views of the individual critic, but an impersonal, reproducible 'truth'. Anyone approaching the text and conducting the same stylistic procedure ought to arrive at the same results.

Nowadays, however, few people would claim that stylistics is totally objective, and not many people would want it to be. Exactly which elements of a text you decide to scrutinize is a subjective decision – not everyone would agree about what the significant elements are. Even more subjective is the process of interpretation. It is now widely acknowledged that your personal history and current circumstances influence the way you interpret what you read. For example, if you were someone who had never studied literature or linguistics before, your interpretation of this chapter would be very different from what it would be if you were either an 'old school' literary critic, or if you had a professional background in linguistics.

Stylisticians can disagree both at the level of interpretation, which is dependent on the reader and context in which the text is read, and also at the philosophical level of how texts should be analysed and for what purpose. For example, in *Feminist Stylistics* (1995), Sara Mills suggests that stylistics can be used to demonstrate the way gender is represented and constructed by texts, and that stylisticians can use this information to uncover the ways in which society operates to the disadvantage of women. Overtly political practices such as these are supported by some stylisticians and opposed by others.

What remains central to the practice of stylistics is the application of linguistic knowledge to describe the ways that writers use language, and the choices that they make in creating texts. This part of stylistics can be seen as systematic and objective, in so far as stylisticians can describe and draw attention to the formal features of a text. Once these features have been identified, however, the interpretive process is much more subjective.

The final part of our definition, that stylistics deals with the aesthetic properties of texts, is also true some of the time but not all of the time. What makes a text attractive (for example, its metre or its metaphors), is an area of interest to many stylisticians. But as we said above, some stylisticians have agenda that are quite different – the exploration of sexism or racism in a text, for instance.

Therefore we will have to stretch our original definition of stylistics somewhat. We will be looking at texts – some will be traditional literary texts, but others will not. We will be looking at the data of the texts (language) and analysing it according to linguistic categories and theories. However, linguists would acknowledge that the preference for some categories or theories over others is not ever entirely objective. We will be emphasizing the aesthetic properties of language, but we will not be exclusively concerned with aesthetics.

1.3 Some debates about the methods and purpose of stylistics

Early examples of stylistic analyses usually started with a text (a poem, for example, or a short story) and used stylistic analysis as a route to accounting for its 'meaning'. We, on the other hand, have usually chosen to start from a description of the 'raw materials' of texts – the linguistic structures out of which the text is composed. We examine this 'data' to find out more about how writers draw upon the range of resources which is the English language, in order to create distinctive texts. One way of describing our approach to stylistics is to say that it is *language*-driven rather than *text*-driven. Our aim is to illustrate the way language works in *any* text, rather than to construct a model which explains an individual text.

One of the main functions of early stylistics was to explain how the 'meaning' of a text was created through the writer's linguistic choices. Pinning down the 'meaning' of a given text is of less concern to us than it has been to stylisticians in the past, because of developments in theories about how we interpret language. Stylistics tended to treat meaning as if it 'resided in the text'; that is to say, all you needed to do to really understand a text was to read or study it thoroughly and carefully enough. Analysis, such as that provided by a stylistic description, would provide the 'ultimate' or 'essential' meaning of the text.

Because of research in the field of pragmatics (which will be discussed in chapter 5) it is now more frequently held that meaning is not a stable and absolute thing, but depends upon the process of interpretation by a reader or hearer. Your interpretation of something you read can depend on many contextual factors, including your cultural background, and the circumstances in which you read it. Thus stylisticians are now less anxious to 'find out what a text means' (although stylistic analysis may help you find meanings in a text which you would otherwise have missed). Instead we are more interested in the systematic ways language is used to create texts which are similar or different from one another, and we also link choices in texts to social and cultural context.

We have therefore departed from traditional stylistics in two significant ways. Firstly, we have incorporated contemporary linguistic theories about the process of reading and interpretation into our analytical models. As we said above, it was a fundamental assumption of stylistics that everything you needed in order to understand the 'true meaning' of a poem or novel or play was contained in the written text. Sufficiently detailed analysis was all that was needed to extract it. Nowadays people are far more aware of the contextual factors which influence interpretation, and make it possible to extract several different 'meanings' from the same text.

The second significant way in which we have departed from traditional stylistics is to have included quite a lot of information about what the constituent parts of language are (i.e. the pieces it is made up of) and what the 'rules' are for the ways in which they can be combined.

To do this, we have drawn on general linguistic models of phonology, morphology, syntax and discourse, which are not unique to stylistics but found in linguistic analyses in many fields. We find these fit our analytical purposes and are more practical and widely applicable than some of the specialist models of language created specifically for stylistic analysis – such as, for example, Halliday's systemic grammar (see Halliday, 1973).

We have left aside the kind of stylistics which involved devising a model of language use which was appropriate only for a narrow range of texts, sometimes even only applicable to a single text. Instead, we have selected models of language which offered flexibility and a wide range of applications, to enable you to use a stylistics approach on any text you might want or be required to analyse.

Analysing language on the levels of phonology, syntax, and so on, and also the ways generations of writers have exploited the linguistic resources available to them, is in our opinion a direct and straightforward way to understand literature better (and not just individual texts).

Having said that, however, we need to put an important caveat in here, because inevitably things are never quite as straightforward as we might hope! When it is actually in use, language is always 'messier' and more diverse than most models, including ours, suggest or can cope with. This is partly because we have restricted how complicated and long this book became, to make it portable and readable, and partly because language in the abstract is so complex that linguists are still trying to name and describe all the variety of structures which are available to its speakers. This phenomenon is sometimes described by the phrase 'all grammars leak', which means that no descriptive system can yet account for all the possible ways language can be used. Another reason for the 'messiness' of real language, when we get down to trying to describe it, is that when people use language they are creative and sometimes respond to situations by doing new things with it which could not always be predicted from what is known by linguists.

The upshot of this is that you may well find that this book does not provide all the answers you need for some questions, and furthermore, there are not always 'right' answers to be found. Your data – written texts or spoken language – won't always fit into neat patterns, and there could well be a shortfall between the theory you are working with and the data you are applying it to. But, on the positive side, it is in exploring this gap between existing theories and actual language use that new things are discovered about the way that language works in general, and more particularly, how language is used to create individual texts.

We are also departing from the purpose of traditional stylistics by using it to look at 'non-literary' texts. However, this has been common practice for many stylisticians since the mid-1980s (see Montgomery, 1986b; Cook, 1992; Mills, 1995; Myers, 1994).

1.4 The background to the study of language and literature

One of the reasons why there may be a considerable amount of linguistic information in this book which is new to you is that since the 1950s, there have been substantial changes in the ways language and literature have been taught in British schools. How best to teach English is still a very live debate. As a result of changes in peda-gogical approaches, most British-educated students who arrive in higher education to study English today have not acquired the same kind of knowledge about literary language, or language in general, as was studied by previous generations of schoolchildren. For example, although grammar is not a large part of school education nowadays, older people may remember being taught the different parts of speech and how to analyse the grammar of a sentence – a process called parsing. A generation or two ago, this sort of knowledge about language was a standard part of education. We both have parents who were taught to identify parts of speech and figures of speech (known as tropes), whereas by the time Shân was in school (1971–84), teaching about the structure of the English language was not part of the syllabus.

However, as we were growing up, despite the reduction in explicit teaching on the structure of language in schools, the study of linguistics was experiencing rapid development. In 1957, the year Joanna was born, linguistics as we now know it arguably emerged into public consciousness, with the publication of Noam Chomsky's ground-breaking *Syntactic Structures*. Debates about the interface between the study of language and the study of literature were also taking place around this time, notably at the 'Conference on Style' held in Indiana in 1958, and published afterwards as *Style in Language* in 1960.

The changes in our awareness of the structures and functions of language that have taken place in the last forty years mean that anyone writing a book about language now, and in particular, a book about stylistics, can draw on a great deal of knowledge which has been built up in the fields of linguistics and discourse analysis. In this book, we have included some of the knowledge and skills of analysis that have largely fallen out of use – for example the knowledge about metre and sentence structure that our parents' generation had – with much more recent theories of language use that have developed in the course of the 1970s and 1980s. We also want to reflect the shifting focus of interests within the field of stylistics, which has undergone considerable changes, from the need to establish stylistic principles in the 1970s, to current concerns about the nature of literature and what should be taught in schools and in further and higher education in a new millennium.

1.5 The purpose of this book

One of the main purposes for this book was to meet the needs of our own students. We have been teaching stylistics at different institutions in the UK to people from a variety of different backgrounds: English Literature courses, English Language courses, students from universities overseas who have studied language and literature from different angles from those adopted in British education, and people not registered at a university but just interested in language and literature. This kind of diversity amongst students in a class or readers of a text is becoming more and more common, as modularity becomes the method by which many higher education institutions organize their courses. If you are taking a course in stylistics, it may well be that you have taken a different selection of courses prior to this one from anyone else in your group. Therefore a textbook needs to be accessible to people with very different experiences and backgrounds, and we have tried to take this into account. You may also be experiencing non-traditional methods of teaching, such as resource-based learning or open learning. For this reason, this book is intended to be both self-contained and reasonably comprehensive, so if you are tackling this subject for the first time, and have a limited range of resources to draw on, this book should help to get you through.

Secondly, syllabuses have changed a great deal in recent years, and if you are studying English Literature, instead of 'great works' written by a limited number of writers, you may also find you are studying texts which were written within the last fifty years or so, are less widely known, and on which not much secondary material is available. With this increasing diversity in the texts studied on degree courses, many people find they need guidelines for reading and analysing texts which, ideally, will work for *any* text, not simply a limited number of traditional 'literary' texts. We have adopted a flexible approach to textual analysis which will lend itself equally well to Milton or an advertisement in a weekly magazine such as *Woman's Own*.

Thirdly, it was our experience that a textbook which satisfactorily used language to find out about literature, and also used literature to explore language did not exist. We thought many of our students – and we ourselves – might benefit from such a book, so we set out to write this one. We have included descriptions of the 'anatomy' and structure of English, and suggestions on how information about the structure of language can be applied to describe and illuminate different types of texts and genres (i.e. kinds) of writing.

1.6 The structure of this book

This introduction has presented an outline of the general aims of the book. In the next three chapters, we introduce some of the components and structures of English. Chapter 2 is an account of the way phonological (sound) and metrical patterns are produced through the sound and stress systems of the language. It also deals with how these features of language are used in poetry, and how to approach the analysis of poems. Chapter 3 deals with syntax (or grammar) and the different word classes, and the ways in which these can combine to form phrases, clauses and larger units of discourse. In this chapter we will also discuss the stylistic concept of *deviation*, i.e. the ways in which literary language is sometimes distinctive through its departure from 'ordinary' or 'normal' linguistic usage (see Mukařowský 1970). Chapter 4 looks at semantics – the meaning of words – and how writers can play with and create meaning through forms such as metaphors and metonyms.

Having established the 'tools' of analysis, the next three chapters look at particular kinds of texts to which these 'tools' can be applied. Chapter 5 focuses on the genre of drama: the ways dialogue imitates and departs from naturally occurring speech, and how stories are told in drama. Chapter 6 examines how different levels of stylistic analysis can be applied to literary styles in fiction – novels, novella and short stories. In this chapter we concentrate on the differences between 'classic realist' texts and modernist and postmodernist writing. Chapter 7 deals with applications of stylistic theory to what can be termed 'popular' texts, showing how the use of 'literary' language is not necessarily confined to texts which are widely recognized as having literary or aesthetic value. We will show here how the resources of language are mobilized in a whole range of different kinds of texts, from advertisements to newspaper headlines. In chapter 8, we summarize the main debates in stylistics, and provide some suggestions for further study in specific areas of stylistics and linguistic theory which we have only been able to mention briefly in other chapters.

You will see that throughout the book there are activities to complete; our suggested answers to some of these can be found at the end of the book. One purpose of these is to make the text more interesting – most people find *doing* something more fun than just 'drifting' through a text, which is what reading can easily become. So you can use the activities to help you keep focused on the topic. Another reason for including them is to give you some idea of how much you already know, and what sort of knowledge and skills you still need to acquire. Sometimes an activity will draw your attention to the fact that you can *already* do something, and that the task in question is one you can take in your stride. On other occasions it is useful to see that there is a gap between what you know or are able to do *now*, and what you *want* to know or be able to do, so that you can reread a section, or look up the same topic in another book, which may explain it in more depth or in terms you find easier to understand.

Activities are also just a good way of finding out about a topic. You will probably understand something in greater depth if you have tried to work through different kinds of analyses, and thought about what was obvious and what was difficult, rather than just reading about it. Not only will your understanding be deeper, you should find you can more easily apply your new skills and knowledge in other, different situations.

Because it can be frustrating to complete an activity and then have no feedback on your work, we have included comments and sometimes suggested answers, usually at the back of the book, but sometimes straight after the activity. This is to make it clearer whether you have understood the topic or not, and also to provide a kind of textual 'dialogue' between you, the reader, and us, the writers – though of course a dialogue with a book will not be as satisfying as a discussion with friends, fellow students, or a tutor. Some activities are very open-ended, so we haven't tried to cover all the possible answers you may think of.

We have also included a glossary at the end of the book which includes those key terms we use from current linguistic terminology which are given in bold typeface in the text. A brief word of warning – be aware that technical words can be used slightly differently in different disciplines (or sub-divisions of disciplines), so the meanings we give may not apply in all contexts. The index at the back of the book will also help you find what you need.

At the end of each chapter is a summary of the main points and suggestions for analytic procedures. These are structured to help you with assignments, if you are undertaking an assessed course.

We hope you find this book useful, practical and enjoyable!

Note

1 We have put 'scientific' in scare quotes to show that the classification of linguistics as a scientific discipline is not always clear-cut. Some areas of linguistics, particularly those involving work on artificial intelligence and theoretical linguistics, are closest to what are generally considered the 'hard' sciences. Most other areas, particularly sociolinguistics, discourse analysis, and areas which have close links to psychology and anthropology, tend to fall into the domain of 'human' or 'social' sciences. However, many departments of language and linguistics have historical links with the humanities, due to the origins of language study (philology, historical linguistics) within departments of English literature. Many still have their academic 'home' within those departments for that reason, even though their interests and methods of study are often very different from other humanities subjects.

Stylistics provides a strong, and we believe, fruitful interdisciplinary link between the study of language and the study of literature, sharing the same object of study – texts in their many and varied forms.

Sound and metre in poetry

2.1 Introduction

In this chapter we look at some of the 'building blocks' of language, from which poetic forms of sound and metre are constructed, and show how these forms have been used to write poetry.

The first aspect of poetry we will be concerned with is sound patterning. This includes rhyme, which most people are familiar with, and also other kinds of sound patterning such as alliteration, assonance, reverse rhyme and consonant patterning. These are features of language which poets and prose writers exploit to create effects such as beauty or emphasis in their writing. In order to analyse some of these features linguistically, we will look at **phonology** in this chapter; phonology is the study of sounds in a language. We will be looking at the definitions of a sound, the difference between sounds and letters, the structure of a syllable, and the ways these parts of language can be arranged to create literary effects.

The second aspect of poetry we will consider is the stress patterns of spoken English. These are used in poetry to create rhythmical effects, and some of the conventional arrangements of rhythm (also called **metre** in this context) and rhyme will be illustrated.

Thirdly, we look at examples of different poetic forms which are defined by the arrangements of sound and metre. This is followed by a discussion of some of the reasons for following formal poetic conventions; this section may be of help if you are writing assignments. The chapter concludes with a checklist of points which are appropriate to cover in an analysis of the structure of a poem.

From experience, we know that sometimes people feel uneasy doing this kind of close analysis and feel that some of the mystery and magic of poetry is lost if they have to pull its workings apart; that 'we murder to dissect', as Wordsworth wrote. Our attitude is that by understanding the linguistic skill demonstrated by a writer in crafting a text, we enjoy it more, and the magic is increased. We hope that you too will find your enjoyment of poetry increased. We also hope you will feel your understanding of language is enriched by studying the sophisticated patterns which writers can make with language. This aesthetic dimension is often ignored in linguistics courses, but it is actually very important to the way people use language.

You will find it useful if you can obtain a copy of *The Norton Anthology of Poetry* to refer to while you are reading this chapter – for details see the References at the end of the book. Many of the poems we quote from are reproduced in *Norton*, and you could then read the whole poem, and compare it to others written by the same poet, or in the same period.

2.2 Sound patterning

2.2.1 Examples of sound patterning

Most people are familiar with the idea of rhyme in poetry – indeed for some, this is what defines poetry. End rhyme (i.e. rhyme at the end of lines) is very common in some poetic styles, and particularly in children's poems:

1 Mrs. *White*
   Had a *fright*
   In the middle of the *night*
   Saw a *ghost*
   Eating *toast*
   Half way up a lamp*post*

2 Little Bo-*peep*
   has lost her *sheep*
   And doesn't know where to
       find them
   Leave them *alone*
   And they will come *home*
   Waggling their tails *behind*
       them

These lines, from Shakespeare and Emily Dickinson respectively, also rhyme:

3 Fair is foul and foul is *fair*
   Hover through wind and
       murky *air*

4 Exaltation is the going
   Of an inland soul to *sea*
   Past the houses, past the
       headlands,
   Into deep *eternity*

Songs often rhyme as well:

5   Hark! the herald angels sing
      Glory to the newborn King!

These are all examples of end rhyme, where the last word of a line has the same final sounds as the last word of another line, sometimes immediately above or below, sometimes one or more lines away. Not all poetry by any means *has* to have end rhyme; these lines by Marge Piercy for example do not:

6   Long burned hair brushes
      across my face its spider
      silk. I smell lavender,
      cinnamon: my mother's clothes.

Many poets do use rhyme, and other kinds of sound patterning as well, some of which are far less widely recognized. A completely different tradition of sound patterning is used by William Barnes in his poem 'Linden Lea', where sounds are arranged in a way very rarely seen in English poetry:

7   To where for me the apple *tree*
      Do lean down low in Linden *Lea*

As well as having end rhyme (*tree* and *Lea*), there is an intricate arrangement of sounds in the last line:

    Do lean down low in Linden Lea
    (D) L N D N L /(N) L ND N L

There are only three **consonants** used in the whole line of seven words (see below for an explanation of the term *consonant* if you are unsure of it), which are **D**, **N** and **L**, and they are arranged into two clusters of **LNDNL**, with an extra **D** and an extra **N**. This patterning of consonant sounds imitates a style of Welsh poetry called *cynghan-nedd* (pronounced 'cun-han-eth'), a different tradition from English poetry, but one used by a few poets writing in English such as Gerard Manley Hopkins and Dylan Thomas.

The lines of poetry below come from 'The Passionate Shepherd to His Love' by Christopher Marlowe. Read these lines aloud, listening for sounds that are repeated. Try to identify any words which:

(a)   start with the same sound as another word
(b)   end with the same sound as another word
(c)   start and end with the same sound as another word
(d)   have different sounds at the beginning or the end, but the same sound in the middle as another word

8   Come live with me and be my love
     And we will all the pleasures prove

Your answers may include:

(a)   *with* and *will* begin with the same two sounds
(b)   *will* and *all* end with the same sound; so do *prove* and *love*
(c)   *live* and *love* start and end with the same sound
(d)   *come* has the same middle sound as *love*

By repeating sounds in words like this, poets can build up very intricate patterns. The sound patterns which are used in these two lines will be considered later on in this chapter in more detail.

2.2.2 Sounds versus letters

In order to be able to analyse the sound patterning in poems, we need a system which lets us talk about sounds of language independently of the spelling system. Notice we were talking about *sounds* rather than *letters* in the analysis of the two lines by Marlowe. One of the advantages of discussing sounds not letters is that we can distinguish between the sounds in *love* and *prove* at the ends of the lines above, which have the same spelling for their last three letters, but are not pronounced in the same way: the sound of the letter *o* is different in each word. In order to describe sounds accurately, a system has been developed which is quite independent of the spelling system. This is called **phonemic notation** (or sometimes **phonetic notation**, a more detailed version); this is the system used in dictionaries to indicate how a word is usually pronounced.

Phonemic notation

If you look up *prove* in the dictionary, you will see next to it /pruv/, or something similar, and this is to tell you that the sound in the middle of *prove* is pronounced nowadays the same as the sound in *zoo* or *you*, and not like the sound in *love, but* or *tough. Love* appears in the dictionary as /lʌv/. The two symbols, /u/ and /ʌ/ represent the two different sounds or **phonemes**. For someone who understands phonemic notation, the symbols specify quite clearly how the two words are usually pronounced. Every phoneme used in English has its own symbol, which is unique to that sound.

Phonemes are represented between two oblique lines: for example /t/, /h/, /s/, or /g/. There are two categories of phonemes: **vowels** and **consonants**. Broadly speaking, consonants are sounds you make by blocking the flow of air from your lungs with a closure somewhere in your mouth or throat (e.g. when you say *m* your lips are closed; when you say *t*, your tongue touches the roof of your mouth).

Vowels are sounds made without any closure – you alter the shape of your lips and change the position of your tongue to make the sounds *oo* and *ee*, but you don't block the air coming out of your mouth. There are problems with this definition – for example, sounds such as *w* as in the word *wait*, for which the phonetic symbol is /w/, are usually classed as consonants while in fact they have at least as much in common acoustically with vowels, because the air flow is not really blocked when you say them. However, in practice this broad definition of vowels and consonants will cover most situations.

We have reproduced a list below of the basic sound symbols for English pronunciation. In actual fact, the set of phonemes most frequently reproduced are usually for only one kind of pronunciation (or **accent**): educated pronunciation from the South East England, known as **RP** or **Received Pronunciation**. If you travel around different parts of the UK or in other English-speaking countries, you will hear many different pronunciations, and for people from some places, such as Scotland, different phonemes are needed.

Phonemes of English

The words selected to illustrate the consonants contain the specified sound twice, except for *reared*, *yews* and *use*, and *witch*. The phonemes shown here are the sounds used by speakers from Southern England.

Consonants			Vowels		
phoneme	e.g. in context	phonemic transcription	phoneme	e.g. in context	phonemic transcription
/p/	pip	/pɪp/	/i/	bead	/bid/
/b/	barb	/bɑb/	/ɪ/	bid	/bɪd/
/t/	tact, tacked	/tækt/	/ɛ/	bed	/bɛd/
/d/	dared	/dɛəd/	/æ/	bad	/bæd/
/k/	cake	/keik/	/ɑ/	card	/kɑd/
/g/	gargle	/gɑgl/	/ɒ/	cod	/kɒd/
/tʃ/	church	/tʃɜtʃ/	/ɔ/	caught, court	/kɔt/
/dʒ/	judge	/dʒʌdʒ/	/ʊ/	good	/gʊd/
/f/	fearful	/fɪəfəl/	/u/	food	/fud/
/v/	vivid	/vɪvɪd/	/ʌ/	bud	/bʌd/
/θ/	thirteenth	/θɜtinθ/	/ɜ/	bird	/bɜd/
/ð/	the brother	/ðə brʌðə/	/ə/	announcer	/ənɑʊnsə/
/s/	cease	/sis/	/ə/	laboured	/leibəd/
/z/	zones	/zəʊnz/	/ə/	vanilla	/vənɪlə/
/ʃ/	sheepish	/ʃipɪʃ/	/ei/	may	/mei/
/ʒ/	treasure	/trɛʒə/	/əʊ/	mow	/məʊ/
/h/	hothouse	/hɒthɑʊs/	/ai/	high	/hai/
/m/	murmur	/mɜmə/	/ɑʊ/	how	/hɑʊ/
/n/	nanny	/næni/	/ɒi/	boy	/bɒi/
/ŋ/	fingering	/fɪŋgərɪŋ/	/ɪə/	rear	/rɪə/
/l/	lull	/lʌl/	/ɛə/	rare	/rɛə/
/r/	reared	/rɪəd/	/ʊə/	Ruhr	/rʊə/
/j/	use, yews	/juz/	/l̩/	battle	/bætl̩/
/w/	witch	/wɪtʃ/	/n̩/	fatten	/fætn̩/

(from Wells & Colson (1971) p. 17)

From the list of phonemes above you can see that there are far more sounds in English than there are letters of the alphabet (about forty-three or forty-four sounds, depending on your accent, compared to twenty-six letters). This is because, as we said above, there is not a one-to-one correspondence between the spelling system and the sounds we use to communicate orally. For example, /t/ and /h/ represent the sounds that begin *train* and *hat*, but we use another symbol for the sound at the beginning of *there*: /ð/. This is because although we just recycle *t* and *h* in spelling, the sound we actually say when we read the letter combination *th* is not at all like the sounds we make when we read either *t* or *h*. We also need another symbol to represent the sound at the beginning of *theatre*: /θ/. If you put your hand to your throat when you say the *th* at the beginning of *theatre* and *there*, you should feel a vibration in your throat for the *th* /ð/ in *there* which you do not feel when you say the *th* /θ/ in *theatre*. This is the feeling of your vocal chords vibrating, and means that the *th* in *there* is voiced (i.e. you make that sound by letting your vocal chords vibrate as the air from your lungs passes through your throat), while the *th* in *theatre* is unvoiced (i.e. you make this sound by not letting your vocal chords vibrate as the air passes through your throat). As this is a difficult difference for many people to detect consciously, you may need to make the /ð/ sound and the /θ/ sound several times before you are confident you can hear and feel the difference. This is a further example of spelling not giving us very much information about the actual sounds of a word.

Consonants

Most people find consonants easier to transcribe into phonemic notation than vowels, as they often share their phonetic symbol with the letter of the alphabet usually associated with that sound in spelling (e.g. /g/, /h/, /m/, /p/, and so on). However, there are some consonants that people do find more difficult.

/ŋ/

This sound is the sound at the end of *fang* /fæŋ/, and also occurs before the sound /k/ in words like *link*, represented phonemically as /lɪŋk/. It is the sound used at the ends of words like *swimming*, *deciding*, *breathing*, if the speaker is in quite formal circumstances

and / or speaks with an RP accent. (In actual fact, many people pronounce this ending differently – for example as /n/ – when they are
more relaxed. In spelling, this more relaxed, non-standard, pronunciation is sometimes indicated by using an apostrophe instead of the
final letter, for example, *swimmin'*, *decidin'*, *breathin'*.)

/ʔ/

This sound represents the glottal stop, which is a way of stopping the
airflow at the top of your throat rather than in your mouth. It is not
really a phoneme, because it does not change the meaning of a word
if it is used instead of a /t/ (it is called an allophone). It is often used
in speech where a 't' is used in spelling, and is sometimes represented
in print with an apostrophe, which is meant to imply a sound is missing. In fact there is no missing sound – speakers simply have a choice
of whether to use /t/ or /ʔ/ in some contexts. Its use can have social
class connotations sometimes: working class speakers are likely to use
it more frequently than middle class speakers. This was why Princess
Diana once made the newspapers for reportedly saying 'there's a lot
of it about' as /ðɛəz ə lɒʔəv ɪʔ əbaʊʔ/.

/j/

This symbol is used for the sound that sometimes occurs initially in a
syllable where there is a *y* in the spelling e.g. *yacht* – /jɒt/; *you* – /ju/;
yes – /jɛs/; *beyond* – /bijɒnd/.

Rather more confusingly, it also appears before the sound /u/
sometimes, even when there is no indication in the spelling, as in: *few*
– /fju/; *tunes* – /tjunz/; beautiful – /bjutəfʌl/. However, this pronunciation is changing – Americans use /j/ before /u/ much less than British
people (US pronunciation of *news* is /nuːz/), and in parts of Britain
it is also being used with diminishing frequency (e.g. *beautiful* is
pronounced /buʔəfʌl/ in Somerset).

Vowels

The phonetic symbols for vowels tend to be less familiar-looking to
the untrained eye than the ones used for consonants. For example,
despite the differences in spelling, the vowel sounds in *I*, *eye*, *aye*, *try*,
and *height* are all the same, and are represented by the symbol /aɪ/.
On the other hand, despite all being spelt with an *o*, the vowel sounds

in the words *or, so, to, how, women* and *off* are all different, and these sounds are represented by the symbols /ɔ/ in *or*, /əʊ/ in *so*, /ə/ in *to* (or, if it is stressed, /u/), /aʊ/ in *how*, /ɪ/ in *women*, and /ɒ/ in *off*. Below are some of the vowels which behave in particularly unexpected ways if you are new to the area:

/ə/

This is a very frequent sound in spoken English – it is known as *schwa*, the so-called 'neutral' vowel that people often use in unstressed syllables, and it is used in many contexts where in spelling you might find different letters being used.

/eɪ/ /əʊ/ /aɪ/ /aʊ/ /ɒɪ/ ɪə/ /ɛə/ /ʊə/

These sounds are all diphthongs. They are represented by two phonemic symbols to show that while you actually say this vowel your mouth moves, changing the sound you make.

/n̩/ /l̩/

These are called *syllabic consonants*. They are unusual in that when they appear in particular contexts, they can stand alone as syllables without a vowel in the pronunciation, as in: *bitten* – /bɪtn̩/; *button* – /bʌtn̩/; *bottle* – /bɒtl̩/.

If you have never had any previous contact with phonemic transcription, a brief summary such as this one is not going to be able to give you everything you need to know. If you are interested and want more information, we recommend: J. C. Wells and Greta Colson (1971) *Practical Phonetics*, Pitman, London.

ACTIVITY 2.2 ━━━━━━━━━━━━━━━━━━━━━━━━━━━━━━━

What common words are represented by the following phonemic notations?

(1) pɛt (2) peɪpəklɪp (3) fɪŋɡətɪp (4) hɛəkʌt (5) bʊk
(6) sɒlt ənd pɛpə (7) vjuz (8) fɪlm (9) tʃɒklʌt (10) pɛtrəl
steɪʃn̩

See the section at the end of the book for our answers to this and some of the other activities in the book.

━━━━━━━━━━━━━━━━━━━━━━━━━━━━━━━━━━━━━━

How would the following words be represented phonemically?

(1) spun	(2) kite	(3) sell	(4) pot	(5) car
(6) tiger	(7) tank	(8) length	(9) cinema	(10) traffic
(11) table	(12) aimless	(13) that	(14) protest	(15) suggestion
(16) belief	(17) persuasion	(18) religion	(19) thank you	

2.2.3 Syllable structure and sound patterning

When we talk about a rhyme in poetry, we are referring to the relationship between the sounds of two words, i.e. a relationship independent of the spelling. Rhyme refers specifically to two words having the same final vowel and consonant sound. For example, these lines from Shakespeare's play *Macbeth* rhyme in pairs, or to use the technical term, couplets:

9   When shall we three meet *again*
       In thunder lightning or in *rain*?
       When the hurley burley's *done*
       When the battle's lost and *won*

A phonetic transcription of the final words of these lines looks like this.

again	/əgeɪn/
rain	/reɪn/
done	/dʌn/
won	/wʌn/

Done and *won* rhyme because they have the same two final sounds: /ʌn/. *Again* and *rain* also have the same two final sounds: /eɪn/. A rhyme occurs when the two final sounds in a **syllable** are identical. While phonemes are the smallest units of sound that we hear as meaningful in a language, syllables are the smallest unit of a sequence of sound which can act as a unit of rhythm (that is, they can be stressed or unstressed in a word or phrase; there will be more on this later). As rhyme and other forms of sound patterning depend on relationships between syllables we will spend some time here on the structure of a syllable.

A syllable typically consists of a vowel, with the option of one or more consonants on either side of the vowel. Thus the basic syllable structure we can assume is:

(consonant) vowel (consonant)
or in 'short hand': cvc

To illustrate the variations possible in syllable structure, let's consider **monosyllabic** words (that is, words of one syllable – *mono* means *one*). *Cat*, *run*, and *hell* are all monosyllabic words, and meet the criteria of a central vowel, bounded on either side by one consonant (remember that a consonant is not the same as a letter, so *hell* ends in one consonant /l/, although in the spelling there are two letter 'l's). In addition to this arrangement, instead of just a single consonant, **consonant clusters** can also often occur, where up to three consonants can form a group in the space reserved for a consonant in the syllable. Examples of this are: *stem*, *trek*, *strain*, *trench*, *talc*, and *rest*. Despite having more consonants, these are still monosyllabic words because they only have one vowel sound.

As we said above, the consonants in a syllable are in fact optional; syllables can exist without them. Monosyllabic words with no final consonants include *pay*, *tie*, and *flow*; monosyllabic words with no initial consonant include: *eat*, *own*, *aim* and *in*. *Eye*, *a* and *owe* are monosyllabic words without either initial or final consonants.

A rhyme occurs when two or more words have the same last vowel and consonant sound (e.g. *dig* and *fig*). This can be represented as cVC; the shared vowel and final consonant (or consonant cluster) are indicated with upper case letters, and the initial consonant (or consonant cluster), which differs, is indicated by a lower case letter.

So far, we have described in detail what a rhyme is, in linguistic terms. Now we will look at the ways poets use rhyme in practice.

In the first four lines of the poem below by Sir Edmund Spenser, *stay* rhymes with *play*, and *sits* rhymes with *wits*.

10   Of this world's theatre, in which we stay,   a
      My love like the spectator idly sits   b

Beholding me that all the pageants play,	a
Disguising diversely my troubled wits.	b

You will be able to see that we have followed the convention of marking the lines that rhyme in a poem by putting a lower case letter *a* at the end of the first line, and at the end of every subsequent line that ends in a rhyme which matches the first line (only the third line in this case). This is then repeated with a letter *b* placed at the end of the next line with a rhyme which is different from *a*, and at the end of every subsequent line ending in rhyme *b* (in this case lines 2 and 4).

ACTIVITY 2.4

Can you complete the rhyming scheme for the rest of the poem? As *fits* rhymes with *wits* it is also a *b* rhyme:

10	Of this world's theatre, in which we stay,	a
	My love like the spectator idly sits	b
	Beholding me that all the pageants play,	a
	Disguising diversely my troubled wits.	b
	Sometimes I joy when glad occasion fits,	b
	And mask to mirth like to a comedy;	
	Soon after, when my joy to sorrow flits,	
	I wail and make my woes a tragedy.	
	Yet she, beholding me with constant eye,	
	Delights not in my mirth, nor rues my smart;	
	But, when I laugh, she mocks, and when I cry,	
	She laughs, and hardens evermore her heart.	
	What then can move her? If nor mirth nor moan,	
	She is no woman, but a senseless stone.	

Some of the rhyming words in this poem fit neatly into our earlier description of monosyllabic words. *Heart* and *moan*, for example, both have the structure cvc. *Cry* is a cv- word, while *eye* is a -v- word. *Fits* and *flits* have the structure cvc. However *tragedy* has the structure:

27

tr a g e d y   (ordinary spelling)
c v c v c v   (vowels and consonants / consonant
                 clusters)
/tr æ ʤ ə d i/   (phonemic transcription)

Tragedy is a 3-syllable word, i.e. it is made up of three cvc segments:

tra ge dy
cv- cv- cv-

Words that have several syllables like *tragedy* are called **polysyllabic** words (*poly* means *many*). To work out how many syllables a word has, you need to identify how many vowels you can hear when it is said. Each vowel will form the heart of one syllable.

1 syllable	2 syllables	3 syllables	4+ syllables
kite	classic	presumption	automatic
spam	kettle	sensation	melodious
bridge	tranquil	tomato	decentralization

Automatic has four syllables; *decentralization* has six. *Melodious* can have either three or four syllables, depending on how it is said. To pronounce four, you would say /mələʊdijəs/. To pronounce it with three, you would elide the last two vowels – that is, reduce them to one sound: /mələʊdʒəs/.

A complication to the rule of counting vowels are words like *sudden* and *kettle*, which have **syllabic consonants**. We treat /n/ and /l/ in these contexts as if they are syllables in their own right, as discussed above.

ACTIVITY 2.5

How many syllables do the following words have?

cupboard	mirror	cat	walls	table
strewn	admirable	elevator	persuasive	honeysuckle
inadvisable	gladiator	oregano	blushed	

Rhymes are not restricted to monosyllabic words, or to the final syllables of polysyllabic words. Two-syllable words can rhyme; these examples are of words which share not only their final vowel and consonant, but their last *two* vowels and consonants: *garden / pardon*, *grieving / leaving*, *sleeping / leaping*, *snooker / lucre*.

Here are the rhymes above returned to their original contexts in extracts from poems by Louis MacNeice, Rupert Brooke, Edwin Morgan, and Gerard Manley Hopkins:

11   The sunlight on the *garden*
     Hardens and grows cold
     We cannot cage the moment
     Within its web of gold
     When all is said and done,
     We cannot ask for *pardon*

12   Now God be thanked who matched us with his hour
     And caught our souls and wakened us from *sleeping*
     With hand made sure, swift eye and sharpened power
     To turn as swimmers into cleanness *leaping*

13   . . . And they,
     trailing five bairns, accepting his omission
     of the foul crumbling stairwell, windows wired
     not glazed, the damp from the canal, the *cooker*
     without pipes, packs of rats that never tired –
     any more than the vandals bored with *snooker*
     who stripped the neighbouring houses, howled, and fired
     their aerosols – of squeaking 'Filthy *lucre!*'

14   Margaret, are you *grieving*
     Over Goldengrove *unleaving*?

Rhymes of more than two syllables usually only appear for comic effect, as they tend to appear very contrived. In the case of 'The Rhinoceros' by Ogden Nash, for example, *rhinoceros* is rhymed with *prepoceros* (i.e. *preposterous*!).

15   The rhino is a homely beast,
     For human eyes he's not a feast.

Farewell, farewell, you old rhinoceros,
I'll stare at something less prepoceros.

Limericks also sometimes make use of triple rhymes, as in the case of *fermented* and *lamented* in the verse below:

16   There was a young woman from Ryde
Who ate green apples and died
The apples fermented
Inside the lamented
And made cider inside her inside

It is more difficult to use a three-syllable rhyme in a serious poem, but you could read 'Don Juan' by Byron for some examples.

You may have noticed in some of the examples given that while we considered the end rhymes of poems, there were sometimes other kinds of rhymes in the lines as well. In the Louis MacNeice poem, for example, where the first and final lines of the stanza are double rhymes (*garden* and *pardon*), the first word of the second line (*Hardens*) also contains many of the same sounds. Except for the final /s/, it is in fact another double rhyme for *garden* and *pardon* (the second and fourth lines have end rhyme, as well). Similarly, in another poem by Gerard Manley Hopkins, 'God's Grandeur', rhyme is not constrained to the ends of lines:

17   Generations have trod, have trod, have trod
And all is seared with trade, bleared, smeared with toil,
And wears man's smudge, and shares man's smell,
The earth is bare now, nor can foot feel being shod.

The words *seared*, *bleared* and *smeared* all rhyme within a single line; this is called **internal rhyme**.

2.2.4 Different forms of sound patterning

At the beginning of this chapter, we looked briefly at two lines of Marlowe's poem 'The Passionate Shepherd'. We identified several different kinds of sound patterning, which we will now consider in more detail. The lines were:

18 Come live with me and be my love
    And we will all the pleasures prove

These two lines, rather amazingly, include examples of almost all the different kinds of sound patterning used in poetry.

- rhyme: *me – be*   *love – prove*
                /mi/ – /bi/   /lʌv/ – /pruv/

We have already discussed rhyme in detail. The *me – be* rhyme is internal rhyme, rather than end rhyme. The words *love* and *prove* would probably have both been pronounced with the same vowel sound by Marlowe (a sound more like our modern pronunciation of *prove* than of *love*). Therefore they would have been a rhyme then, although to us they sound like a half-rhyme, or like consonance.

- alliteration: *me – my*   *pleasures – prove*
                /mi/ – /maɪ/   /plɛʒəz/ – /pruv/

The initial consonants are identical in alliteration. As you can see, *pleasures* and *prove*, though both start with /p/, have consonant clusters initially: /pl/ and /pr/. Therefore they are not completely alliterative, because the consonant clusters are not identical.

- assonance: *live – with – will   come – love*
                /lɪv/ – /wɪð/ – /wɪl/   /kʌm/ – /lʌv/

Assonance describes syllables with a common vowel.

- consonance: *will – all*
                /wɪl/ – /ɔl/

Syllables ending with the same consonant/s are described as having consonance.

- reverse rhyme: *with – will*
                /wɪð/ – /wɪl/

Reverse rhyme describes syllables sharing the vowel and initial consonant (rather than the vowel and the final consonant as is the case in rhyme).

- pararhyme: *live – love*
  /lɪv/ – /lʌv/

Where two syllables have the same initial and final consonants, but different vowels, they pararhyme.

- repetition

Although there are no examples in the lines from 'The Passionate Shepherd', it is of course possible to have a complete match of CVC, for example *the sea, the sea*. This is called repetition.

ACTIVITY 2.6 _____

What different forms of sound patterning can you find in the first stanza of the poem, 'Easter Wings', by George Herbert (who lived 1593–1663)?

19   Lord, who createdst man in wealth and store,
                  Though foolishly he lost the same,
                        Decaying more and more,
                              Till he became
                                Most poore:
                                With thee
                              O let me rise
                        As larks, harmoniously,
                  And sing this day thy victories:
            Then shall the fall further the flight in me.

2.3 Stress and metrical patterning

2.3.1 Word stress

We looked above at some examples of double rhymes: *garden / pardon, grieving / leaving, sleeping / leaping, snooker / lucre*. In all these cases, the second syllable sounds fainter and less significant than the first syllable when you say the word.

In English words of two syllables, one is usually said slightly louder, slightly higher, held for slightly longer, or otherwise said slightly more forcefully than the other syllable in the same word, when the word is said in normal circumstances. This syllable is called the **stressed** syllable. Not all languages have stressed syllables in their words; in some, such as Japanese, all syllables in a word have more or less equal stress. In this book, we'll be using an accent over a vowel to indicate the stressed syllable and a dot over unstressed syllables (though you will see different ways of indicating stress):

kitten   important

Words of three syllables or more can have a main stress and in addition, a secondary stress on another syllable. In these cases, numbers are sometimes used rather than just accents. 1 indicates the main stress, and 2 indicates the secondary stress. The word *unimportant* for example has the main stress in the same place as *important*, but a secondary stress on the first syllable:

unimportant

However, stress does depend in part on the context in which a word is said. For example, if someone had said that being punctual was important and you disagreed, you might say:

That's unimportant

with the main stress and the secondary stress in the opposite order.

If you can't tell automatically which syllables in a word are stressed, try saying the word aloud and holding different syllables in turn for slightly longer than the others. A syllable which can be drawn out longer than the others without the word sounding very peculiar is probably a syllable on which the stress naturally falls.

ACTIVITY 2.7

Mark the syllables in the following words with a dot over each one, and then go back and mark the stressed syllable in each word (as it is pronounced in your variety of English; there are sometimes differences, for example between American and British English, in where the stress is placed) with an accent over the syllable. The first word is done as an example.

perförm	mirror	walls	unkind	strewn
admirable	persuasive	cupboard	honeysuckle	inadvisable
gladiator	oregano	blushed	elevator	

2.3.2 Stress in longer units

In addition to stress within an individual word, when we put words together in utterances we stress some more strongly than others. Where someone puts the stress depends partly on what they think is the most important information in their utterance, and partly on the inherent stresses in the words which we looked at above. Read the sentence below, first trying to put equal stress on each syllable, and then in a way that seems comfortable. Mark which syllables you would stress.

I need to buy a pair of purple shoes, and a new red hat.

It is possible to read this sentence putting stress on different words in turn, so as to suggest the speaker wants to *buy* the shoes and hat (as opposed to borrowing, stealing or hiring them); that the *speaker* wants to buy them (as opposed to someone else buying them); that the speaker wants a *new* hat (instead of an old one); that they want a *pair* of shoes (instead of just one), and so on. By putting the stress on the final word, 'hat', you create the meaning that the speaker is correcting a misunderstanding on the part of someone they are addressing, who perhaps thought they were going out to buy a red coat.

Poetry can exploit the way we use stress when we speak to create rhythms. When stress is organized to form regular rhythms, the term used for it is **metre**.

2.3.3 Analysing metre

To work out the metre of a poem, first of all you need to work out the number of syllables in a line, as in this example from the play *Romeo and Juliet*, by Shakespeare:

20   For saints have hands that pilgrims' hands do touch
     = 10 syllables

You should then read the line aloud in quite a relaxed way. Being relaxed will prevent you from trying to create extra emphasis which isn't 'natural' to the line. As you read it, you should be able to hear or feel that some of the words you say are with a slightly more forceful puff of air. These are the stressed syllables. Sometimes it helps to tap your hand in time with the syllables you produce more forcefully:

20a For saints have hands that pilgrims' hands do touch

It is sometimes possible to read a line of poetry in more than one way, which can make it difficult to fix on a pattern for the stresses. The line of poetry above has been marked as having alternate stressed and unstressed syllables, but you could actually read it slightly differently. For example:

20b For saints have hands that pilgrims' hands do touch

Reading the line with this rhythm would change the meaning slightly. The emphasis on 'do' implies that there are things which pilgrims' hands do not touch, or that there are parts of saints which are not touched. When an actor interprets a line in a play, one thing they take into account is where they place the stresses, since this can affect the meaning.

To return to the line of poetry in question, if you read it aloud without thinking too hard about the meaning, you will probably find you have read it in the stresses marked in 20a because of the way it is constructed. A ten-syllable line like this, with stress on alternate syllables and which starts with an unstressed syllable, is a very specific and popular form in English poetry known as **iambic pentametre**. *Iambic* refers to the pattern of unstressed and stressed syllables: an unstressed syllable followed by a stressed one is an **iamb**.

An iamb is an example of a unit of metre. Units of metre are called **feet**, and these are combinations of unstressed and stressed syllables which can be repeated in a poem. The term 'pentametre' refers to the number of feet in the line. The line from *Romeo and Juliet* is in pentametre because it contains five feet; *pent* comes from the Greek word for *five*.

2.3.4 Different types of feet

The names of the different types of feet most frequently found in English poetry are as follows:

iamb

an iambic foot contains two syllables, an unstressed syllable followed by a stressed one:

21   And palm to palm is holy palmer's kiss

trochee

a trochaic foot contains two syllables as well, but in this case, the stressed syllable comes first, followed by an unstressed syllable:

22   Willows whiten, aspens quiver

anapest

an anapestic foot consists of three syllables; two unstressed syllables are followed by a stressed one:

23   Without cause be he pleased, without cause be he cross;

dactyl

a dactylic foot is similar to an anapest, except reversed – a stressed syllable is followed by two unstressed ones:

24   Óne for thě mástěr, ǎnd óne for thě dáme

spondee

a spondaic foot consists of two stressed syllables; lines of poetry rarely consist only of spondees:

25   ǎnd ǎ bláck-/Báck gúll bént lǐke ǎn íron bár slówly̌.

pyrrhic

a pyrrhic foot is two unstressed syllables, as in 'like an' in line 25 above.

S. T. Coleridge devised a verse to illustrate the different types of metrical foot, which if you want to remember which metre has which name, can work as a mnemonic (that is, as a memory aid):

26   *Metrical Feet*

Tróchěe trǐps from lóng tǒ shórt.
From lóng tǒ lóng in sólěmn sórt
Slów spónděe stálks; stróng fóot yět íll áb/lě
Évěr tǒ cǒme úp wǐth thě dáctyl trǐsýllǎblě.
Iǎmbs márch from shórt tǒ lóng.
With ǎ leáp ǎnd ǎ bóund thě swíft ǎnǎpésts thróng.

2.3.5 Different types of metre

We said above that a line that contains five iambs is in iambic pentametre. Similarly, lines that contain two feet (of any kind) are described as dimetre, those with three feet as trimetre, and those containing four feet are described as being in tetrametre. Lines with six feet are hexametres, with seven are heptametres, and with eight are octametres (the first part of each term relates the Greek word for the appropriate number).

ACTIVITY 2.8 ─────────────────────────────

Can you identify the metres in the following lines? (27 is completely regular, but 28 and 29 have variations in their metre)

27 Wild Nights – Wild Nights!
         Were I with thee
         Wild Nights should be
    Our luxury!

28 He is not here; but far away
            The noise of life begins again,
            And ghastly through the drizzling rain
    On the bald street breaks the blank day.

29 Nobody heard him, the dead man,
         But still he lay moaning:
         I was much further out than you thought
    And not waving but drowning.

2.4 Conventional forms of metre and sound

At different times, different patterns of metre and sound have developed and become accepted as ways of structuring poems. These conventional structures often have names, and if you are analysing poems, it is worth being able to identify the more frequent conventions that poets use.

Couplets

Couplets are two lines of verse, usually connected by a rhyme. Rhyming couplets have been popular throughout most periods of English poetry. Poets in the eighteenth century in particular made frequent use of them, as in this opening to a poem by Lady Mary Wortley Montagu, written in 1747:

30   *The Lover: a ballad*

At length, by so much importunity pressed,
Take, C–, at once, the inside of my breast;
This stupid indifference so often you blame
Is not owing to nature, to fear or to shame;
I am not as cold as a virgin in lead,
Nor is Sunday's sermon so strong in my head;
I know but too well how time flies along,
That we live but few years and yet fewer are young.

Wordsworth and Coleridge in the late eighteenth century also deployed rhyming couplets. This is an extract from 'The Mad Mother' by Wordsworth:

31   Her eyes are wild, her head is bare,
The sun has burnt her coal-black hair,
Her eye-brows have a rusty stain,
And she came from far over the main.

Quatrains

Stanzas of four lines, known as quatrains, are very common in English poetry. Oliver Goldsmith's poem, 'When Lovely Woman Stoops to Folly' written in 1766, is in quatrains. The layout on the page highlights the rhyming scheme, and also the metrical pattern. The lines are iambic, with lines of nine and eight syllables, alternately. The nine-syllable lines end in unstressed syllables, forming double rhymes as discussed earlier:

32   When lovely woman stoops to folly,
    And finds too late that men betray,
What charm can soothe her melancholy,
    What art can wash her guilt away?

The only art her guilt to cover,
    To hide her shame from every eye,
To give repentance to her lover,
    And wring his bosom – is to die.

Blank verse

Blank verse consists of lines in iambic pentameter which do not rhyme. These are very common in English literature: Shakespeare's characters (late sixteenth century) frequently speak in blank verse, and other examples include Milton's epic poem, *Paradise Lost* (seventeenth century), Wordsworth's *The Prelude* (late eighteenth century), and some of Robert Browning's dramatic monologues (mid-nineteenth century). This example is from Browning's poem 'Andrea del Sarto' (1855):

33   But do not let us quarrel any more,
       No my Lucrezia; bear with me for once:
       Sit down and all shall happen as you wish.
       You turn your face, but does it bring your heart?

Sonnet

The sonnet is a poetic form which has been used in English since the mid-sixteenth century. Many poets have experimented with its quite rigid formal constraints. The basic form is fourteen lines, each of ten syllables, and usually in iambic pentametre. A variety of rhyming schemes are possible, and the rhyming scheme usually indicates the progression of ideas through the poem. In the seventeenth-century sonnet below by Michael Drayton, for example, the rhyming scheme indicates the stages of the narrator's thought:

34 1 Since there's no help, come let us kiss and part;   a
      2 Nay, I have done; you get no more of me;   b
      3 And I am glad, yea, glad with all my heart   a
      4 That thus so cleanly I myself can free;   b
      5 Shake hands for ever, cancel all our vows,   c
      6 And when we meet at any time again,   d

```
 7 Be it not seen on either of our brows              c
 8 That we one jot of former love retain.             d
 9 Now at the last gasp of love's latest breath       e
10 When, his pulse failing, passion speechless lies,  f
11 When faith is kneeling by his bed of death,        e
12 And innocence is closing up his eyes,              f
13 Now, if thou woulds't, when all have given him o'er, g
14 From death to life thou might'st him yet recover.  g
```

The poem is organized into three groups of quatrains with alternately rhyming lines, and a final rhyming couplet. The first two quatrains are similar in content: the speaker is acknowledging the end of a relationship between the speaker and the addressee. The third quatrain describes in allegorical terms the end of the relationship (i.e. the emotions of love, passion, and the qualities of faith and innocence are represented as if they were people). The final couplet is a 'twist'; despite the preceding lines, the speaker would like the addressee back! The metrical pattern is mostly iambic pentametre, with slight variations in lines 9 and 10, and an extra unstressed syllable in line 14.

Sonnets which consist of three quatrains and a rhyming couplet usually end with a reversal or a challenge to the preceding ideas in the final two lines. Sonnets structured in this way are referred to as Shakespearean sonnets. The sonnet by Spencer used to illustrate rhyming schemes (extract 10) is also an example of a rhyming scheme linked to the progression of ideas.

Another common sonnet form is the Italian (or Petrarchan) sonnet, where lines are rhymed in a group of eight (an octave) and a group of six (a sestet). A poem rhymed in this way usually looks at an idea from one angle for the first eight lines, and then from another angle for the last six. Milton's sonnet 'When I consider how my light is spent' is an example of a sonnet structured like this.

Free verse

This is a form of verse (also called *vers libre*) that uses little or no conventional rhyme or metre. It has been very popular in the twentieth century. 'Pin Money' by Valerie Sinason is an example of free verse:

35   *Pin Money*

On Friday mornings
the whole estate smelt of glue.
The women were sticking tassels on to lampshades,
earning their pin money.

On Friday evenings
queuing for their pay,
the women stood,
legs thin as pins,
While the men waited in the pubs,
thick and powerful as magnets.

Limericks

Limericks are five-line verses in which generally the first, second and fifth lines rhyme, and the second and third lines rhyme. The lines are usually anapestic (two unstressed syllables, followed by a stressed) with three feet in the first, the third and the fifth lines, and two feet in the second and the third. Notice that the word 'ordinary' in the limerick below needs to be pronounced with three syllables in order to scan – this is elision which was discussed earlier.

36   There was a young lady named Wright
Who could travel much faster than light
She started one day
In the ordinary way
And came back the previous night

Though the ones mentioned here are possibly the most common, many other verse forms appear quite regularly in English poetry. A very good summary is given by Jon Stallworthy in an essay on versification in *The Norton Anthology of Poetry*.

All these forms may give the impression that poetry can be a very rule-bound activity. This is partially true. At some moments in history, poetry has followed very strict conventions, and though many poets today use free verse forms, poems are still written which conform to strict conventions. However, poets have always played with conventions as well, and you will come across poems from all periods which are experiments with structural forms. The limerick below demonstrates an experiment with metre for the purpose of humour!

37   There was a young man from Japan
      Whose limericks never would scan.
          When his friends told him so,
          He said, yes I know
      But I always try to get as many words into the last line as I
         possibly can.

2.5 The poetic functions of sound and metre

Having explored how sound patterning and metre work linguistically, and how they have been employed by poets, we come to a very important question – *why* do this? What is gained by this very elaborate patterning in the forms of language?

Different poets have different reasons; we have identified some possible reasons here, you may think of others that have not occurred to us. The reasons given here will not all apply to every poem you come across, but they can give you an idea of the range of effects sound and metre can have.

Reasons for poets using sound and metrical patterning include:

- for aesthetic pleasure – sound and metrical patterning are fundamentally pleasing, in the way that music is; most people enjoy rhythms and repeated sounds. Children in particular seem to like verse for this reason.
- to conform to a convention / style / poetic form – as with clothes and buildings, poetry has fashions, and different forms of sound patterning have been popular at different times. The time at which they were writing has a great influence on why poets selected the forms they did. For example, consonant patterning (alliteration) was very common in very early poetry, written in Old English. One of the most famous and beautiful alliterative poems from the Middle English period is 'Pearl'; its author is unknown.

38	(translation)
Perle, plesaunte to princes paye	Pearl, pleasing and delightful for a
To clanly clos in golde so clere:	prince to set flawlessly in bright gold:
Oute of oryent, I hardlye saye,	among the pearls of the orient, I
Ne proved I never her precious pere	assuredly say, I never found one of
So rounde, so reken in uche araye,	equal value. So round, so radiant
So smal, so smothe her sydes were,	in every setting; her sides so narrow,
Quere-so-ever I jugged gemmes gaye,	so smooth; wherever I judged gems
I sette hyr sengeley in synglere.	gorgeous before, I set her apart as unique.

If you mark the alliteration in this extract from the first stanza, you will see how important it was to the structure of this poem.

- to experiment or innovate with a form – poets innovate to create new poetic forms, and also to challenge assumptions about the forms of language which are considered appropriate to poetry. In the sixteenth century, Sir Philip Sidney's innovations included the use of English rather than Italian for his poetry, at a time when English was not regarded as sufficiently 'dignified' language for poetry. Wordsworth wrote his *Lyrical Ballads* in very simple language at the end of the eighteenth century, to express his belief that the language of 'ordinary people' could be poetic too. Tom Leonard, a contemporary poet, writes in Glasgow dialect, to challenge the assumption that standard southern English is the only appropriate variety of English in which to write poetry.

- to demonstrate technical skill, and for intellectual pleasure – there is a kind of satisfaction to be derived from the cleverness of some poems and the magic of form and meaning being perfectly combined. Poets show their skill with words in the same way as athletes demonstrate their ability to run fast or leap hurdles. Welsh poets in the thirteenth and fourteenth centuries developed ever more complicated arrangements of consonants (*cynghannedd*, mentioned at the beginning of the chapter) to show how clever they were, and to impress the Welsh nobility by whom they were employed.

- for emphasis or contrast – some metrical patterns, such as 'slow spondees', or sudden changes in a previously regular pattern, draw your attention to that place in the poem. It could be where a concealed meaning is suddenly made plain, where there is a shift in mood, or where the main idea suddenly changes direction.

- onomatopoeia – when the rhythm of a line or its sound imitates the sound of what is being described, this is known as **onomatopoeia**. In Wilfred Owen's poem 'Anthem for doomed youth', the sound of gunfire is imitated:

39   Only the stuttering rifles' rapid rattle
     Can patter out their hasty orisons

In Keats's 'Ode to a nightingale' the sound of bubbles bursting is mimicked in the line:

40   With beaded bubbles winking at the brim

Examples of onomatopoeia are actually quite rare, so be wary of leaping to it as an explanation for the use of sounds and rhythms in a poem.

2.6 Analysis of poetry: checklist

This is a checklist of areas you might want to cover, when analysing a poem.

- Information about the poem

If this information is available to you, somewhere in your analysis give the title of the poem, the name of the poet, the period in which the poem was written, (either the date, for example, the mid-eighteenth century, or a name, for example, the Augustan period), the genre to which the poem belongs, if you recognize it – for example, whether it is lyric, dramatic, epic, nonsense, sonnet, elegy or satire – these categories are not mutually exclusive; a lyric poem can also be a sonnet. You can get this information from one of the reference books listed at the end of this chapter. You might also mention the topic, for example, whether it is a love poem, a war poem or a nature poem.

- ## How is the poem structured

  These are structural features that you should check for; there may well be others we have omitted. Don't worry if you don't find any examples of reverse rhyme, or a regular metrical pattern in your poem. What matters is that you looked, so if they had been there, you wouldn't have missed them.

  You don't need to write about all the headings below. Working through them is the process of getting to know the poem. After that you can select which are the interesting features you want to discuss.

  (a) Layout – are the lines grouped into stanzas of equal / unequal lengths?

  (b) Number of lines.

  (c) Length of lines – count the syllables; are lines of regular syllabic length?

  (d) Regular metre – which syllables carry stress? Are there an equal number of unstressed syllables between the stressed ones? How many feet (stressed syllables) to a line? Comment on the type of foot and the number of feet per line – or say that there is no regular metrical pattern. Finding no regular metre is not to say that there is no exploitation of metre however. A poem can be written in free verse and can occasionally use particular metrical patterns for emphasis, or onomatopoeic effect.

  (e) End rhyme – plot the end rhyme, if there is any. You could check with a reference source such as the essay by Jon Stallworthy at the end of the *Norton Anthology*, to see if the metre and end rhyme conform to a particular style of poem (e.g. a ballad, a sonnet or a villanelle).

  (f) Other forms of sound patterning – assonance (*come, love*), consonance (*will, all*), alliteration (*me, my*), pararhyme (*live, love*), reverse rhyme (*with, will*), half rhyme (*love, prove*), and repetition (*the sea, the sea*).

Comment on the effect of these forms, using the list of reasons we suggested above for reference.

You should also check for literal and figurative uses of language, interesting uses of syntax, punctuation and register, and for intertextual allusion. These are all discussed later in this book.

Suggestions for further reading

Durant, Alan and Nigel Fabb (1990) *Literary Studies in Action*, London: Routledge.

Leech, Geoffrey (1969) *A Linguistic Guide to English Poetry*, London: Longman.

Stallworthy, Jon (1983) 'Versification', *The Norton Anthology of Poetry*, New York: Norton, 1403–22.

Wells, John C. and Greta Colson (1971) *Practical Phonetics*, London: Pitman.

Chapter 3

Grammar and literary style

3.1 Introduction

In this chapter we will address the question of why we should be interested in undertaking a grammatical analysis of literary texts, and what this level of analysis can tell us about different kinds of literary style. As we mentioned earlier, many people resist the idea of analysing the grammar of sentences in a poem or a novel, because they feel it destroys their enjoyment of the text as an entity. However, knowing how something works does not necessarily always entail losing pleasure in it. This certainly doesn't seem to be the case as far as other aesthetic objects are concerned. Think of a beautifully crafted clock and its component parts. If you knew how it was put together, and understood how all the parts interconnected with each other, would this mean you could no longer take pleasure in it as an aesthetic object? Some clocks even overtly display the way that they work as part of their aesthetic appeal, and some texts do just the same, as we will see later.

Stylistic analysis of a text allows us to do a similar kind of thing – to examine the workings of a text. This breaking down of the text into component parts enables us to analyse each component on its own terms, and understand how it fits together with other components. When it's put back together again, into a sentence, or a set of sentences, we can then see more clearly the relationships between them which will increase our understanding and consequently our appreciation of the text as a whole.

In this chapter we introduce the basic grammatical structures and word categories of English in order to describe how sentences are made up of smaller components: clauses and phrases. Through some practical examples, we show how knowledge about these grammatical components can be used in an analysis of 'literary' language, which is often distinguished from other, more 'ordinary', forms of language use. This difference, or 'deviation' from what are taken to be the structural 'norms' of non-literary language can only be described and accounted for once we are able to identify the grammatical structures of the language.

Throughout this chapter we will use the term 'normal' to refer to ordinary, everyday conversational use of language, and the term 'deviant' to refer to language use that is structurally more unusual and literary, although this may not always be a useful distinction to maintain, as we will discover. The term 'deviation' in language was originally used by the Prague School linguist Jan Mukařowský (1932) to describe the ways in which literary language can be said to differ from more everyday, non-literary language. However, the distinction between literary and non-literary language forms is not always clear cut, and many people prefer to think of a sentence that in some way deviates from a grammatical norm as being **marked** (as opposed to deviant) while sentences which follow the more usual pattern are **unmarked**.

Marked forms of language use can be found in conversational contexts as well as in literary contexts, when speakers want to create particular effects or meanings. For instance, the sentence:

She was fast asleep

is grammatically unmarked, as the words are arranged in a way that doesn't draw attention to any specific element within it. However, if we move some of the words around the sentence reads:

Fast asleep she was

then we have a sentence which is grammatically marked, with a shift in emphasis on to these particular words. If we change things even more, to:

She fast asleep was

then we have disrupted the grammatical pattern even more, and we would probably agree as speakers of English that this sentence is one that we probably wouldn't use in our everyday speech.

3.2 What is grammar?

There are many different approaches to grammar, all of which serve different kinds of purposes. First of all, there is the approach those people who have learned a language formally will recognize, which can be found in the 'grammar books' that are used in schools and second language classrooms, and which are designed to show you the 'correct' way to write and speak a language. This pedagogical approach is probably the most widely held notion of what a grammar is and does. Secondly, there is 'traditional' grammar, which generally refers to grammatical study from classical Greek and Roman scholars through to the end of the eighteenth century, when modern linguistics began to develop as a more scientific area of study (see section 1.2 of the Introduction above).

'Grammar' can also be used to refer to the knowledge that every speaker has of the language that they speak. We might not be aware of this knowledge, or able to describe it to someone else, but we have an intuitive grasp of the structures and forms of the language (or in the case of bi- and multi-lingual speakers, the languages) that we speak. Theoretical linguists, like Chomsky in the 1950s, are interested in discovering the rules that underlie these linguistic structures, including the rules governing the way words are put together to form sentences, known as **syntax**, and in building a theoretical model of the way that languages work. They are also interested in looking for similarities between different languages in order to understand more about how the human mind might work.

Another approach to grammar is one which aims to provide a comprehensive description of the structures and categories of a language; the best known British English example is probably Randolph Quirk *et al.*'s (1985) *A Comprehensive Grammar of the English Language*. It is this notion of grammar that we work with in this chapter and which has informed our analyses of the texts discussed here.

3.3 Attitudes to grammar: prescription and description

A prescriptive approach to grammar is based on the notion that a native speaker's language usage can be right or wrong. The function of traditional grammar books was to provide a set of instructions that had to be adhered to if a sentence was to be considered stylistically correct. You are probably familiar with some of these, such as:

don't start a sentence with 'and'
don't split infinitives
don't end a sentence with a preposition
don't use third person plural pronoun *they* to refer to a non-specific singular third person (e.g. someone)

all of which are sometimes considered to be stylistically 'bad form'. So the well-known split infinitive of the Star Trek mission '*to boldly go* where no man has gone before' would be quite unacceptable to a prescriptive grammarian. Non-standard features of the language, such as the use of the double negative (e.g. 'you ain't seen nothing yet') which is a feature of many dialects of English, would be considered to be just plain wrong.

The other way of looking at grammar is from the descriptive viewpoint. A descriptive grammar, as the name suggests, aims to describe what happens when language is used by recording what it actually is that native speakers do with language, rather than what somebody says they should be doing. However, even descriptive grammars have tended to focus on standard forms rather than on non-standard varieties of English.

The prescriptivist notion that there are right and wrong ways of using language is frequently the subject of public debate, where people air strong views about the 'correctness' or 'sloppiness' of language use and complain about falling standards in the use of English, like the Conservative politician Gillian Shepherd who, along with the newsreader Trevor Macdonald, initiated a 'Campaign for Better English' in 1994, to try to 'improve' the way that people speak.

In practice, most people, including writers, use language in various ways depending on who is being addressed, where they are, and what kind of effect they want to produce. In literary language particularly, the structures of grammar can be 'stretched' or disrupted in various ways to produce different effects, while still being recognizable as a version of English. In the following extract, two of the prescriptive 'rules' listed above are being broken quite deliberately:

1   You spent your childhood on the road, here today, gone
    tomorrow; you grew up a restless man. You loved change.
    And fornication. And trouble. And, funnily enough, towards
    the end, you loved butterflies. Peregrine Hazard, lost among
    the butterflies, lost in the jungle, vanished away as neatly and
    completely as if you had become the object of one of those
    conjuring tricks you were so fond of.

In this passage Angela Carter has three sentences that begin with
'and'. Two of those sentences are incomplete, and she ends the last
sentence with the preposition 'of'!

There are other interesting structures in this extract, too.
Whatever approach we take to grammar, we need a way of naming
different grammatical components, and of identifying what words are
doing in a sentence, before we can analyse them in detail and start to
say how they might affect what this text means. So we will return
to this example later in the chapter, once we have established some
criteria for describing sentences and their component parts.

3.4 Two levels of grammar: morphology and syntax

Grammar works on two levels. **Morphology** is the part of grammar
which provides rules for combining the linguistic units that form
words. The smallest unit that carries grammatical information in a
language is called a **morpheme**. For example, we can transform an
adjective into an adverb, or an adjective into a noun, by combining
two morphemes. The morpheme (and adjective) *quiet* plus the
morpheme *-ly* becomes the adverb *quietly* (a word now made up of
two morphemes); *quiet* plus *-ness*, becomes the noun *quietness*. The
word *quiet* is a 'free' morpheme, which means it can be used on
its own, while *-ly* and *-ness* are 'bound' morphemes, which have to be
attached to another word. These kind of morphemes are called
derivational morphemes, because they are used to build up new
words. Although they do not carry any semantic meaning on their
own, they do indicate some important information when attached to
a free morpheme, for example, we know that a word ending in *-ness*
indicates a state of some kind, i.e. *quietness* is a state of being quiet.
The *-ly* ending for adverbs indicates how something was done, e.g.

'she talked *quietly*'. In the following examples, identify the different morphemes, and decide whether they are 'free' or 'bound':

inconvenient	deliberately
truthfulness	icily
indefinitely	levelheaded

You could have listed *-in*, *-ful*, *-ness*, *-ly* and *-i* as bound morphemes, while *convenient*, *truth*, *definite*, *deliberate*, *ice*, *level* and *head* fall into the free morpheme category. You may be wondering what to do about the *-ed* morpheme in *headed* – this should become clear in the next paragraph!

In English, one of the ways we signal a change in **tense** is by adding the past tense morpheme *-ed* to a verb stem, which is realized phonetically as /d/ as in flow*ed*, /ɪd/ as in want*ed*, or /t/ as in stretch*ed*. So 'Jane wants to be a movie star' can be changed into a past tense sentence by adding an element to the main verb: 'Jane want*ed* to be a movie star'. We can also give grammatical information about **number** through morphological combinations and changes: we can add the morpheme *-s* (which is pronounced in different ways depending on the phonological context; for example, it is realized as /s/ as in cat*s*, /z/ as in dog*s*, and /ɪz/ as in horse*s*) to make words plural. In standard English, (but not in all non-standard varieties of English), the morpheme (s) also carries information about **person**, in relation to the subject of a verb (I want, Jane want*s*; he jump*s*, they jump). These second types of morphemes are called **inflectional morphemes**, and the *-ed* of *headed* in the activity above falls into this category.

Morphology also gives us rules for combining free morphemes, that is to say, morphemes which carry meaning in their own right. *Play* and *ground* or *grave* and *yard* are examples of free morphemes which can be combined to form *playground* and *graveyard* respectively. Some writers use this linguistic potential of combining words to create new and sometimes ambiguous meanings. In the following stanza from a poem by E. E. Cummings, the writer creates an adjective *moonly* out of the morphemes *moon* and *-ly*, and a new verb, *unbe*, out of the morphemes *un* and *be* (the *it* refers to *love*):

2   It is most mad and moonly
    and less it shall unbe

> than all the sea which only
> is deeper than the sea.

James Joyce is another writer who experimented with the relationship between morphological structures and meaning in his work, for example, in the following (at first sight rather daunting!) passage from *Finnegans Wake*:

3   What a zeit for the goths! vented the Ondt, who, not being a
     sommerfool, was thothfully making chilly spaces at hisphex
     affront of the icinglass of his windhame, which was cold anti-
     topically Nixnixundnix.

While this may seem like unreadable nonsense on one level, if we focus on analysing the morphological structure of the unfamiliar words, we can perhaps make a little more sense of the extract, and at least have a little linguistic fun in the process.

Much of Joyce's linguistic inventiveness arises from the way he plays with possible combinations of morphemes, not just from English but other languages too. For example, *sommerfool* is made up of two identifiable free morphemes, *sommer* and *fool*, and you may recognize *sommer* as the German word for *summer*. *Thothfully* looks like a mixture of the free morphemes *thought* and *sloth*, combined with the two bound morphemes -*ful* and -*ly*, while *hisphex*, and *windhame* are all possible morphological combinations in English, albeit not familiar words to be found in a dictionary. *Antitopically* is formed from a combination of the morpheme *anti*-, the word *topic* and the bound morpheme -*ally*. The word *cold* can be interpreted as a verb, *called*, because of the similarity in the pronunciation of the two words. Once we have got this far with a morphological analysis, we can then make some further associations on a semantic level. For instance there seem to be 'hot' words (arguably *sommer* and *sloth*) and 'cold' words (*chilly*, *icing*, *cold*), as well as words to do with time and the weather: *summer*, *wind*, *chilly*, *cold* and *zeit*, the German word for time. *Vented* would also fit in this field if we consider that Joyce might be using it as an English word here, as in 'to vent one's anger'; he might also be making a pun with the French word for *wind*, which is *vent*, by turning it into a past tense English verb form with the past tense morpheme -*ed*. In this way, we can begin to appreciate what Joyce is doing with the raw materials of language, and increase our understanding of the text too.

The second level of grammar is the syntactic level. **Syntax**, as we noted above, provides rules for combining words to make sentences. So for instance, we know that we can combine the words *my*, *name*, *is* and *Jordan*, in various possible grammatical ways:

My name is Jordan.
Jordan is my name.
Is my name Jordan?
Is Jordan my name?

but not:

• Is name Jordan my

or

• name Jordan my is

The syntax of English allows us to make any of the first four combinations above, but not the last two. There is a fifth combination:

• Jordan, my name is.

which is arguably slightly more unusual than the others, but which is nevertheless grammatically acceptable as a way of emphasizing, or foregrounding, the name itself by moving it up to the front of the sentence (see section 3.1 above). Similar examples are:

Snowing, it was.
Black, my cat is.

As speakers of English, we recognize these examples as being grammatical or not. If however we want to explain in what way they are grammatical, or in what way they are deviating from a grammatical norm, we need to know more about the different kinds of words that are available in the language, and the possible places where they can occur in a sentence.

3.5 Word classes

There are several different categories or classes of words available in the grammar. The main classes of words that you may already be familiar with in English are:

nouns
verbs
adjectives
adverbs
prepositions

Being able to recognize the class of a word is particularly helpful in stylistic analysis since it will enable you to identify and describe the various structural components in texts. Once you can label these components, you will then be able to identify not only regular ways in which they combine, but also to recognize changes in those patterns and variation between texts. This knowledge will give you some basic analytic tools for describing the relationship between words and phrases in a text (what we call its formal features) and the meaning of that text; for talking about how we read a text and the kind of inferences we might make about what kind of text it is.

3.5.1 Identifying word classes

How do you decide what category a particular word should be assigned to? One way of doing this is to establish what its grammatical form is; in other words, what it is actually doing and where it occurs in a sentence. For example, we know that adverbs typically come after verbs, as in:

Jim typed *slowly*.
The baby cried *loudly*.

The presence of a **determiner** (the, a, an, some etc.), indicates that one of the words following it will be a noun. The noun may occur next to the determiner, i.e. in a structure *the* + *x*, the *x* will probably be a noun. For example:

the *caterpillar*
a *leaf*
some *salami*

It may however be separated from the determiner by some other words, typically adjectives, as in:

the *furry* caterpillar
a *wrinkled brown* leaf
some *disgusting* salami

One way to find out which is the noun is to see which one is essential and 'belongs' with the determiner; e.g. you can say *the caterpillar* but not *the furry*, and *a leaf* but not *a wrinkled brown*; *some salami* but not *some disgusting*.

Another characteristic of nouns is that they can also be inflected for number by adding the plural morpheme *-s*, pronounced in this example as /z/:

Ten furry caterpillars

However (confusingly!), words don't always stay in a particular class and depending on their position in a sentence, can sometimes change their syntactic category. We can experiment with this idea by taking a sentence and substituting other possible words in a particular slot, and see what happens. In the following headline, two words are being used in classes other than the ones someone writing a grammar book might assign them to:

Six questioned over 'plot to make weapon deals with criminals'.

Six is usually described as a particular kind of adjective, called a *numeral* in grammar books, and its position in a sentence is often before a noun: *six EGGS*; *six PRINCESSES*; *six very fat and happy KITTENS* (the nouns in these phrases are in upper case). In other words, we usually need to know six *what* are being talked about. However, in the headline, the word *six* is not behaving like a numeral, but more like a noun (similar examples are *The Birmingham Six, The Guildford Four*). We have to infer that *six* refers to six people, rather than six eggs, princesses or kittens.

The word *weapon* on the other hand, from our experience, usually belongs to the noun class, as in *the weapon*; *three weapons*; *the dangerous weapon* (i.e. the determiner *the* can be put in front of *weapon*; it can be made plural by adding an -*s* morpheme, and an adjective, such as *dangerous*, can be inserted between *the* and *weapon*). However, in this example it **modifies** the word *deal*. In other words it tells us what kind of deal was made: a *weapon* deal rather than a *fair* deal or a *dirty* deal, so it is syntactically doing the work of an adjective in this case. Thus both the words *six* and *weapon* are being used in categories other than the ones they might usually be expected to belong to. This is actually a very common linguistic feature of newspaper headlines, and is due to constraints on space and the need to provide a succinct, often eye-catching, lead to a news story (see chapter 7 for more on the use of language in headline texts).

To summarize the point we have been making here: as these examples show, words may look as if they belong in one grammatical category, like noun or verb or adjective, but in practice can change categories when they are shifted around to occupy different structural positions in sentences. This means that we can call a word a noun, or a verb, or an adjective, but it is the position it occupies in the sentence which really counts. Another extract from the poem by e. e. cummings we quoted from above illustrates how writers exploit these categories. What grammatical categories do you think the words *always* and *never* belong to in these lines?

4   love is less always than to win
     less never than alive

Always and *never* are usually categorized as **temporal adverbs**, i.e. they provide further information about the time something happens. In these lines however they are used where you would expect to find an adjective of some kind, as in *less complicated*, or *less wonderful*.

We can illustrate this further with a poem by Dylan Thomas called 'Do not go gentle into that good night'. In this title line, there are some words which in standard English usage would not normally occur in the place that they occur here. First of all, think about what kind of word *go* is.

Once you have identified it (it is a verb), make a list of the words which you would most likely expect to find immediately after this word.

You probably have words like *slowly, carefully, quickly* or *quietly*. These are **adverbs**, and one of the slots that adverbs can occupy in a sentence is the slot immediately after a verb. You can test this out with other verbs:

She slept deeply
He ate hungrily
She screamed loudly

In the Dylan Thomas poem, the phrase *go gentle* would usually be *go gently*. The poet has used an adjective in this particular slot in the sentence instead of an adverb. He also uses another adjective, *good*, in an unusual way in this line. What are the kinds of adjectives you would usually use to describe the noun *night*? *Dark, scary, moonlit* or *frosty* spring to mind, but probably not *good*, except within the context of a farewell. So in this line we have two unusual combinations of words that would not occur in standard English usage.

To recap, we have the (grammatically) unusual combination of the words *go* and *gentle*, and the combination of *good* and *night*, which is (semantically) odd in this particular context. When patterns of word combinations are disrupted in this way, the effect is often to make the language seem more literary, and the meaning appear more subtle and more complex. If we were to read this poem in depth, we might want to look closely at how Dylan Thomas is using adjectives in combination with other types of words to create a literary effect, or achieve a particular meaning.

It should also be noted that in many non-standard varieties of English, it is quite normal to use the same form for both adjectives and adverbs, as in *drive careful*, or *run quick*. For more information on the grammar of English **dialects**, you could look at *Real English* by James Milroy and Lesley Milroy (1993).

Not all types of word class can be manipulated in this way, however, and in the following section, we will describe the different types of word classes, and what writers can do with them, in more detail.

3.5.2 Open and closed class words

As we have mentioned before, native speakers of a language have grammatical knowledge which enables them to distinguish between possible combinations of words in a sentence, and impossible combinations, even when the words themselves are unfamiliar. We can illustrate how this knowledge works by using the following sentence (found in language classes everywhere!) from Lewis Carroll's poem 'Jabberwocky':

5   Twas brillig and the slithy toves
      Did gyre and gimble in the wabe.

Here, we recognize that *wabe* is a noun because it is preceded by a determiner, *the*. As we have seen, our knowledge of English grammar tells us that in any structure made up of *the* + *x*, *x* will be a noun. Similarly, we recognize *the slithy toves* as having the structure of determiner + adjective + noun, because of the positions of the words in relation to each other: *The* comes first, *toves* comes last, and *slithy* is between the two, so this fits our knowledge of similar combinations such as *the slimy toves* or *the muddy toves*. The fact that *toves* also carries the inflectional plural morpheme *-s* indicates that it is a noun, while *slithy* carries the adjectival morpheme *y*.

Our native speaker knowledge also allows us to recognize *gyre* and *gimble* as verbs. One structural feature that enables us to do this is the presence of the word *did*, as in similar structures like *they did run*, or *they did jump*, which marks these verbs for past tense. We know that in the structure *x* + *did* + *y*, whatever goes in the *y* slot will probably be some form of verb, so *gyre* and *gimble* belong to the same class of word as *run* and *jump*. Other ways of recognizing verbs is that they carry inflectional morphemes like *-ed* and *-ing*. So if we see the words *the toves gimbled* or *the toves were gyring* then again, we would know that *gimbled* and *gyring* were verbs.

ACTIVITY 3.1 ━━━━━━━━━━━━━━━━━━━━━━━━━━━━━━━━━

Using the same procedure as we have done above for *wabe*, *slithy toves* and *gyre and gimble*, can you identify the word class of *brillig* in the same extract?

You may have noticed that in both this example and the extract from *Finnegans Wake* above, only certain types of words have been experimented with. The class of words that writers can use to experiment with in this way are **open class** words, or those that carry semantic meaning. Writers tend not to interfere with the structural words that we have used to identify the open class words, such as *the* and *did*. This is because they carry important grammatical information, and if writers did not put them in their usual position in a sentence, it would become practically impossible to interpret their texts at all. These kinds of words, which include determiners, prepositions (i.e. words like *up* and *under*), and conjunctions, (i.e. words like *and*, *but* and *because*) are called **closed class** words.

Similarly, it is the derivational morphemes that writers use creatively, rather than the inflectional morphemes which carry grammatical information about tense and number. If we go back to the James Joyce example again, we can see that the grammatical structure of the sentence is maintained through the occurrence of closed class words like *the*, *who*, *at*, *of* and *which*, and structures like *was -ing*, whereas the deviation occurs in the open class words: nouns, adjectives and adverbs.

ACTIVITY 3.2

The following is a poem by Fleur Adcock. Make a list of all the words that you can clearly assign to the category of nouns, verbs, adverbs and adjectives. What are the words you have left over, and how would you try to classify them?

6   *Immigrant*

> November '63: eight months in London.
> I pause on the low bridge to watch the pelicans:
> they float swanlike, arching their white necks
> over only slightly ruffled bundles of wings,
> burying awkward beaks in the lake's water.
> I clench cold fists in my Marks and Spencer's jacket
> and secretly test my accent once again:
> St James's Park: St James's Park: St James's Park.

3.6 Describing noun and verb phrases

In the section above we have given you some ideas about how to categorize words into classes, and how to distinguish between open and closed class words. In the following section we will look at how nouns and verbs can form part of larger units called **noun phrases** and **verb phrases**, before moving on to describe how they can combine to form sentences.

3.6.1 The noun phrase

A basic definition of a noun is that it is a word that refers to something in the world, which can be concrete, like *table* or *house*, or abstract like *love* or *idea*, or a person, like *John Lennon*. Often we need to do more than just refer to something by name, we need to qualify it or differentiate it from other similar things. We can do this by making it more specific, or more elaborate, through a process called **modification**. Nouns are often preceded by a determiner such as *the* (see section 3.5.1 above). They can be premodified further by adding some information before the main noun itself. They can also be postmodified, by adding information after the noun. Look at the following examples: the main noun (often referred to in grammar books as the head noun) in each one is *stick*, and the extra information is in upper case.

> stick
> THE stick
> THE OLD stick
> THE stick WITH THE IVORY HANDLE
> THE stick THAT BELONGS TO MY GRANDMOTHER

All the examples above are known grammatically as **noun phrases**. They can be premodified by an adjective, such as *old*, by a prepositional phrase (i.e. a phrase that begins with a preposition) such as *with the ivory handle*, and by a whole new clause such as *that belongs to my grandmother* (we will discuss clauses in more detail in section 3.7 below). We can even put all these pre- and post-modifying elements together to make a very long noun phrase:

THE OLD stick WITH THE IVORY HANDLE THAT BELONGS
TO MY GRANDMOTHER

You may well be able to think of further modifications to make it longer still!

Noun phrases can refer very explicitly to a person or thing by name (John Lennon, Buckingham Palace) or much less explicitly, in the form of a pronoun (he, it) where the information about who 'he', or what 'it' is, is given earlier or sometimes later on in the text. In spoken language, this information is often recovered from the context of an utterance, rather than from the surrounding text. For instance,

It's got an ivory handle

means very little if you don't know what it refers to (these referring words that derive their meaning from the context they are used in are called **deictic** expressions, and we will discuss them more fully in chapter 4).

ACTIVITY 3.3

The passage below contains a high proportion of various types of noun phrases. How many of them can you identify, and which is the 'head' noun in each one?

7   A succession of hands, dry, cold, moist, reluctant or firm clasped his. Grace Willison, the middle-aged spinster, a study in grey; skin, hair, dress, stockings, all of them slightly dingy so that she looked like an old-fashioned, stiffly jointed doll neglected too long in a dusty cupboard.

3.6.2 The verb phrase

Verbs are very complex grammatical entities. One way of describing a verb is as a type of word that enables you to say something about the subject of the sentence. Verbs are sometimes referred to as 'doing' words, but this is misleading as many verbs have no relation to 'doing' anything at all! In the following examples, only two verbs, *eat* and *drive*, could be said to describe an action of some sort:

> John EATS oranges.
> Jan's house IS at the end of the street.
> That red car BELONGS to my mother.
> Susan's idea TURNED OUT to be a disaster.
> He DRIVES to work every day.

The verb forms *is*, *belong* and *turn out* describe a state, or attribute, rather than an action. For more on categories of verbs, see Halliday (1967).

A **verb phrase** can contain different kinds of grammatical information. Firstly, the **lexical verb** carries the meaning content, which in the above examples are respectively *eat*, *be*, *belong*, *turn out* and *drive*. Within the verb phrase there is also information about **tense** (past and present). In the above examples, *drives* is a present tense verb form (marked by the -*s* morpheme), while *turned out* is a past tense form (marked by the -*ed* morpheme). Verb phrases can also carry information about **mood** (or modality). This is the category of grammar that gives us information about a speaker's attitude towards their utterance. Modality can convey degrees of possibility, certainty or doubt, as well as information about obligation, permission or suggestion. We can change the modality of *John eats oranges* by adding modal words like *should*, *can't* and *won't*, each of which gives us more information about John and the oranges, contained within the verb phrase:

> John should eat oranges (i.e. they are good for him)
> John can't eat oranges (i.e. they are bad for him)
> John won't eat oranges (i.e. he doesn't like them)

Verb phrases can also give us information about **aspect**; this is the category of grammar that indicates whether an action or state of affairs is completed or not, for example:

> I'm watching EastEnders (the activity is not yet complete)
> I watched EastEnders last night (the activity is over and complete)

For more information on tense, aspect and mood in English sentences, see Palmer (1979) and Coates (1983).

Can you identify the lexical verb in each of the following sentences? The first one is capitalized for you:

> Six North Africans were PLAYing boule beneath Flaubert's statue.
> We should buy her some flowers.
> It was an uncertain spring.
> Versace has come up with a feisty new fragrance.
> I've been to London.

The other lexical verbs are *buy*, *was*, *come up with* and *been*. You will notice that in the case of *was*, the lexical verb is also inflected for the past tense. The other elements in the verb phrase which carry information about tense, mood and aspect are called **auxiliary verbs**. In the above sentences, the auxiliaries are *were*, *should*, *has*, and *'ve* (a contraction of *have*) – can you say what kind of extra information they are providing in these verb phrases?

3.6.3 Non-finite verb phrases

So far, the verb phrases we have been discussing have all carried information about tense, modality, and aspect. These are called **finite verb phrases**, because they contain a finite, main verb. There is another category of verbs, called **non-finite verbs**, which do not carry this kind of information. These verbs can be in the form of an infinitive, as in *TO see*, *TO boldly go*; a gerundive, as in *seeING*, *boldly goING*, or a past participle, as in *as SEEN on TV*.

In the extract below, the first sentence contains examples of both a finite and a non-finite verb phrase:

8   He *stood* at the hall door *turning* the ring, turning the heavy signet ring upon his little finger while his glance travelled coolly, deliberately, over the round tables and basket chairs scattered about the glassed-in veranda. He pursed his lips – he might have been going to whistle – but he did not whistle – only turned the ring – turned the ring on his pink, freshly washed hands.

The first verb phrase, *stood* is finite, (i.e. it is marked for tense; the action described happened in the past). The second one, *turning*, is non-finite (i.e. it carries within it no information about when it happened). Non-finite verb phrases do particular kinds of work in a sentence; for example, they are often used as post-modifiers of noun phrases and thus could be said to have more in common with adjective phrases than they do with other kinds of verbs. An example of this kind of non-finite verb phrase in the above extract is *scattered*, which gives us more information about the *round tables and basket chairs*.

ACTIVITY 3.4

Read extract 8 again, and underline all the verb phrases. Can you differentiate between the finite and non-finite verb phrases? What kind of criteria have you used to make your distinction?

In the passage below, (which you have already encountered in section 3.3) Angela Carter uses a series of non-finite verb phrases in an unusual way:

9 You spent your childhood on the road, here today, gone tomorrow; you grew up a restless man. You loved change. And fornication. And trouble. And, funnily enough, towards the end, you loved butterflies. Peregrine Hazard, lost among the butterflies, lost in the jungle, vanished away as neatly and completely as if you had become the object of one of those conjuring tricks you were so fond of.

If we look closely at the way *vanished* is used in this sentence, we can see that it occurs as the third element of a sequence of non-finite verb phrases, consisting of the past participle of the verb *lose*, which are used to post-modify the head noun phrase *Peregrine Hazard*:

Peregrine Hazard	lost among the butterflies
	lost in the jungle
	vanished away

So if *vanished* is to fit into the pattern which has been established by the first two elements of the sequence we can read it as a non-finite verb. However, it could also be interpreted as a finite verb if we analyse the sentence structure as follows:

Peregrine Hazard vanished away

which can be read as a complete sentence with *vanished* as the main verb.

This would probably have been the most likely interpretation if *vanished* had not occurred as the third part of a descriptive sequence of non-finite verb phrases. As it is, there does not seem to be a main verb here at all, which makes this sentence ungrammatical in the normal sense. The sentence is further complicated by a change in the noun which is the **subject** of this sentence (for more on subjects, see 3.6 below), which changes from third person *Peregrine Hazard* (which might be replaced with the pronoun *he*) to second person *you*. This again produces an unusual sentence structure, as the writer shifts from using direct address to her character:

you loved change
you grew up a restless man

to referring to him in the third person:

Peregrine Hazard, lost among the butterflies

These changes in the formal structure of the sentence seem to signal a change in the register of the text at this point. The change is from personal memory to the kind of language associated with another form of remembrance – that found in tombstone inscriptions, where a dead person is identified by name, followed by some information regarding how they died (if appropriate), such as *lost at sea*.

Just by looking at one short piece of text, we can see how writers explore and exploit the categories and structures available in the grammar of English to produce particular effects, and we have used our knowledge of how sentences usually work in English as a basis for describing what is unusual and different about this text in terms of its grammatical structure. To conclude this section on verb phrases, try the following activity:

ACTIVITY 3.5 _____

The text below contains a wide variety of verb forms. First of all, underline all the verb phrases in this extract. Now decide which of them contain main verbs (i.e. are finite verb phrases) and which are the non-finite verb phrases. Lastly, what could you say about how the non-finite verbs are being used in this text?

10   Mumtaz Aziz began to lead a double life. By day she was a single girl, living chastely with her parents, studying mediocrely at the university, cultivating those gifts of assiduity, nobility and forbearance which were to be her hallmarks throughout her life, up to and including the time when she was assailed by the talking washing chests of her past and then squashed flat as a rice pancake; but at night, descending through a trap door, she entered a lamplit secluded marriage chamber which her secret husband had taken to calling the Taj Mahal, because Taj Bibi was the name by which people had called an earlier Mumtaz – Mumtaz Mahal, wife of Emperor Shah Jehan, whose name meant 'king of the world'.

In this section we have begun to describe what verbs do in a sentence, and distinguished between finite and non-finite verb phrases. There is of course much more to say about what verbs can do, and the various types of verbs that exist, so we suggest further reading on this at the end of the chapter. In the final section, we will deal with how noun phrases and verb phrases can be combined to form sentences.

3.7 Describing sentences

First of all we need to point out that a **sentence** is primarily a unit of written language. People do not speak in sentences but in **utterances** which may or may not be formed by what we generally think of as a 'complete' grammatical sentence. A grammatical sentence usually consists of a **subject** and a **predicate**. The subject is the noun phrase which starts the sentence, and the predicate is everything that comes after it. So in the sentence:

John eats oranges

the subject is *John*, and the predicate is *eats oranges*. In the following sentences the subject is on the left, and the predicate on the right:

The train	/	was late
Chocolate	/	is good for you
It	/	snowed in the morning

There are many different types of sentences, as we will see shortly, but most sentences will always contain at least one unit of subject and predicate, and this unit is called a **clause**. Can you identify the subject and predicate in the following sentences?

Six North Africans were playing boule beneath Flaubert's statue.
We'll visit your relatives for you for a small fee.
It was an uncertain spring.
Versace has come up with a feisty new fragrance.
I've been to London.

The subject in each of these sentences is respectively: *six North Africans*, *we*, *it*, *Versace* and *I*. The predicate in each sentence is everything to the right of these words, including the contracted forms of *will* (*'ll*) in *we'll* and have (*'ve*) in *I've*.

3.7.1 Simple and complex sentences

Sentences can be of several types. A simple sentence is one which consists of a single clause, like the ones above. Clauses can also be joined together to form complex sentences. There are various ways of combining clauses, and we discuss some of these below.

Firstly, a coordinated sentence is one which consists of two or more clauses joined by a conjunction like *and* or *but*, as in the examples below:

John eats oranges BUT he won't touch bananas
(2 clauses)

John eats oranges BUT he won't touch bananas AND apples are out of the question
(3 clauses)

ACTIVITY 3.6 ━━━━━━━━━━━━━━━━━━━━

The following extract from a short story by Ernest Hemingway contains mainly simple sentences. Can you identify the subject and predicate in each one?

11 The king was working in the garden. He seemed very glad to see me. We walked through the garden. 'This is the queen,' he said. She was clipping a rose bush. 'Oh, how do you do,' she said. We sat down at a table under a big tree and the king ordered whisky and soda.

Another way of combining clauses is through a subordinate (rather than a coordinate) relationship. In this kind of relationship, the link between the clauses in the sentence is rather different. To explain this further, using the Hemingway example again, the two clauses which are joined by 'and' in this coordinated sentence both form a complete sentence on their own:

We sat down at a table under a big tree.
The king ordered whisky and soda.

Now look at the following complex sentence from a short story by Kate Chopin:

12 As the day was pleasant, Madame Valmonde drove over to L'Abri to see Desiree and the baby.

The two clauses in this sentence are:

As the day was pleasant
Madame Valmonde drove over to L'Abri to see Desiree and the baby.

What is the difference between these two clauses and those in the Hemingway example? The main grammatical difference is that the first clause, *as the day was pleasant*, cannot occur on its own. It is incomplete until it is attached to the second part of the sentence. This type of clause is called a **subordinate clause**, and the relationship between the two parts of this sentence is established by the subordinating conjunction *as*. This word not only links the two clauses, but it defines the nature of that link. In this example, the conjunction *as* produces a causal link between these two clauses. There are many other types of words that can function to link clauses in this way. Can you identify the subordinate clauses in the following sentences? What sort of link they do they have with the main clause?

> When I get home I'll cook the supper.
> Helen was wearing red, which had always been her favourite colour.
> If you can't stand the heat, you should get a fire extinguisher.

In the first example, the subordinate clause is *when I get home*, and the link between the two clauses is temporal, established by the conjunction *when*. The subordinate clause in the second sentence is called a **relative clause**. Relative clauses are often linked to the main clause by a relative pronoun such as *who*, *which* or *that*, and typically give more information about some element of the main clause (in this case, the red colour of the dress). In the final example, the relationship between the two clauses is conditional, where the conjunction *if* establishes the link between two states of affairs. Written, as opposed to spoken, language frequently consists of long strings of complex sentences made up of embedded subordinate clauses of this type.

ACTIVITY 3.7

The following sentences are both complex, and contain one subordinate clause. First of all identify the clauses, then decide what you think the link between them is.

13   Miss Brooke had that kind of beauty which seemed to be thrown into relief by poor dress.

14   In Devonshire where the round red hills and steep valleys
     hoarded the sea air leaves were still thick on the trees.

One of the problems with written language is that sentences
sometimes get so packed with subordinate clauses that it becomes
very difficult to work out the links between them. Consider this
example taken from the introduction of a student's essay:

> This project is based on the language used by first generation
> Jamaicans who have been living in the UK since the 1950s.
> Given that they are first generation Jamaican as opposed to
> their children who may have been born in England their speech
> will be explored to see whether there is a constant use of
> Jamaican Creole or if there are any other influences such as
> London Jamaican a term used by Mark Sebba which describes
> how young people some of whom are not of Jamaican descent
> use a linguistic variety which is in part similar to Jamaican
> Creole as well as being the English which is spoken by White
> London contemporaries.

ACTIVITY 3.8

How would you break the paragraph above into more manageable
'chunks' of clauses if you had to rewrite it?

You would probably need to leave the first sentence as it is,
then proceed to separate the rest into shorter sentences with fewer
clauses in each one. Our rewritten version is in the suggested answers
to activities at the end of the book.

In certain areas of language use, a high number of embedded
relative clauses is a prominent stylistic feature. Legal documents
are an example of one such area, where the extensive use of relative
clauses can lead to problems of interpretation, particularly for
non-specialists.

So far in this section we have analysed the structure of

sentences in terms of their basic units of subject and predicate, which make up a clause. The subject is typically (though not always) a noun phrase of some kind, and the predicate is everything that follows, (minimally a verb phrase). We have also looked at how these clauses combine in different ways to form simple and complex sentences, and we have briefly outlined the difference between the grammatical relationships of coordination and sub-ordination.

3.8 Foregrounding and grammatical form

Throughout this chapter we have been dealing with some of the fundamental grammatical categories and structures of English, and exploring some of the ways that these can be used in an analysis of what makes language 'literary'. We have also discussed the concepts of 'normal' and 'deviant' use of language in relation to levels of liter-ariness, and how these may correspond to unmarked and marked grammatical forms. What seems to distinguish literary from non-literary usage may be the extent to which the grammatical structure of a sentence is salient, or **foregrounded** in some way, to use another of Mukařowský's terms (see section 3.1). Consider the following examples, both of which describe inner city decay. The first is from the *Observer*, (29 November 1995):

> The 1960s dream of high rise living soon turned into a
> nightmare.

In this sentence, there is nothing grammatically unusual or 'deviant' in the way the words of the sentence are put together.

However, in the following verse from a poem, the grammatical structure seems to be much more challenging, and makes more demands on our interpretive processing of these lines:

15 1 Four storeys have no windows left to smash,
   2 but in the fifth a chipped sill buttresses
   3 mother and daughter the last mistresses
   4 of that black block condemned to stand, not
      crash.

The sentence in line 2 of this verse that starts *but in the fifth* ... is unusual in that the predicate of the sentence is made up of a sequence of embedded elements, as we can see if we write them out in a full form:

> a chipped sill buttresses mother and daughter
> who are the last mistresses of that black block
> which is condemned to stand, not crash.

Furthermore, the main verb in this sentence is *buttress*. This word can be either a noun or a verb, but we would argue that it is more likely to occur as a noun in less literary contexts.

In literary texts, the grammatical system of the language is often exploited, experimented with, or in Mukařowský's words, made to 'deviate' from other, more everyday, forms of language, and as a result creates interesting new patterns in form and in meaning. One way that this happens is through use of non-conventional structures that seem to break the rules of grammar. In the following extract, what is the rule that has been broken in the first sentence?

16 The red-haired woman, smiling, waving to the disappearing shore. She left the maharajah; she left innumerable other lights o' passing love in towns and cities and theatres and railway stations all over the world. But Melchior she did not leave.

We have seen that sentences normally consist of a subject and a predicate, and that the predicate normally contains a verb phrase. However, the first sentence here contains no main finite verb, and therefore should not occur as an independent unit, but looks as though it should be linked to another clause. Yet here it does occur on its own.

Another way in which literary language can deviate from other kinds of language use is by disrupting the usual order of words in a sentence. We can illustrate this by looking at an extract from Shakespeare's *Richard II*, which contains some sentences which could be described as having normal syntactic structure (according to modern usage), and some which definitely could not!

17 GREEN: 1 Well, I will for refuge straight to Bristol Castle.
            2 The Earl of Wiltshire is already there.

BUSHY:	3	Thither will I with you; for little office
	4	Will the hateful commoners perform for us,
	5	Except like curs to tear us all to pieces.
	6	Will you go along with us?
BAGOT:	7	No I will to Ireland, to his majesty.
	8	Farewell: if heart's presages be not vain
	9	We three here part that ne'er shall meet again.

We can quite easily identify the lines which follow the usual structural pattern: these are 2 and 6. The others, lines 1, 3, 4, 5, 8 and 9, all contain some disruption to normal syntactic organization, while line 7 follows the normal structure, but like 1 and 3, seems to be missing the main lexical verb (see section 3.5 above). We can show how this disruption occurs by rewriting these lines in a different way, according to the rules of modern English syntax, as follows:

1   Well, I will for refuge straight to Bristol Castle.
     Well, I will (go) straight to Bristol Castle for refuge.

3   Thither will I with you; for little office
4   Will the hateful commoners perform for us,
5   Except like curs to tear us all to pieces.
     I will (go) thither with you, for the hateful commoners will perform little office for us except to tear us all to pieces like curs.

8   Farewell: if heart's presages be not vain
9   We three here part that ne'er shall meet again.
     Farewell, if heart's presages be not vain, we three part here that shall ne'er meet again.

Although there is clearly still some of the 'literariness' left in these rewritten versions, this is due mainly to the **register** of some of the words, e.g. *thither*, *farewell*, *presages* (for more on register, see chapter 4), and to the use of verb forms which are now archaic in most dialects of English, such as the *be* form instead of *are* in the conditional clause which starts *if heart's presages be not vain*. What we have done is to move certain parts of the sentences around to make them sound more like ordinary, modern English, and we can do this because we recognize the ways in which these lines from

Richard II are deviating from what can be considered as the normal syntactic pattern. For example, we know that *like curs* in line 5 should usually come at the end of the sentence rather than right near the beginning, before *to tear us all to pieces*. We also know that *we three here part* should be *we three part here* and that *ne'er shall* would ordinarily be *shall never*. In grammatical terms, we can say that the adverbial *here* usually comes at the end of a clause, as in:

we'll leave you here
we stop here
we can have lunch here

and we can also say that the negative particle *never* (or *ne'er* in this case) usually comes after the auxiliary verb, as in:

I shall never see you again

So from these examples, we can see how the 'literariness' of language doesn't just depend on the type of words used (i.e. on the register) but also on the arrangement of those words into sentences.

It is not only in poetry or dramatic texts that words get moved around to make different patterns in sentences. Fictional texts also frequently contain unusual grammatical patterns, as we can see by looking again at the extract from *Wise Children*:

The red-haired woman, smiling, waving to the disappearing shore. She left the maharajah; she left innumerable other lights o' passing love in towns and cities and theatres and railway stations all over the world. But Melchior she did not leave.

In this extract, Carter not only has a sentence without a main verb in it, she also uses a marked syntactic structure in the final one:

But Melchior she did not leave

You may recall this structure from the discussion in section 3.1 above, where we pointed out that it was rather more marked than the more usual word order for English sentences, which is *S*ubject, followed by the main *V*erb, followed by the *O*bject (often referred to as *SVO*). By placing the direct object (Melchior) before the subject and main verb here (she did not leave), Carter produces a structural contrast between this and the previous two clauses which reinforces the contrast in meaning:

> she left the Maharajah
> she left innumerable other lights o' passing love
> Melchior she did not leave

3.9 Analysis of grammar: checklist

In this chapter we have been looking at some of the basic grammatical components of English, and describing how these combine to make sentences, both simple and complex. We have also introduced the linguistic units of noun phrases and verb phrases, and suggested some ways in which a grammatical analysis of literary language can enhance our understanding of a text and our pleasure in reading.

After reading this chapter, there are various ways that you should be able to approach the analysis of grammatical structures in literary texts, both poetry and prose. Depending on the kind of text you are dealing with, some of the following procedures may be appropriate:

- where there seems to be foregrounding on the level of lexis, you can use morphological analysis to look at new combinations of words.
- where there is foregrounding on the level of word order and syntax, you can use your knowledge of word classes (i.e. nouns, verbs, adjectives etc.) to analyse unusual or 'marked' combinations.
- again on the grammatical level, you can look for combinations and patterns in the use of different types of phrases: noun phrases and verb phrases which may contribute to a more literary usage of language, as well as analysing the structure of sentences.
- in all cases, you should find that being aware of the systems of the language, the rules which govern the combination of a range of grammatical elements, will make it possible for you to identify the more 'deviant', 'marked' or literary structures, from more 'everyday', non-literary usage of language, and thus be able to say more about the structural patterning in a text.

Suggestions for further reading

Our discussion of the grammar of English has of necessity been limited, and sometimes over simplified. This is a vast area, and we suggest that for further information about syntax, phrase structure and morphology, you refer to the following texts:

Graddol, David, Jenny Cheshire and Joan Swann (1994) (2nd edn) *Describing Language*, Buckingham: Oxford University Press.

Kuiper, Koenran and W. Scott Allan (1996) *An Introduction to English Language*, London: Macmillan Press.

Milroy, James and Lesley Milroy (eds) (1993) *Real English*, London: Longman.

Quirk, Randolph and Sidney Greenbaum (1973) *A University Grammar of English*, Harlow: Longman.

Wardaugh, Ronald (1995) *Understanding English Grammar: A Linguistic Approach*, Oxford: Basil Blackwell.

Finally, a word of warning: when you are working with constructed examples, as grammarians frequently do, you can usually make things fit neatly into the categories they are supposed to go into. When you are using examples from real data (as you will have seen from working through some of the activities in this chapter), matters are not always so clear cut, although as a result, it could be argued, much more interesting!

Meaning

4.1 Introduction

Most of us cannot remember a time before we could communicate our meanings to others, or before we could understand others' meanings when they talked to us, but despite this the concept of 'meaning' is surprisingly difficult to define or explain. It has been approached from many very different angles by linguists, by literary theorists and by philosophers. Theories of meaning can be very complex, and are often hotly disputed: entire books are written proposing certain hypotheses and discrediting others.

If meaning is complicated in language which is primarily concerned with transmitting information or establishing social relations (writing in a scientific journal, or greeting a friend, for example) then it is inevitably going to be very complicated in literary uses of language, where writers may deliberately explore the edges of possible meanings in a language and try to push them a bit further to see what kind of effect they can get. In this chapter, we will first consider some of the different ways linguists have thought about meaning. We will then look at some of the ways of creating meaning which have been exploited in literature, though these are far from being unique to literary texts.

4.2 Semantics

When we want to know the meaning of an unfamiliar word, we look it up in the dictionary. Discussions of meaning at the level of single words usually come under the scope of **semantics**, the study of word meaning. Semantics considers how the meanings of words in a language relate to each other: the system of meanings into which words fit and by taking their place in the system, acquire their meanings.

For example, semantics is concerned with the relationships between words such as between the words in the sequence *pool – lake*

– *sea* – *ocean* or in *village* – *town* – *city*. A town is smaller than a city but bigger than a village, and so the word *town* occupies the 'semantic space' between the words *village* and *city*. *Village, town* and *city* have a semantic relationship, in which, at least to some extent, the meaning of each word depends on the meanings of the other two words. This way of thinking about language sees it like a patchwork quilt, where every little separate patch – or word – fits in with every other patch exactly, with no gaps between the patches and with no overlaps, each patch – or word – taking up its own space and no more or less, all fitting together to make the overall pattern. This can be a useful way to start thinking about meaning in language, but it is easy to think of aspects of word meaning to which the patchwork quilt model of language cannot apply.

4.2.1 Gaps and overlaps

For one thing, there actually *are* overlaps and gaps in word meanings. Gaps in meaning can be difficult to identify, but that does not mean that they do not exist. If you know another language well, you will soon realize that there are some words other languages have that English has no equivalent for, and vice versa. German, for example, has the word *Schadenfreude*, which means getting pleasure from someone else's misfortune, and although the idea can easily be expressed in English (as has just been done), there is no single English word that has the same meaning, i.e. there is a gap (sometimes called a **lexical gap**) in English where German has the word *Schadenfreude*. For the most part, however, we are unaware that our language has meaning gaps in it.

In a science fiction novel by Suzette Haden Elgin, *Native Tongue*, women in a futuristic society make up their own language to fill in the gaps in the existing language, which represents masculine, rather than feminine values. The new meanings for which they invent words include *wonewith*: 'to be socially dyslexic; uncomprehending of the social signals of others', *ramimelh*: 'to refrain from asking, with evil intent, especially when it is clear that someone badly wants the other to ask'; and *radiidin*: 'non-holiday, a time allegedly a holiday but actually so much a burden because of work and preparations that it is a dreaded occasion; especially when there are too many guests and none of them help'. These meanings cannot be expressed in English using just one word! Having a word for a concept means speakers of that language are more likely to acknowledge the possible existence of whatever the word refers to. In the case of these invented words, attention is drawn to the experiences and perspectives of women in the novel, and the fictional society they inhabit in fact changes as a result of this recognition.

ACTIVITY 4.1

Gender is a notorious area in English for what are called **asymmetries** in the lexis, i.e. there are often words to describe women that do not have an equivalent which can be used to describe men, and vice versa. However, language does change, and sometimes different groups of people use language in different ways, so some of these 'gaps' may be filling up, or disappearing as words change their meanings. Can you think of English words to fill the following lexical gaps, or are there 'holes' in the language at these points?

- a female equivalent of *emasculate*
- a female equivalent of *virile*
- a male equivalent of *nymphomaniac*
- an insult for a woman that is the equivalent of calling a man an 'old woman'
- a description of a boy who has some feminine attributes that has equivalent connotations to 'tomboy'

Overlaps in meaning are much easier to identify: *teenager* and *adolescent* overlap in meaning; so do *cash* and *money*, and *watched* and *observed*. In these cases we appear to have at least two words with very similar meanings – pairs of words like these are called **synonyms**.

However, complete synonymy is actually very infrequent – even if words appear to have the same meaning in some contexts. You can equally well *watch the grass growing* and *observe the grass growing*, but while you might have *observed three statues in the corner* you are less likely to have *watched three statues in the corner*, unless you thought the statues were about to move or that someone was hiding behind them. The verb *to watch* seems to be applied more to moving or changing things than to stationary things, while the verb *to observe* applies equally well to stationary objects as to moving or changing objects.

Although we have been concerned to show that language is not just a patchwork quilt of interlocking meanings because gaps and overlaps do occur, it is still worthwhile looking at the structural relationships between word meanings.

4.2.2 Opposites

Some words have opposites (or **antonyms**, their formal name) in English: *go* and *stop*, *single* and *married*, *alive* and *dead*. What is interesting about these particular opposites is that they are mutually exclusive – i.e. they are absolute opposites. If you have *stopped* you cannot be *going* at the same time. You could say 'that married man is nice' but 'that married man is single' is a contradiction, and would only be said in relatively unusual circumstances. Someone might still say it if there had been a misunderstanding, for example; perhaps if the person addressed had assumed the man in question to be married, but the speaker actually knew that he wasn't.

Not all words are absolute opposites though. *Old* for example is not the absolute opposite of *young*, since someone who is thirty years of age may be 'young' to someone of seventy, but 'old' to someone of seven. These are known as comparative opposites.

For some purposes, you might deliberately want to exploit the contradiction of two opposites; for example, the possibility of being happy and sad at the same time. In Shakespeare's play, *Romeo and Juliet*, Romeo responds to the feud between his family and Juliet's with contradictions:

1   Here's much to do with hate, but more with love.
    Why then, O brawling love! O loving hate!
    Of anything of nothing first create!
    O heavy lightness! Serious vanity!
    Mis-shapen chaos of well-seeming forms!
    Feather of lead, bright smoke, cold fire, sick health!
    Still-waking sleep, that is not what it is!

Romeo's speech brings together contradictions – *lightness* that is *heavy*, *health* that is *sick*, *sleep* that is *waking*. One purpose the speech might have within the play is to draw attention to the irony that love between family members can bring about fighting and bloodshed between families. It is also a kind of prophecy of what will happen later in the play. The love between Romeo and Juliet will bring them great joy and great sorrow. Juliet will take a drug that will make her appear dead but from which she will wake. The combination of contradictory words or images is a well-established device in literature known as an **oxymoron**.

4.2.3 Hyponyms and superordinates

Other important relationships between words, other than opposites and synonyms, are classificatory relationships. For example, if someone asks you *would you like a drink?* in order to respond you would need to establish what kind of drink was on offer as well as what kind you wanted. The type of drink on offer is often signalled by the context. In a pub or at a party *would you like a drink?* is likely, at least in Britain, to be taken to refer to an alcoholic drink. In a café it is more likely to be taken to refer to a hot, non-alcoholic drink. On a beach beside an ice-cream van, it is most likely to be taken to mean a cold non-alcoholic drink. This range of choices could be presented in a diagram like this:

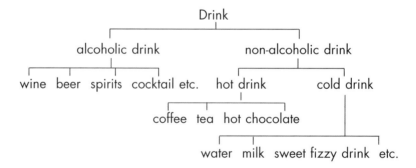

In most cafés in Britain until quite recently, asking for a coffee in a café was a relatively simple business. Now however, a new layer of subcategories exists. You can have a large or a regular coffee. It can be filter, decaff, cappuccino, espresso, café latte, or a flavoured coffee. This set of choices could be represented as part of the diagram above as:

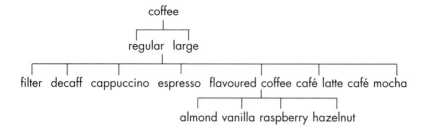

All these different categories of drink can be described in terms of their relationship to each other, and the technical terms are **hyponyms** and **superordinates**. A superordinate is an overarching term which embraces all the words below it on the diagram. Thus *coffee* is a superordinate for *cappuccino, filter, espresso* and *decaff*. A hyponym is the opposite: a word that can be included in the category above it on the diagram. *Decaff* is a hyponym of *coffee*, and *coffee* is a hyponym of *drink*.

A literary example of this can be found in Gerard Manley Hopkins' poem:

2   Glory be to God for dappled things
     For skies of couple colour as a brinded cow
     For rose moles in all stipple upon trout that swim
     Fresh fire coal chestnut falls, finches' wings.

Here the superordinate is *dappled things*, and the hyponyms are *skies, trout, chestnuts* and *finches' wings*.

The relationships of hyponym and superordinate are to some degree fixed: *dogs, cats, cows* and *polar bears* are always hyponyms of *animals*. However, there is also scope for individual interpretations about relationships between things, as in the Hopkins poem.

ACTIVITY 4.2

Suggest hyponyms for the following:

the media, jewellery, soup, fastenings for clothes, stationery

Suggest superordinates for the following:

> jazz, wheat, fountain pen, central heating, igloo, dictionary, suitcase

---

4.3 Context

The purpose of this chapter so far has been to introduce some of the issues which need to be taken into account when considering meaning. Just looking at semantics however would still leave a lot to explain about how meaning in a language actually works. Word meaning in fact explains only a fraction of how we use words to make meanings. The crucial element that semantics does not consider is context. This word 'context' is deceptively straightforward – in fact it refers to an infinite number of factors which could influence how an individual interprets a chunk of language; the area of linguistics that is concerned with the effect of context on meaning is **pragmatics**. Factors that need to be included in the context when we are interpreting language are discussed in the subsections below.

4.3.1 Deixis

Some words take part of their meaning from the context. A famous illustration of this aspect of meaning is an anecdote about a message found inside a bottle washed up on a beach. The message reads:

> Meet me here at the same time tomorrow with a stick this long.

Many of the words in this message do not have a useful meaning because they are not accompanied by other information. These words are *me*, *here*, *the same time*, *tomorrow* and *this long*. All these words do have a meaning (for example *me* means the person speaking / writing; *tomorrow* means the day after today), but they need contextual information to make their meaning complete. Words like these are called **deictics**. The name for the process is **deixis**.

If, instead of finding the message washed up on the shore, it had been handed to you by a the writer of the message, the meanings of *me*, *here*, *the same time* and *tomorrow* would all be clear. *Me* would refer to the person who gave you the message, *tomorrow* would refer to the day after the one you received the message on, and *here* would refer to the place where you were standing at the time (though the writer of the message would still have to indicate to you how long a stick they wanted you to bring!). In this case, the deictics would be clarified by exophoric reference, i.e. by information you had obtained from outside the text.

This information could also have been provided by the text. For example, the message might have read:

> My name is Hitomi, and I need a stick the same height as the railings. I am standing at the end of Brighton pier and it is 3pm on August 16th 1996. Meet me here at the same time tomorrow with a stick this long.

The second part of the message now makes more sense, because of the information given in the first half (although you would probably still consider it a strange request!). The words *me*, *here*, *the same time*, *tomorrow* and *this long* are all explained by the earlier information. This second version of the message is an example of anaphoric reference, i.e. the information we need to understand the meaning of the deictic words like *me* has been given earlier by the text (in this case, it refers to someone called Hitomi).

The message could also have been written in a different order:

> Meet me here at the same time tomorrow with a stick. I am standing at the end of Brighton pier on August 16th 1996 at 3pm. My name is Hitomi, and I need a stick the height of the railings.

In this case the referencing process works in the other direction – we can supply the meanings of *me* and *tomorrow* from information that comes later in the text. This is known as cataphoric referencing.

4.3.2 Homonyms

Some words have more than one meaning, and you have to rely on the context to decide which meaning is intended. For example, the sentence *the pitch is all wrong* could refer to a badly planned football stadium, a piece of music played out of tune, or the rigging of a rowing boat. Without more contextual information, you wouldn't know which was meant because the word *pitch* can mean all of these. The technical term for words with more than one meaning is **homonyms**.

Ironically for linguistic terms, you will find the words 'text' and 'discourse' themselves have more than one meaning. In this section, we are using 'text' to refer to written language and 'discourse' to refer to spoken language. However, sometimes 'text' is used to refer to a particular book / poem / play, and 'discourse' can mean a particular conversation, or even someone's set of beliefs about life. Generally which of these different meanings applies will be made clear by the context.

An illustration of the importance of the context to the meaning of a word appears in these lines by George Herbert:

3   Only the pure and virtuous soul
     Like seasoned timber never gives

If you were asked to explain the meaning of the word *gives* without these lines, you would probably say it means something like *to pass something to someone else* as in *I gave her a box of chocolates*, or *she gave me the flu*. You probably would not say it means *to bend or break* – which is its meaning in this context. The desk dictionary we are using offers twenty-one meanings for the word *give*, and *to yield or break under force or pressure* is the eighteenth meaning it presents. It is only the context of the rest of the two lines which guides us to select one possible meaning rather than another.

4.3.3 Other similar texts / discourses

Many of our conversations take the form of routines. We know what to expect because we've taken part in them so many times before. When someone says 'Knock, knock', you know you are supposed to reply 'Who's there?'. If someone you knew slightly greeted you with 'Hello, how are you?' you would most probably respond with a variation of 'Fine, and you?'. You would probably interpret the same question completely differently if it came from your GP at their practice. So we bring our past experience of similar interactions to bear when we decide how to interpret some utterances.

In literature, our experience of detective fiction leads us to expect the murderer to be revealed at the end. Only our knowledge of different kinds of cigarette adverts allows us to recognize an advert for Silk Cut or Benson & Hedges. And in poetry we have expectations of certain kinds of structures – which can be subverted for comic effect as in this limerick, quoted already in chapter 1:

4   There was a young man from Japan,
     Whose limericks never would scan.
     When his friends told him so,
     He said 'yes, I know,
     But I always try to get as many words into the last line as I possibly can!'

4.3.4 Your prior knowledge

As a listener or reader, you bring all your past experiences of the world to everything you hear or read. These experiences influence how you interpret language; to some extent you have experiences in common with people from the same cultural background as you, and to some extent, your experiences are unique to you. William Golding gave an illustration of the role this kind of experience can have in interpretation, using his novel, *The Lord of the Flies*. On visiting a South Seas island, similar to the one on which his novel was set, he realized that the inhabitants of this island had acquired an interpretation of his book which he had not intended when he wrote it. The conch shell, which in Golding's book is blown by the characters to call meetings, and is used as a symbol of who has the right to speak, was believed to summon island spirits by the indigenous people. So when they read the book, they interpreted some parts of the book differently from British readers, because of their different cultural background.

As members of a largely secular society, reading *Paradise Lost* more than three hundred years after Milton wrote it, most of us miss many of the allusions to religious issues of the time, and so it might be said we read a very different poem from the one Milton's contemporaries read – because of our different background knowledge.

The field of pragmatics is an area of linguistics which holds a particular fascination for many people, because it is clear that the human mind does something we still do not fully understand when it selects which aspects of the context are relevant to the interpretation of a text or discourse. It is one of the aspects of language use that artificial intelligence experts still have not fully explained, and one of the reasons why computers still cannot talk to us. Apocryphal illustrations of the problems which computers have had in imitating this ability of humans include a computer translation of 'out of sight, out of mind' as 'invisible idiot', and of 'the spirit is willing but the flesh is weak' as 'the vodka is good but I don't recommend the meat'.

4.4 Register

Finally there is a further dimension to word meaning to consider – the meaning words acquire through the ways they are used – and the people who use them. This is the sociolinguistic aspect of meaning, and it is another reason why many words that might semantically appear to be synonyms are not actually synonymous in use. *Home*, *abode* and *residence* all mean 'the place where I live'. However, you are not likely to use these words interchangeably. You might invite a friend *home* with you any day of the week; you might invite them to your *abode* if you were making a joke, but you would probably not invite them to your *residence*. The difference between the words is in the degree of formality / informality. *Home* is the least formal word and therefore the word most likely to be used in ordinary conversation. *Residence* is the more formal, and only likely to be used frequently in legal documents or when talking about a very high status member of society – you will hear news broadcasters observe that *the Queen is in residence at Buckingham Palace*, or refer to *the Prime Minister's country residence of Chequers*, for example.

Most formal English words are derived from Latin and Greek roots, while many of the most ordinary and informal ones have Germanic origins. *Home* for example, resembles the German word *Heim*, while *residence* comes from Latin. Word length is also closely connected to how formal a word is, and often to its origins. *Home* has just one syllable (i.e. it is monosyllabic), while *residence* has three (i.e. it is polysyllabic).

The difference between formal and informal language is also called a difference of **register**. Register refers to a style of language appropriate for a specific context. Thus a formal register is appropriate for legal documents and official occasions like the opening of Parliament, while an informal register is appropriate for casual conversations.

To take an illustration from a novel, consider the following extract from *Small World* by David Lodge:

5   For more *elaborate ablutions*, or to answer a call of nature, it was *necessary* to *venture* out into the draughty and *labyrinthine* corridors where baths and showers and toilets were to be found – but little *privacy* and *unreliable supplies* of hot water.

The italicised words are derived from Latin or Old French; some of them (*labyrinthine, ablutions*) are relatively infrequent in casual speech; all of them have more than one syllable. Compare the effect of these words on the passage with a rewritten version below which omits them:

If you wanted to have a bath or a shower, or to use the loo, you had to go out of your room, and the corridors were draughty and hard to find your way around. The bathrooms weren't terribly private, and there wasn't always hot water.

The rewritten passage, while carrying substantially the same meaning as the original is much more informal, much more like casual speech. We have not only changed some of the lexis (from *elaborate ablutions* to *have a bath or shower*; from *to venture out* to *to go out*) to create this effect of course; we have also changed the word order, changed the passive form into the active and used the second person 'you', which is a less formal form, and turned the one long sentence into two shorter ones. All of these contribute to making the text less formal and more like speech.

How close are the meanings of the two passages? In terms of the information they carry about the place being described, they are very close in meaning. But other kinds of meaning have been lost and created in the rewriting. The very fact that Lodge's original version is more compact, elegant and formal than ours, carries meaning; one interpretation of his choice of register is to have comic effect. The rather grand register contrasts with the mundane subject matter to create humour, which is lost in our rewritten version when the register is changed.

As with the other aspects of language considered in this book, people do deliberately experiment and play games with meaning and with register. Such experiments and games are frequent, and sometimes extreme. They are to be found in the literary language of poems, novels and plays, and in language use which is non-literary as well. People often attempt to create new and unique meanings by manipulating factors relating to meaning that have been considered here – by combining words with opposite meanings, by using synonyms and emphasizing the slight differences in meaning between the words, and by changing register.

ACTIVITY 4.3

In section 4.1, we argued that there were few true synonyms in English because of differences in the ways we actually use words. Below are a list of words, and their synonyms as given by a thesaurus. Identify which words are in your opinion:

(a) synonyms which could be used interchangeably
(b) synonyms, but because they belong to different registers could not be used interchangeably
(c) not really synonyms

discommode / inconvenience   journalist / newspaperman
sadness / sorrow   question / inquire
intelligent / clever   remember / recollect
nervously / apprehensively   scold / admonish

The rest of this chapter will look at specific ways of creating new meanings, through the use of figurative language.

4.5 Literal language and figurative language

At the beginning of this chapter, we talked about one way of identifying the meaning of a word being to look it up in the dictionary. The first meaning for a word that a dictionary definition gives is usually its literal meaning. The literal meaning of the word *tree*, for example, is a large plant. However, once we start talking about a tree in the context of *a family tree* for example, it is no longer a literal tree we are talking about, but a figurative one. The literal use of the word *tree* refers to an organism which has bark, branches and leaves. A family tree shares some of these qualities – graphically, a plan of a family and a representation of a tree can look similar, and in a way they are both a process of organic growth, so we use the same term for both. But when we use the term for a plant it is a literal usage, and when we use the term to describe our ancestry, it is a figurative usage.

Another word for the figurative usage of language is **trope**, which refers to language used in a figurative way for a rhetorical purpose. To illustrate a trope, consider one of the most famous pieces of rhetoric in English Literature, Mark Antony's speech from *Julius Caesar*:

Friends, Romans and Countrymen, lend me your ears . . .

Lend me your ears is a trope, used figuratively for rhetorical ends in order to make more impact than a literal variation such as *listen to me for a moment*. We do not interpret the line literally as a wish to borrow the flesh-and-blood ears of the audience, but as a figurative request for attention. Tropes are frequent in most language use. The rest of this chapter will consider different forms of tropes, starting with similes.

4.5.1 Similes

A **simile** is a way of comparing one thing with another, of explaining what one thing is like by showing how it is similar to another thing, and it explicitly signals itself in a text, with the words *as* or *like*. The phrase *as cold as ice* is a common simile; the concept of coldness is explained in terms of an actual concrete object. The word *as* signals that the trope is a simile.

6   O, my love's like a red, red rose,
     That's newly sprung in June:
     O, my love's like the melody
     That's sweetly played in tune.

The first line of the poem above, *O, my love's like a red, red rose*, is a simile. To communicate his feelings, the poet invites the reader to perceive in his sweetheart some of the properties of a rose. Properties this might include are beauty, freshness, scentedness, specialness and rarity. Greenfly, thorns or blight, also common properties of roses, are less likely to seem appropriate points of comparison, bearing in mind what we know of the context.

This process of transferring qualities from one thing to another is fundamentally how another type of trope, **metaphor**, works too. There is a formal difference however, in that the words *like* or *as* do not appear. Because they are not explicitly signalled, metaphors can be more difficult to identify.

4.5.2 Metaphor

Metaphor is another linguistic process used to make comparisons between the attributes of one thing/person and something else. Metaphors can be very simple, but there are many ways in which they can also be extremely complex, so we will be considering this feature of language in detail.

Metaphor as transport

In the example of the Robert Burns poem above, the process of transferring qualities from one object to another, from a rose to a person, was discussed. The concept of a 'transfer' is actually embedded in the etymology (i.e. the linguistic background) of the word *metaphor*, which is Greek for 'transport'. Perceiving a metaphor as a kind of transport draws attention to the way a metaphor transports a concept from where it is normally located, to somewhere else where it is not usually found. Thus a metaphor allows you to create correspondences in the world which did not exist before, and allows new meanings to occur. To look at this process in a text, consider this poem by Emily Dickinson:

7   The Clouds their Backs together laid
     The North began to push
     The Forests galloped till they fell
     The Lightning played like mice

     The Thunder crumbled like a stuff
     How good to be in Tombs
     Where Nature's Temper cannot reach
     Nor missile ever comes.

At one level, the poem is an observation of the shelter which the grave provides from the ferocity of the forces of nature. The aggression and violence of nature is communicated by means of metaphors and similes. Applying the idea of metaphor being a kind of 'transport' to the line *The Forests galloped till they fell*, you might say that the word *gallop* is more usually found in the context of horses, and it has been 'transported' to the context of forests. A consequence of 'transporting' a word from its usual context is that the reader may connect the word not only with its new context (in this case, *forests*) but also with its old context (in this case, *horses*). Thus reading the word *gallop* may introduce into the reading of the poem other qualities the reader associates with galloping horses to the context of the forests. The reader may attribute the forest of the poem with the movements, strength and wildness of galloping horses, creating for the reader an image of trees tossing wildly, apparently no more rooted to the ground than horses are.

Different readers do of course have different backgrounds and different ways of reading poetry. No one can predict what every reader will do. What we have demonstrated here is the way *we* read the poem.

Collocation

Another useful term for discussing metaphors is **collocation**, which refers to words which are associated with each other. The word *green* for example, is often found next to other words: *green with envy*, *green politics*, or *village green*. The word *green* is 'co-located' with these other terms, that is, they are found in the same places.

More generally, you could make a list of words which broadly collocate with the word *green*, for example, you might come up with *grass, trees, countryside* and so on, because a text which contained the latter three words is quite likely also to contain the word *green*. On the other hand, depending on how you interpreted the word *green* you might equally come up with a list of words from contemporary politics – *consumer, global warming, ozone-friendly, bio-degradable*. One list of words might be described as drawn from the context of rural images, the other from the context of environmental concern.

Metaphors occur when a word is taken, or 'transported', from the area in which it is usually located to a new context. An effect of this is that the word can still remind us of all the other words it usually collocates with, as the word *gallops* in the Dickinson poem is able to remind us of horses.

Vehicle, tenor and ground

Another way of describing how metaphors work is to use the terms of vehicle, tenor and ground, which were coined by I. A. Richards, a literary scholar who taught at Cambridge in the 1930s. Tenor is the term he uses to describe the subject of the metaphor – in the example above this would be the forests. Vehicle is the term he uses for the 'transported' part – in this case, the horses. Ground is the common properties of the two concepts or objects – the properties of movement and power and wildness.

4.5.3 Simile versus metaphor

There is a literary argument that similes and metaphors are fundamentally different. Because a simile explicitly says something is like something else, it is clearly establishing a comparison. A metaphor, on the other hand, according to this argument, draws attention to one or two features shared by two very dissimilar things. The pleasure in metaphor, it is claimed, comes from a similarity discovered in the midst of differences, while in similes the pleasure comes from the extensive similarities.

We do not hold the view that there are any categorical differences between similes and metaphors except for the very straight-forward formal linguistic differences. To us, the difference really seems as simple as the fact that similes contain *like* or *as* while metaphors don't. For example, if someone said, *your hands are as cold as ice* one day and *your hands are blocks of ice* the next, we do not think there would any significant difference in meaning to be found between the two comments, although the first is a simile and the second a metaphor.

However, metaphors are often harder to identify than similes as a rule of thumb, and can be used in more varied, intricate and subtle ways, since they can appear as almost any part of speech. We will look at this in more detail in the next section.

4.5.4 Explicit and embedded metaphors

One aspect of metaphors which can create confusion is the difference between explicit and embedded metaphors. We have been dealing with both so far, without making a distinction, but it is helpful to differentiate between them if you are conducting an analysis of a text.

Explicit metaphors are often easier to identify than embedded ones. Explicit metaphors take the form **X is Y**, as in the examples below. In these, the tenor (the subject of the metaphor) and the vehicle (the thing or person introduced for the purpose of comparison) are in bold; they are both nouns. The tenor comes first in each sentence:

You are my **knight in shining armour**
You are my **sunshine**
You are a **pain in the neck**
He is the **apple of her eye**
She was my **worst nightmare**
The **house** will be **paradise**
That **pudding** was an absolute **dream**
You're a **brick**!

In all these examples, something or someone is being compared to something/someone else through a construction using the appropriate part of the verb *to be* (i.e. *am, are, is, was, were, will be*). Other verbs are also possible, as long as the person / thing being compared and the person / thing they are being compared to are explicitly stated. For example:

> The **children** made **pigs** of themselves
> My **angel** of a **father** said he would help
> (the vehicle – *angel* – comes before the tenor – *father* – in this sentence)

In contrast, embedded metaphors are far less predictable. Sometimes the tenor and / or the vehicle are not always actually stated. Consider:

> The **cash machine** ate my card

The cash machine in this example is the tenor, the thing about which the comparison is being made. It is being compared to something which is not explicitly stated, by means of the verb *ate* (the ground of the metaphor, i.e. the attribute which the vehicle and the tenor have in common). Since machines do not usually eat but animals do, this metaphor compares the cash machine to an animal which devours things, via the verb not the noun, as was the case with the explicit metaphors.

Another example of an embedded metaphor is a description of the pop singer Björk given in a music review in the *Guardian* newspaper, which described her as *pixieing around on stage*. The reviewer has invented a word, the verb *to pixie*, to describe Björk's actions. *Björk* is the tenor, and *pixie* is the vehicle. The ground of the comparison are the properties Björk allegedly shares with a pixie, such as being small, looking extraordinary, and having fierce, spiky, energetic movements.

The writer has turned the noun *pixie* into a verb in order to make the sentence more interesting. A simile such as *Björk moves around on stage like a pixie* would have been less unusual, as would an explicit metaphor, such as *Björk is a pixie on stage*.

The poem below by Sylvia Plath is full of explicit metaphors, and also contains some similes.

(1) Identify the metaphors, and their ground, tenor and vehicle
(2) Identify the similes (these also can be explained in terms of ground, tenor and vehicle).

8 *You're*

> Clownlike, happiest on your hands,
> Feet to the stars, and moon-skulled,
> Gilled like a fish. A common-sense
> Thumbs-down on the dodo's mode.
> Wrapped up in yourself like a spool,
> Trawling your dark as owls do.
> Mute as a turnip from the Fourth
> Of July to All Fools' Day,
> O high-riser, my little loaf.
>
> Vague as a fog and looked for like mail.
> Farther off than Australia.
> Bent-backed Atlas, our travelled prawn.
> Snug as a bug and at home
> Like a sprat in a pickle jug.
> A creel of eels all ripples.
> Jumpy as a Mexican Bean.
> Right, like a well-done sum.
> A clean slate, with your own face on.

'The Snowstorm', by Ralph Waldo Emerson, contains some good examples of implicit metaphors. Words or phrases in italics are implicit metaphors in some way – some are very complex. Decide what the vehicle, tenor and ground might be in each of the italicised instances.

9   *The Snowstorm*

Announced by all the trumpets of the sky,
Arrives the snow, and, driving o'er the fields,
Seems nowhere to alight: the whited air
Hides hills and woods, the river, and the heaven,
And veils the farmhouse at the garden's end.
The sled and traveller stopped, the courier's feet
Delayed, all friends shut out, the housemates sit
Around the radiant fireplace, enclosed
In a tumultuous privacy of storm.

Come see the north wind's *masonry.*
Out of an unseen quarry evermore
Furnished with tile, *the fierce artificer*
Curves his *white bastions* with projected roof
Round every windward stake, or tree, or door.
Speeding, the myriad-handed, his wild work
So fanciful, so savage, nought cares he
For number or proportion. Mockingly,
On coop or kennel *he hangs Parian*[1] *wreaths;*
A swan-like form invests the hidden thorn;
Fills up the farmer's lane from wall to wall,
Maugre[2] the farmer's sighs; and, at the gate,
A tapering turret overtops the work.
And when his hours are numbered, and the world
Is all his own, retiring, as he were not,
Leaves, when the sun appears, astonished Art
To mimic in slow structures, stone by stone,
Built in an age, the mad wind's night-work,
The frolic architecture of the snow.

---

1 Parian = as if made from fine white marble from the Greek island of
Paros
2 maugre = in spite of

4.5.5 Types of metaphor

Although there is a limited usefulness in attempting to categorize every form of metaphor you might encounter – because there would always be some we had missed, and there would always be room for disputing our classification – we will mention the types which occur frequently.

The Extended Metaphor

One common literary use of metaphor is the extended metaphor. 'The Love Song of J. Alfred Prufrock' by T. S. Eliot uses an extended metaphor to describe fog, which is compared to a cat:

10　　The yellow fog that rubs its back upon the window-panes,
　　　The yellow smoke that rubs its muzzle on the window-panes,
　　　Licked its tongue into the corners of the evening,
　　　Lingered upon the pools that stand in drains,
　　　Let fall upon its back the soot that falls from chimneys,
　　　Slipped by the terrace, made a sudden leap,
　　　And seeing it was a soft October night,
　　　Curled once about the house, and fell asleep.

The shared properties of cats (the vehicle of the metaphor, to use I. A. Richards's terminology) and the fog (the tenor of the metaphor) are yellowness (if we are prepared to accept that cats may be yellow!), playfulness, wrapping around things, pressing against glass, wriggling into corners, moving silently and curling up to sleep. These are the grounds of the metaphor, which is extended because the comparison works at more than one level: the fog shares more than one quality with a cat. Another example of an extended metaphor is the Alice Walker poem 'I'm really fond':

11　　I'm really very fond of you,
　　　he said.

　　　I don't like fond.
　　　It sounds like something you would tell a dog.

Give me love,
or nothing.

Throw your fond in a pond,
I said.

But what I felt for him
was also warm, frisky,
moist-mouthed,
eager,
and could swim away

if forced to do so

I don't like fond. / It sounds like something you would tell a dog is a simile; it introduces the vehicle of a dog into the poem; the narrator perceives the emotion her lover declares as more appropriate to a dog than a human. Although she uses the image of a dog to indicate her dislike of his emotion, she then turns the image to her own ends. This is done first by suggesting that he *throw[s his] fond in a pond*, playing with the idea of throwing sticks for dogs. Second, she elaborately compares herself to a dog, emphasizing her playfulness and her independence from him: *warm, frisky, moist-mouthed, eager, and could swim away/ if forced to do so*. This metaphor therefore is exploited at length, with the different grounds for comparison between the narrator and a dog drawn out.

Anthropomorphic metaphors

When animals, objects, or concepts are given specifically human attributes, **anthropomorphism** is said to have taken place. Anthropomorphism occurs very frequently in children's books, where trains and animals have personalities and can talk. Animated cartoon films like *Tom and Jerry* are also anthropomorphic. Writers make use of this device, as in the following opening line to a sixteenth-century sonnet by Sir Philip Sidney:

12   With how sad steps, O Moon, thou climb'st the skies

The narrator of the poem addresses the moon as if it were a person slowly climbing stairs. Another term used to describe this phenomenon is **personification**. Another poet, W. B. Yeats, describes the emotion love as a person, treading the skies like Sidney's moon:

13   When you are old and grey and full of sleep . . .
    . . . And bending down beside the glowing bars,
    Murmur, a little sadly, how Love fled
    And paced upon the mountains overhead
    And hid his face amid a crowd of stars.

Pathetic fallacy

Another form of metaphor that attributes human responses to the environment is pathetic fallacy. This refers to the practice of representing the world as a mirror reflecting human emotions. This was a device particularly exploited by writers in the late eighteenth century and throughout the nineteenth century, when the beauty and the power of nature was often a strong theme in literature. The effects produced can be very forceful, as the surrounding world echoes the feelings of the protagonists, as in this extract from *Middlemarch*, by George Eliot. The characters, Dorothea and Will, who are in love with one another, believe they are parting for ever:

14   He took her hand, and raised it to his lips with something like
    a sob. But he stood with his hat and gloves in the other hand
    and might have done for the portrait of a Royalist. Still it was
    difficult to loose the hand, and Dorothea, withdrawing it in a
    confusion that distressed her, looked and moved away.
      'See how dark the clouds have become, and how the trees
    are tossed', she said, walking towards the window with only a
    dim sense of what she was doing. . . .
      While he [Will] was speaking there came a flash of
    lightning which lit each of them up for the other – and the
    light seemed to be the terror of a hopeless love.

The dark clouds and the tossing trees can be read as metaphors for the unhappiness and confusion of the characters, while a simile is used to make explicit the connection between the lightning and their *hopeless love*.

The mixed metaphor

This is usually a less praised device; it refers to switching metaphors in the middle of a description so some kind of incongruity is produced. To say someone was being taken *on a wild goose chase up the garden path* would be a mixed metaphor, or that *a bottle neck is strangling the traffic flow*. If the terms tenor, vehicle and ground are applied, what happens in a mixed metaphor is that the tenor – the subject of the metaphor – stays the same, but the vehicle and ground change. It is usually thought, in literary writing, to show a lack of control, or language awareness, but it can be used for deliberate effects, as in the Liz Lochhead poem in the section below.

The dead metaphor

Another type of metaphor usually referred to with little admiration is the dead metaphor: a metaphor which has been absorbed into everyday language usage and become naturalized, so that most language users are not aware of it as a metaphor any more. Common examples include *the foot of a bed*, or *the foot of a page*, a *table leg*, the *arm of a chair*: usages so everyday that their metaphorical origins are forgotten. The meaning of some words has expanded to include their metaphorical usages, as is the case for the word *clear*, for instance. The literal meaning of *clear* is that light can pass through, as in *clear water* or *clear glass*. When an idea or an explanation are described as being clear, a mental process is being compared with the passage of light through something. *Is that clear?* doesn't mean *can you see through it?*, but metaphorically, *is it comprehensible?* This metaphor continues when we talk about ideas or a speaker being lucid or opaque. Our language is full of words which have been taken from one area of experience and used to describe another.

Dead metaphors tend not to be considered poetic: some literary critics are scathing about them, and people sometimes regard them as a sign of poor writing in other contexts – but since a lot of the language we take for granted derives from dead metaphors, perhaps we cannot afford to be too squeamish about them.

Resurrecting the dead metaphor

It is possible to bring dead metaphors 'back to life', however. Two ways this can happen are through poetry and through politics.

• poetical resuscitation

The poet Liz Lochhead is a good example of someone who takes everyday figures of speech, and makes them seem strange by breaking them down so that the reader has to think of them again, in a new way. In the poem 'Bawd' she writes:

15   It'll amaze you, the company I keep –
       and I'll keep them at arm's length –
       I've hauled my heart in off my sleeve.

There are two metaphors which would usually be considered 'dead' here: *to keep at arm's length* and *to wear your heart on your sleeve*. The two are combined in such a way as to call attention to themselves and to their exact phrasing. *Keep* is used twice, in the first line to suggest proximity, and in the second to suggest distance. The word *arm* in the second line and the word *sleeve* in the third draw attention to themselves because they collocate when they are used in their literal senses. The metaphorical usages of both words refer to emotional distance or availability. The words of the metaphors are being explored, instead of being taken for granted. Further on in the poem are the lines:

16   I'll shrug everything off the shoulder,
       make wisecracks, be witty off the cuff.

The process of making familiar expressions strange continues with the combination of *to shrug something off* and *off the shoulder*. *Off the shoulder* is not usually a metaphor, because it is generally used literally to describe a low-cut top or dress; *to shrug something off* however is a dead metaphor which is usually means *to ignore something*. By splicing these two expressions, attention is drawn to these well-worn phrases and dead metaphors are resurrected – so to speak! Similarly attention is called to the dead metaphor *off the cuff* because *cuff* in its literal sense collocates with *sleeve* and *arm* when they are used in their literal senses.

- politically motivated resuscitation

Another way we can become conscious of the literal meaning of dead metaphors is through someone, or a group of people, objecting to a particular language usage or deliberately introducing an alternative. This happens quite frequently, and today is often called *political correctness*. For example, the word *black* has all sorts of negative associations in English in its metaphorical usages, which are not linked with its literal meaning of a colour. A lot of people find expressions such as *to blacken someone's name*, *blackleg*, *blacklist*, *black magic*, *a black look*, *black-hearted* or *the black market* racially offensive. In an effort to dispel these connotations, phrases such as *black is beautiful* were coined. Writers such as Toni Morrison, the Nobel prize-winning black writer, use positive and beautiful images in association with black skin, working against a whole tradition of metaphorical language usage.

Another area where political intervention occurs is when words develop a range of metaphorical meanings in English that are apparently non-gender specific, but where their literal meaning is gendered. An example is the word *master*, in the sense of to *master* something, or in the sense of an academic qualification: Master of Science or of Arts (MSc / MA). The literal meaning of master is a male person in authority, the male-gendered equivalent of *mistress* (e.g. *the master and mistress of the house*). The metaphorical meaning of *master* is that one has achieved a level of proficiency or expertise, and it is used of males or females: a woman can be said to have mastered the art of car maintenance, and can hold a Master of Science degree. Comparing the metaphorical usages of *master* to the metaphorical uses of *mistress* (e.g. *his wife met his mistress*) provides an illustration of what typically happens to gendered terms in English. When a male term develops metaphorical meanings, these tend to be positive, while if the female term develops metaphorical meanings, they tend to be pejorative. *Master* has a range of uses that are quite different from the range of uses of *mistress*. Another reason for becoming aware of the metaphorical ways in which words are used, therefore, is that pressure groups pick up on certain usages and draw attention to the embedded inequalities contained within them.

4.5.6 Metonymy

We have looked in some detail at how metaphors are formed and how they function. There are other forms of trope, or figurative language, which are frequently found in literary and non-literary texts; the two which will be considered here are metonymy and synecdoche.

Metonymy, like metaphor, is a figurative use of language rather than a literal one. As *metaphor* is Greek for *transport*, *metonymy* is Greek for *a change of name*. In this case, the name of a referent (or thing referred to) is replaced by the name of an attribute, or entity related in some semantic way, or by spatial proximity, or another kind of link, i.e., the ground of the substitution is not similarity as it is in the case of a metaphor, but association.

A very well-established metonymy is illustrated by the activities of 14 February. If you are one of those who run to the door on the morning of 14 February, looking for a Valentine or five, you would doubtless be more than surprised if what came through the letter box was a dead saint. Two saints called Valentine were martyred in the reign of the Roman Emperor Claudius. Their festivals fall on 14 February, and are commemorated with various pagan forms of behaviour. Cards with hearts on are sent because the name of the saint has been transferred to an object associated with that date; the name of one concept has been transferred to another associated concept, which finds its way into our everyday language usage.

The association can also be of many kinds, including physical proximity. We talk about the kettle boiling when, literally, it is the water in the kettle that is boiling; the metonymy is a result of the proximity of the water to the kettle. Further examples of metonymy in common usage are: *the press* to describe newspapers on account of the printing press used to produce them; *the crown* to describe the monarch on account of their headwear; *cardigan* to describe a garment (on account of Lord Cardigan who famously wore them), *wellingtons* for boots, again on account of having been worn by a famous person, the Duke of Wellington; *burgundy* to describe a colour, on account of the colour of the wine which comes from that region of France (there are two levels of metonymy at work in that example); *giving someone a ring* or *a bell* to describe making a telephone call to them, on account of the sound a telephone makes. Another example was used at the beginning of the chapter, *lend me your ears*, where *ears* represent the process of *listening*.

4.5.7 Synecdoche

A further kind of figurative language is **synecdoche**, which is usually classed as a type of metonymy. Synecdoche refers to using the name of part of an object to talk about the whole thing, as when *black tie* is used to mean formal wear for men (and women!), *strings* is used to mean stringed instruments in an orchestra, and *wheels* is used to mean a car. It is a subdivision of metonymy because it also involves using the name of something connected with an object or concept to replace the original name of the object, or concept. But in this case, you take one part of the whatever it is, and use that name to label the whole thing. A newspaper headline that stated *19 hands lost as cement freighter sinks* was using metonymy – *hand* refers to a whole person, not just part of their body, as it does also in *farm hand*, *stage hand* and *hired hand. Giving someone your hand in marriage* is another example of using *hand* metonymically for the whole person.

ACTIVITY 4.6 _____

The following extracts are taken from newspaper cuttings, which are often a rich source of figurative language. Identify the type of trope employed by each extract, and if appropriate, analyse it in terms of collocation or vehicle, tenor and ground.

* Buckingham Palace has already been told the train may be axed when the rail network has been privatised.

  Daily Mirror 2 February 1993, p. 2

* Ted Dexter confessed last night that England are in a right old spin as to how they can beat India this winter.

  Daily Mirror 2 February 1993, p. 26

* ***Pet Rabbits put in peril by red tape on vaccine***

  The pet rabbit population is at risk from the killer disease myxomatosis because the one man who supplied all of Britain's vaccine has ceased production in the face of costly new Ministry of Agriculture regulations and red tape.

  Daily Telegraph 2 February 1993, p. 1

4.6 Metaphor and language change

This chapter began with looking at meaning as a literal construct, using examples where there was a direct correspondence between the name and the object or concept referred to – the word *book* is agreed by speakers of English to refer a book rather than a newspaper, journal or magazine. This kind of language use usually appears quite stable. It is unlikely that we will wake up tomorrow and find the word *book* being used to refer to a car instead, for example. However, many of the illustrations discussed in the second part of the chapter, devoted to figurative uses of language, have demonstrated that meaning is not always very stable, and there is a lot of scope for creativity. Figurative language use is one way in which the phenomenon of language change takes place, as words acquire metaphorical or metonymic meanings different from their original literal ones, and the new usages become absorbed into the language as commonplace.

4.6.1 New ideas or areas of knowledge

Language change and metaphorical / metonymic usages are evident when there are new developments, in art, for example, or science. When we have a new object or concept, terms of reference are needed to discuss it. Completely new words are relatively rare; mostly words are borrowed from somewhere else. Thus art movements are named metaphorically: the *Fauvists* ('the wild beasts'), or the *Cubists*, for example. In these cases, a word has been transferred from one area to another, recycled in fact. In terms of new technologies, films were called *the talkies* when sound was introduced – a metonym, referring to an aspect of the film. The terms *net* and *web*, used to describe the revolutionary new systems of electronic communications, are metaphors to allow us to talk easily about transporting language and pictures through fibre-optic cables to anywhere in the world, immediately. They are a tiny part of a new vocabulary developed over the last few years to allow people to talk about inventions and experiences new to the world.

4.6.2 Abstract ideas made concrete

Another reason for language change through metaphor and metonymy is that an area of shared experience may be relatively abstract, and in order to be able to talk about it, terms are drawn from another, more concrete, area. Newspapers are a good place to observe this happening: headlines frequently use metaphors as bold, simple and direct ways of conveying an abstract idea.

These two headlines contain examples of the same kind of metaphor: *Green party drifts becalmed* and *Poland sails into uncharted waters*. Both involve groups of people represented as ships, which move spatially with varying speed. The second headline actually contains a metonymy as well, since it is not the geographical zone which we call Poland which is being referred to, but the Polish people who inhabit the area, and even this is itself a metonymy, since the headline probably refers not so much to the entire population as to its government, or on a yet more abstract level, to its economic policies.

The same kind of metaphor is at work in the headline: *Gorbachev reversal puts German unity into gear*. The metaphor is once again of a mode of transport. The concept of Gorbachev, then President of the USSR, changing his mind was expressed in spatial terms, a physical change of direction, and as if he were a car or some kind of engine. To an even greater degree of abstraction, the concept of German unity is being denoted metaphorically as an engine.

When German unity happened, it did have a material reality; the Berlin Wall was physically dismantled; families who had been separated were able to be together – but it was also an intangible event concerned with financial statistics, a common monetary unit, a lifting of working restrictions, a change in how people planned their lives. What it certainly was not, was a car engine, which can be put into gear and driven forward. However, because abstract ideas are so difficult to talk about, particularly in the short headlines used by newspapers, metaphors are used to make the abstract accessible.

4.7 Functions of figurative language use

It is worth noting that the use made of figurative language by the media, for referring to concepts which are abstract in readily accessible terms, usually has the effect of making the concepts under discussion tamer, more domestic, more acceptable. We can be presented with a picture of the world from which much of the uncertainty, the fuzziness, the ambiguity has been wiped.

Not all journalists use figurative language to serve this function: many after all are driven by a sense of social justice to use language in a way that will bring home to people the effect of atrocities such as war and famine, in an attempt to bring about change.

Undoubtedly, metaphors are extraordinarily powerful and pervasive, and some linguists such as George Lakoff and Mark Johnson argue that much of our perception of the world and ourselves is shaped by figurative uses of language.

4.8 Analysis of meaning: checklist

When you are exploring the meaning of a text, or part of a text, you may find the following suggestions helpful.

- If you are not sure where to start on a text, you might try rewriting it, as we did with the extract from the David Lodge novel (extract 5). By comparing the differences between the original text and your rewritten version, you should be able to comment on the degree of formality or informality of the original (i.e. its register), and its effect on the reader. Rewriting a text is also a very good way to identify other significant features in the original.
- What structural aspects of the meaning are being exploited, if any? For example, are overlaps in word meaning, or lexical gaps, being explored? Is the text using opposites or oxymorons, or hyponyms and superordinates in a playful or unusual way?
- How significant is the context of the text to your understanding of it? Might readers with different background knowledge from yours form a different interpretation?
- Does the literal meaning of a particular word or phrase apply here? If not, you are dealing with figurative language. Check for similes, metaphors, metonymy and synecdoche. What is the function of the figurative use of language? It might be to make the abstract seem concrete; to make the mysterious or frightening seem safe, ordinary and domestic, or to make the day-to-day seem wonderful and unusual.

Suggestions for further reading

Lakoff, G. and Johnson, M. (1980) *Metaphors We Live By*, University of Chicago Press, Chicago.

—— (1989) *More Than Cool Reason: A Field Guide To Poetic Metaphor*, University of Chicago Press, Chicago.

Leech, Geoffrey (1969) *A Linguistic Guide to English Poetry*, Longman. See chapter 9: 'Figurative Language'.

Steen, Gerard (1994) *Understanding Metaphor in Literature*, Longman, London.

Wales, Katie (1989) *A Dictionary of Stylistics*, Longman, London. See entries under 'metaphor', 'metonymy', 'simile'.

Chapter 5

Stylistic applications
to drama

5.1 Introduction

The next three chapters in this book are concerned with particular areas of textual language use: drama, fiction and media texts. In this chapter, we will be applying methods of linguistic analysis to the literary genre of drama. Stylistics has tended to have less to say about drama than about the two genres of literature with which it has been principally concerned, fiction and poetry. There are several reasons why this has been the case.

One reason is that a play exists in two ways – on the page, and on the stage; this presents something of a dilemma for the literary critic, since the two manifestations are quite different and need different analytic approaches. When stylistics has focused on drama, it has almost invariably been concerned with the text, rather than the performance. The text, after all, is static and unchanging, (although different editions of a play might contain textual variations). The stylistician may easily turn back the pages to a previous scene, and make comparisons between speeches in different parts of the play, or even reach for another book, and make comparisons between different plays.

The (live) performance of a play, on the other hand, is transient. A speech only partially heard through inattention cannot be heard again on that occasion. Actors may differ in their performances from one night to the next, and a half-empty house mid-week, compared to a packed house at the weekend, will also affect the experience. The director's interpretation can alter the play from one staging to another at many, sometimes fundamental, levels. Shakespeare's plays in particular are continually being interpreted in different ways – *Macbeth* can be set in the time of World War II, *All's Well that End's Well* can be set in modern society; settings can be naturalistic, or formal and abstract.

5.1.1 The significance of context

When you watch a live performance of a play, the importance of context to the process of interpretation which we have discussed earlier in this book (see chapter 4), becomes strikingly apparent. Your interpretation of what is performed before you will be strongly affected by a number of factors. For example, how well you know the play will influence whether or not you pick up certain nuances in the performance. If you are tired, looking for the actors' names in the programme, or eating sweets – all relatively common states or activities for theatre audiences – you may miss the backward glance thrown by one actor to another, which suggests a change in the relationship of the characters. If you are admiring the costumes or the set, you may be less aware of a tone of voice, a posture. These kinds of factors influence our reading of all texts; live performances simply emphasize their importance.

When we take all these elements into account – the variations which may occur between different performances of the same play, and the variations in the conditions under which a member of the audience can experience a performance – it becomes clear why most analysts prefer to devote their labour to written copies of the play.

5.1.2 Drama on film

Of course, now that much drama is filmed and televized, and can be obtained commercially on video, or recorded at home, the conditions described above for live performances do not always apply for many filmed productions of plays. Video allows us the privilege of reviewing speeches we want to hear again, of watching the same scene many times, maybe once for the content and delivery of a speech, once to watch the behaviour of other actors in the background. The process of filming also does some of the job of interpreting for us. The camera may focus on one character's expression as they speak, the tension in the hand of another, and then move to the sky, to show the fading light. These are all elements which might be present on stage, but which we might miss if our gaze was not being directed by the camera in this way.

Having pointed out the differences between a live performance of a play and the text, it is important to emphasize that from a linguistic perspective it clearly is both possible and easier to analyse a play as a written text, than to analyse it as a live performance. Mick Short (1996) discusses the problem of whether to analyse the text or the performance, and argues that there are 'a number of considerations which suggest that the object of dramatic criticism should not be the theatrical performance'. That is, the text of a play is indeed a legitimate object of study, and there are reasons why the text of a play should be studied, rather than a performance of the play:

(a) Teachers and students have traditionally read plays without necessarily seeing them performed and have still managed to understand them and argue about them.

(b) A special case of this is the dramatic producer, who must be able to read and understand a play in order to decide how to produce it. . . .

(c) There is a logical and terminological distinction between a play and a performance of it. Coming out of the theatre, people can be heard making comments of the form 'that was a good / bad production of a good / bad play'. . . .

(Short 1996: 159)

Short proposes that people automatically distinguish between the text and the performance for different purposes. We agree that the text of a play *is* a legitimate and interesting object of study, and also with a point Short makes later, that discourse analysis is a way of analysing the text which can take account of its dramatic properties. However, this is not to say that performance can never be analysed, particularly now we have access to recorded performances.

5.2 How should we analyse drama?

In the following sections, we describe some of the approaches that have been used to analyse dramatic texts, and explore some of the more recent applications of linguistic theory to drama.

5.2.1 Drama as poetry

Stylistic analysis of dramatic texts has tended to follow one of three approaches. The first of these is to treat an extract of the text as a poem – as we have already done in chapter 2, where lines from the sonnet which is Romeo and Juliet's first conversation are analysed in exactly this way. Since sound and metre are as relevant in many dramatic texts as they are in poetry, everything to do with metre, sound patterning, syntax and figurative language already discussed in chapters 2, 3 and 4 might be appropriate areas to analyse.

5.2.2 Drama as fiction

Secondly, the play can be analysed for character and plot, treating it more or less like fiction. The two components of plot and character clearly are as significant in dramatic texts as in fiction, so again, this is an obviously relevant way to proceed; some of the approaches described in chapter 6 can be used to do this.

Drama however differs fundamentally from fiction in that it usually lacks a narrative voice, and this absence can make a novel difficult to dramatize successfully. One of the recognized problems in dramatizing Jane Austen's *Pride and Prejudice*, as was done by the BBC in 1995, is that the ironic narrative voice offers a different perspective on characters and events from the one the characters in the novel necessarily perceive or comment on. Thus the information and the attitude conveyed in the narrative voice must be translated into other aspects of the dramatization.

There are ways, in drama, of attempting to deal with the function of the narrative voice. A chorus, as was used in Greek Tragedy, has also been used in plays by T. S. Eliot (*Murder in the Cathedral* and *The Cocktail Party*, for example), and can give another perspective on the actions of the characters or plot development. Dylan Thomas used a narrative voice reading over the play in *Under Milkwood*, and Dennis Potter, in the television play *The Singing Detective*, uses a voice-over technique.

Information about the plot and the characters is sometimes given through explicit interjections by the playwright in the text of the play, as stage instructions. George Bernard Shaw, for example, gives very precise instructions about the appearance of his characters and the set. The following extract is taken from the opening stage directions to *Arms and the Man*:

1   The window is hinged doorwise and stands wide open. Outside, a pair of wooden shutters, opening outwards, also stand open. On the balcony, a beautiful young lady, intensely conscious of the romantic beauty of the night, and the fact that her own youth and beauty are part of it, is gazing at the snowy Balkans. She is in her nightgown, well covered by a long mantle of firs, worth, on a moderate estimate, about three times the furniture in the room.

Explicit notes such as these can be interpreted by the director, actors, costume and set designers into audible signals through the choice of accent and other features of the speech of the characters, and into visual signals such as clothing, posture and movements, which can give the audience information about character not dissimilar to that which a narrative voice might deliver.

It is the analysis of character and plot with which *traditional* dramatic criticism has been typically concerned. Andrew Bradley, the author of a well-known textbook (1905) used by schoolchildren sitting exams in Shakespeare, which gave rise to a saying: 'If you've read Bradley, you won't do badly!', concentrated on this aspect of Shakespeare's plays. In doing so, he perpetuated what was later viewed as a critical fallacy: the idea that the characters had some kind of identity beyond the boundaries of the play. It is sometimes referred to as 'How many children had Lady Macbeth?', because one of Lady Macbeth's speeches refers to her having breast-fed a child, but no child of the Macbeths' is mentioned or appears in the play. This anomaly has given literary critics much food for thought and debate and raised questions about whether Lady Macbeth had children in a previous marriage, or whether they had died young, and this was what had hardened her to the extent she could urge her husband to commit murder.

These kind of questions can only arise if characters are regarded as having a 'life' outside the text. Most critics nowadays regard them as inappropriate, although it is still not unusual to read analyses of drama that discuss characters as if they were psychologically complex living people with histories, rather than creations borne of their author's observations of how people are.

5.2.3 Drama as conversation

We have said that stylistics has approached the texts of plays as if they were poetry, and as if they were a kind of fiction. This does not really account for aspects of drama that are different from poetry and different from fiction; the qualities that make it a genre in its own right. One crucial aspect in which drama differs from poetry and fiction is in its emphasis on verbal interaction, and the way relationships between people are constructed and negotiated through what they say. This is where linguistics really comes into its own, since there is an enormous amount of work on what people do when they talk, and on how communication and miscommunication occur.

Linguistics, and techniques of discourse analysis in particular, can help us analyse the exchanges between characters, in order to:

(a)   help us to understand the text
(b)   help us understand how conversation works
(c)   allow us to appreciate better the skill a playwright has demonstrated in the way they have written the speeches of their characters
(d)   help us to see things in the text that other forms of analysis might have allowed us to miss.

The rest of this chapter is about the different aspects of language use which playwrights can draw upon as a resource. Each aspect is illustrated, and as usual, there are activities to try.

5.3 Differences between speech and writing

It may appear a self-evident truth that speech in plays is quite unlike naturally occurring conversation – especially if you think 'Shakespeare' when you read the word 'play'. However, even apparently naturalistic contemporary dramas usually use language in a way which is quite unlike the language of ordinary, private conversations.

Below is an extract from a naturally-occurring conversation between two women who are preparing for an evening event to inform people about African culture. Because spoken language, particularly in conversations, is very different from ordinary written language, we need special conventions to represent it in a written form. This written representation of speech is called a **transcript**, and there are many different ways of transcribing a conversation, although none of them can claim to capture every detail of the talk. The transcription conventions we have used here are:

> M = words spoken by Mary; S = words spoken by Susan
> The lines are numbered and follow on from one another without a pause.
> Where the two speakers speak at the same time, their words have the same line number (e.g. line 3).
> Pauses less than half a second long are shown as a full stop in brackets.
> Where speech was indecipherable, it is shown as '(unclear speech)'.

Mary and Susan's Conversation – part 1:

1	M:	ok (.) so we can have some tea (.) what else (.) and
2	M:	then I've got a a book on Zambezi (.)
3	M:	just just a wildlife book em
	S:	yeah (.) that's quite a lot already (.)
4	S:	I'll see what Ricky's got she's got a em
5	S:	(.) (unclear speech)
6	M:	em (.) and then I suppose we can have baskets and
7	M:	things but (.)
	S:	yeah
8	M:	how (.) those are just things tha. that gonna stand kinda
9	M:	like stand up on the workbench but what about like on the
10	M:	walls or (.)
11	S:	are we meant to have something
12	M:	I don't know I just thought how are we gonna make it cos

13 M: the (.) the actual recipe isn't that Africany really

14 S: no (.) (unclear speech)
        (recording and transcript made by Karen Eatock 1996)

A common reaction to seeing a transcript of a conversation for the first time is that it doesn't seem to make sense! It often looks very messy and it's hard to see how the people having the conversation could have understood each other. This is partly because a lot of the information is given through intonation and non-verbal communication in real conversations. In the transcript above, a lot of the information Mary and Susan had about what the other person meant is missing – for example, we can't see their eye contact, hear if their intonation was questioning or emphatic, can't hear which words they stress. There are ways of showing this information on a transcript (like a musical score that carries all the information about how an orchestra should play a composition), but the more information is given, the more complicated the transcript is to read and analyse.

The transcript demonstrates some of the common features of conversations, which we look at in more detail below.

5.3.1 Pauses and pause fillers

There are some short pauses in this extract (lines 1 and 3, for example), which are very common when people speak; we often pause while we organize our thoughts. There are also some pause fillers: the noises we make when we have not finished what we want to say, but are hesitating. Sounds we make in those circumstances include *umm*, *uh*, *mmm* and *er*. In this transcript, Mary and Susan use *em* (lines 3 and 4). Pauses and *umms* and *ers* do occur in drama too, of course, but usually in controlled ways. On the radio, recordings of people who *umm* and *er* too much when they are interviewed are often edited before they go on the air, so they sound smoother, briefer, faster-moving and more confident.

5.3.2 Unclear speech

Natural conversations often have unclear parts to them, especially when they are recorded – because speakers turn away from the microphone, because they laugh or cough or eat while they are talking, because they whisper or mutter to themselves or to someone very close to them, because they pronounce words or phrases in a way unfamiliar to the hearer / transcriber, or because they speak very quickly. In contrast, on the stage or in films, it is usually the actor's job to make sure that every word the audience is supposed to hear is clear and audible.

5.3.3 Repetition and recycling

A lot of repetition takes place when we talk. For example, at line 2, Mary says *a* twice, and at line 8, she says *tha.* before she says *that*, the word she probably intended to say. At line 3, she says the word *just* twice. At lines 8 and 9, she repeats part of a clause *those are just things tha. that gonna stand kinda like stand up on the workbench.*

When we speak, we generally make a lot of what might be termed 'production errors', which we repair as we go along. It is common to repeat the first sound of a word (*b. b. biro*), especially if we are momentarily distracted from what we are saying, or haven't quite made up our mind which word to use. Recycling occurs when we get halfway through a phrase or an utterance and decide we need to amend some aspect of the grammar; we then return to the beginning and repeat it with the amendment in place. An example of this in Mary's speech is at line 8 when she says:

tha. that gonna stand kinda like stand up

recycling her choice of verb *stand* as *stand up*. False starts are also frequent in talk – in line 8 again, Mary begins her utterance with *how* then changes it to *those are just things tha*. These last two features are also so common that most of the time we don't notice people doing them.

These features occur seldom in scripted plays, but are evident in some modern films, in which the dialogue is ad-libbed, or deliberately made to appear like natural speech. Directors such as Mike Leigh and Woody Allen do this in their films – if you are not used to the technique, they can be relatively hard to follow.

5.3.4 Turn-taking

One of the linguistic features of conversations which tends to be modified in dramatic texts is the way turns are taken, i.e. the way people having a conversation organize who is going to speak next. For example, in the extract, Mary and Susan usually take it in turns to talk – when one finishes, the other starts, usually without a perceivable gap; this kind of organization of talk is called 'no gap, no overlap' (Sacks *et al.*, 1974). However, at line 3, they both talk at the same time:

3   M: just just a wildlife book em
        S: yeah (.) that's quite a lot already (.)

Simultaneous talk is sometimes described as 'interruption', but this isn't an interruption by Susan, but rather an agreement (*yeah*) which is followed by a comment on the stage of their preparations (*that's quite a lot already*), while Mary finishes describing her book on Zambezi (*just a wildlife book*). Overlap like this is frequent in conversations, but usually relatively short-lived. If one speaker constantly talked at the same time as the other, over long stretches of the other one's turn, then the talk would probably become less of a collaborative conversation, and more of a confrontation. There are no real examples of interruption in this extract between Mary and Susan.

In plays, compared to in naturally occurring speech, there is usually a reduction in interruptions and overlaps. In scripted dialogue, the writer has already decided which character is going to speak next; it is not the participants, in this case the actors, who are organizing their turns at talk. Moreover as an audience, rather than as an active participant in the talk, we can only really understand one speaker at a time. We can usually manage to understand a speaker despite some background noise, such as shouting or whispering, but even these can be distractions. Interruptions and overlapping speech therefore tend to be quite carefully organized in plays, to appear to be overlapping and competing for the floor without making the speeches difficult to follow.

Research suggests (Coates, 1994, Wareing forthcoming) that overlapping speech is a more common feature in the conversations of women than of men. Caryl Churchill is an example of a playwright who has experimented with overlapping speech in all-women conversations such as those in her play *Top Girls*. In a section that prefaces the text of the play, Churchill explains how overlap between the characters is shown in the text, using examples from the play as illustrations:

2   when one character starts speaking before the other has finished, the point of interruption is marked /.

> e.g. ISABELLA: This is the Emperor of Japan? / I once met the Emperor of Morocco.
>   NIJO: In fact he was the ex-Emperor.

a character sometimes continues speaking right through another's speech:

> e.g. ISABELLA: When I was forty I thought my life was over./ Oh I was pitiful. I was
>   NIJO: I didn't say I felt it for twenty years. Not every minute.
>   ISABELLA: I was sent on a cruise for my health and I felt even worse. Pains in my bones, pins and needles . . .

In this play, the actors and director need a key to interpreting the written text, rather like the way we gave you a description of the transcription conventions at the beginning of this section.

5.3.5 Back channel support

When we are listening closely to someone, or when we want to indicate that we are listening, we signal our attention to the speaker in a number of ways. We may turn towards them, lean towards them slightly, nod and / or make sounds which are called back channel support, or sometimes **minimal responses**. These are speech sounds such as *uhuh*, *yeah*, and *mmhmm*. At line 7, Susan says *yeah* which is a minimal response to Mary's suggestion *I suppose we can have baskets and things*.

On stage, an actor might indicate that they are listening through body posture, but they are less likely to have back channel support scripted in for them – their listening is more likely to take place in silence. If you try not giving any back channel support, and not nodding when someone is talking to you in real life, what usually happens is that the speaker will become increasingly hesitant and unsure of themselves. This is not what usually happens on the stage, although there is no reason why this type of interaction cannot be dramatized.

5.3.6 Discourse markers

In ordinary conversations, people frequently use words and phrases that have various, and sometimes rather ambiguous, functions. These include items like *well*, *you know*, *like* and others. At lines 8 and 9, Mary uses *like* twice: 'that gonna stand *kinda like* stand up on the workbench but what about *like* on the walls'. She also uses *kinda* (*kind of*).

These markers can signal a number of things, such as uncertainty, or the wish to disagree but politely, or they can be 'in-group markers' (if all your friends use a particular expression, you may use it too, to show you are part of the group), or even all three things at the same time. These expressions are often imitated in plays – they can be important features of characterization and are one of the devices that writers use in pursuit of verisimilitude (i.e. when they are trying to create a replica of reality to 'deceive' the audience into believing what they see/hear on the stage).

5.3.7 Discourse cohesion

The term 'cohesion' literally means 'sticking together'. For a conversation or indeed any text to be understandable, it must be cohesive. In other words, the different parts of the text must relate to one another. If it lacks cohesion, it will appear very disjointed, and won't seem to make sense. One of the things that makes a conversation or text 'cohesive' is that all the information in it relates to something we've already been told or know anyway. In the transcribed conversation between Mary and Susan, one of the things which makes it rather confusing is that there is quite of lot of information which they, as participants, are taking for granted, but which we (as readers of the transcript) are not actually aware of. In a scripted exchange, the writer or writers usually make sure that everything the reader or member of the audience needs to know is made explicit.

ACTIVITY 5.1

Below we have rewritten the transcription of Mary and Susan's conversation to make it look more like scripted language. We've guessed what the speakers meant to say (we could be completely wrong – we just wanted to make it *look* as if it made sense!), and tried to make it sound more cohesive by making all the information given more explicit. Read our version through and compare it to the original above. What are the things we have changed?

Rewrite of Mary and Susan's Conversation – part 1

1   M: OK, so we can make some African-style tea, and I've got a a book on Zambezi as well although it's just a wildlife book. What else do we need?

2   S: Well, that's quite a lot already. I'll see if Ricky has anything though, I think she's got some things she brought back from that holiday in Africa she might be prepared to lend us.

3   M: Oh yes, and then I suppose we could have African baskets and things

4   S: yeah

5   M: But those are all just things that will stand up on the workbench. What about the walls? We need something to give it atmosphere because the actual recipe we're going to make for the meal isn't really distinctively African.

6   S: No, you're right.

Here is another extract from the same conversation a bit later. First of all, note which features make it more typical of a naturally occurring conversation than a scripted one, and then rewrite it to be more like a piece of scripted dialogue, keeping a record of what alterations you make, and why you make them. A number in brackets, such as at line 22, indicates a pause – the number in the brackets is the length of the pause in seconds.

Mary and Susan's Conversation – part 2

20	M:	do you think it's worth having like a write-up on them (.)
21	M:	or (.) something like that (.) or do you think (.) people
22	M:	aren't really not gonna be interested they're gonna eat the
23	M:	food and go (2. 0) do you think they're actually gonna
24	S:	that's the thing
25	M:	walk up to the front and flick through a book or (.) or read
26	M:	about (.) birds or (.) trees or
	S:	yeah yeah
27	S:	well I think if it's something very short it's not like you'd
28	S:	have to wade through a whole lot of (.) information or
29	M:	yeah sure
30	S:	that'll be cool
31	M:	ok (.) so can you think of anything else (.) that's worth
32	M:	taking (3. 0)
33	S:	not really (.)
34	M:	cos it seems quite criminal (.) having like an African
35	M:	theme but the food isn't African
36	M:	so we've
	S:	isn't African (.) yeah
37	M:	got to try and make it up with (.)
38	S:	yeah
39	M:	surroundings or (.)
40	S:	yeah
41	M:	whatever

Remember – in your version you can make things up if you need to for clarity – though don't depart too far from what appears to have been meant. You will find our suggestions in the section at the end of the book.

5.4 Analysing Dramatic Language

In the previous section we have discussed the differences between language which occur naturally, and language which imitates speech in dramatic texts. In this section we look at the speech in dramatic texts and show how analytic techniques which linguists have applied to naturally occurring conversations can be applied to dialogue in plays to explore the interaction between characters.

5.4.1 Turn quantity and length

How much a character talks can be indicative either of their relative importance in the play, or of how important they appear to think they are. Generally, central characters have longer and more speeches than minor characters. However, Bennison (1993: 82–4) argues that as the main character, Anderson in Tom Stoppard's play *Professional Foul*, develops as a character, he has fewer long speeches – indicative of his increased ability to listen to others.

5.4.2 Exchange sequences

A model frequently proposed as a common structure for exchanges between speakers is the **adjacency pair**, a concept originally developed during the late 1960s in the work of American sociologist Harvey Sacks (1995), and used subsequently in much work in **conversation analysis** (see Hutchby & Wooffitt, forthcoming). Typical adjacency pairs are two-part exchanges such as greeting – greeting:

A: Hi, good to see you.
B: Hello, I'm glad I could make it.

question – answer:

A: What time's the train?
B: Half past seven.

and request – response:

A: Pass the mustard please.

B: Here you are (*passes mustard*).

Another model for structuring conversational exchanges is the so-called IRF model, developed in the approach to discourse analysis of Sinclair and Coulthard (1975) who identify a three-part exchange structure. Examples of this type of exchange are commonly found in teaching situations, when a teacher may ask a question (the *initiation*, coded I), to which the student replies (the *response*, coded R). The teacher then gives feedback on the student's answer (*feedback*, coded F):

Teacher:	Can anyone explain the meaning of the word 'pragmatic'?	**I**
James:	Practical.	**R**
Teacher:	Yes, practical, good.	**F**

Another frequently observed variation is what Sinclair and Coulthard term 'skip-connecting', which is similar to the pattern of insertion sequences (see Levinson 1983), where one exchange pair is embedded within another:

A:	So where did you get your handbag?	(Q 1)
B:	Promise you won't tell anybody?	(Q 2)
A:	Promise.	(A 2)
B:	I found it in my aunt's wardrobe.	(A 1)

Attempts have been made to catalogue many of the patterns of exchanges which are considered appropriate by speakers of English (e.g. an invitation can appropriately be followed by an acceptance or a refusal), but as there is so much scope for variation in context this is really a fruitless task. However, the model of exchange structure can be useful when analysing a dramatic dialogue which doesn't seem to conform to the expected pattern of exchange. Harold Pinter's plays, for example, are famous for the very strange dialogues between characters, where these expected patterns do not occur. The extract below is from *A Night Out*. The characters, Albert and a Girl, are in the Girl's flat, where she has brought him back with her after picking him up on the street.

3   *His hand screws the cigarette. He lets it fall on the carpet.*
GIRL [*outraged*]:   What do you think you're *doing? She stares at him.* Pick it up! pick that up, I tell you! It's my carpet! *She lunges towards it.* It's not my carpet, they'll make me pay –

His hand closes upon hers as she reaches for it.
GIRL: What are you doing? Let go. Treating my place like a pigsty . . . Let me go. You're burning my carpet!
ALBERT [*quietly, intensely*]:   Sit down.
GIRL: How dare you?
ALBERT: Shut up. Sit down.
GIRL: What are you doing?
ALBERT: Don't scream. I'm warning you. . . .
GIRL: What are you going to do ?
ALBERT [*seizing the clock from the mantelpiece*]:   DON'T MUCK ME ABOUT!

This dialogue does not 'fit' our model of exchange structure in several respects. First, Albert does not respond to the girl's exclamations about the dropped cigarette, and her commands to pick it up. Second, she asks him a series of questions ('How dare you?', 'What are you doing?', and 'What are you going to do?'), none of which he gives a direct answer to. Ignoring her questions and commands is one way he demonstrates the unequal distribution of power between them, which culminates in his threat of physical violence.

Although people's real life conversational exchanges do not necessarily always conform to the type of models described above that analysts build for them, the analysis of exchange structure in dramatic texts can nevertheless be a useful approach to exploring aspects of characters' relationships with one another through the kind of interactive talk that they do.

5.4.3 Production errors

Above we have suggested that so-called production errors such as hesitations, repetitions and incomplete turns are common in ordinary, naturally occurring conversation, but less typical of dialogue in plays (except, as in the example given above, in films which deliberately imitate natural discourse). However, sometimes a writer will deliberately use forms such as hesitations to convey something about the character – that they are distracted, for example, or uncertain or shy, or confused, or embarrassed. In this example from *Professional Foul* by Tom Stoppard, the character Anderson meets one of his footballing heroes and offers advice on the opposition in a forthcoming match, a situation in which he demonstrates signs of embarrassment, shown in bold:

4   ANDERSON: I've seen him twice. In the UFA Cup a few seasons ago . . . I happened to be in Berlin for the Heel Colloquium, **er**, bunfight **. . . (In a rush)** I realize it's none of my business – **I mean** you may think I'm an absolute ass, **but** **– (pause)** Look, if Hahas takes that corner he's going to make it short **– almost certainly –** . . .

5.4.4 The cooperative principle

The philosopher Grice (1975) developed the theory of a cooperative principle, which he asserted people used to make sense of their conversations by enabling them to distinguish between 'sentence-meaning' and 'utterance-meaning', i.e. between what a sentence 'means' (out of context) and what the speaker 'means' when they say that sentence (in a particular context).

For example, take the words 'nice earrings'; on the page, these words have a straightforward meaning, a statement of approval about items of jewellery. However, imagine someone twirling in front of you, saying 'how do you like my new outfit?'. If you then responded 'nice earrings', the person in the new clothes would probably assume that rather than just complimenting them on their jewellery, you were also communicating your dislike of what they were wearing. Grice claimed that this meaning can be inferred by the hearer, as participants in conversations expect each other to do certain things, in other words their talk is governed by the cooperative principle, which is made up of four conversational maxims:

the maxim of quantity:	give the appropriate amount of information – not too much or too little

the maxim of quality:	be truthful
the maxim of manner:	avoid ambiguity and using obscure expressions; give information in an appropriate order.
the maxim of relevance:	be relevant.

Grice suggested that people actually break these maxims quite often when they talk – for example, when we deliberately tell a lie we are not 'being truthful'. He suggested that speakers also flout them in a way that is apparent to the addressee, but that we take this for granted in the way we conduct our conversations. For example, in another extract from Pinter's *A Night Out*, Albert apparently flouts the maxim of relevance when he responds to the Girl's questions:

5   GIRL: And what film are you making at the moment?
      ALBERT: I'm on holiday.
      GIRL: Where do you work?
      ALBERT: I'm freelance.

Albert's replies do not directly answer the Girl's questions – he does not tell her what film he is working on nor where he works. However, most people would probably make sense of this exchange by assuming that the answers were relevant to the questions at an underlying level. This would result in the response 'I'm on holiday' being understood to mean 'I'm not making a film at the moment because I'm on holiday', and the response to the second question meaning 'I don't have one single place I can identify, because being freelance, I work all over the place.'

    Grice's point is that we tend to assume that the Conversational Maxims are being acknowledged, even when they appear not to be, and so we would interpret the information offered by Albert as relevant to the Girl's questions. However, we would probably still consider that these responses flout the Maxim of Quantity, even if we assume that they are obeying the Maxim of Relevance indirectly. By flouting the Maxim of Quantity, and not giving out personal details as requested, he keeps the Girl at arm's length, and communicates clearly that he is not inviting intimacy.

5.4.5 Speech acts

The philosophers Austin and Searle were very interested in the way language can be described as action, and Speech Act theory is an account of what we use language for. For example, we can make promises ('I will marry you'), threats ('I'll never speak to you again if you tell anyone'), give orders ('Leave the room!'), make suggestions ('Why don't we leave work early and all go down the pub?'). Sometimes saying an utterance explicitly accomplishes an action, like when someone says 'I declare this supermarket open', or 'I name this ship Clara'. This type of action cannot be accomplished by anybody though. Opening supermarkets and naming ships is usually done by people with some publicly recognized status, whereas promising and making threats can be accomplished by most of us, given the right conditions. The sets of contextual conditions which have to be in place if a speech act is to work are called **felicity conditions**, and if a speaker produces an utterance in a context where the appropriate conditions do not hold, then their speech act will be infelicitous.

Speech acts can be quite explicit; for example, if a character in a play says: 'Take this letter to the post', it is clear an order is being given (which the addressee can chose to obey or disobey). The fact that one character gives an order to another gives the reader / audience information about the relationship between the two characters (i.e. that one may have, or assumes they have, higher status than the other). Speech acts like this which are intended to produce some form of action as a response are called **directives**.

Directives can also be considerably less explicit, and generally, the less obvious they are, the more polite they are. Consider the following:

(1) Take this letter to the post.
(2) Would you mind posting this letter?
(3) Are you going past the post box?
(4) What time does the post go today?

These might all be interpreted as directives in particular contexts. (4) is a 'hint' – neither the letter nor the person who it is hoped will carry out the action are mentioned explicitly, but it might nevertheless be interpreted as a covert request to post the letter.

One of the challenges for a dramatic critic is to identify speech acts and the ways characters respond to them. Characters may produce speech acts which are appropriate to their status within the play, relative to other characters, or ones which appear inappropriate, which mark either a misapprehension on the part of the character about their status, or a change in their status.

5.4.6 Presuppositions

When we talk, we are constantly making assumptions about what kind of knowledge is available to our addressee(s), and what we have to make explicit in our utterances. Sometimes this knowledge is described in terms of 'given' and 'new' information – i.e. what is already known, and what has to be made known to the addressee. One way of encoding given information is through semantic presupposition, for example, in the sentence:

Jane was late for school yesterday

the information that there is someone called Jane, and that she went to school yesterday, is presupposed, or 'given' information, while the assertion that she was late is the new information.

The concept of presupposition has been widely discussed in both linguistic and philosophical literature, sometimes in a highly technical way (see Levinson, 1983 for a thorough discussion of the issues involved). For our purposes, however, we find it useful to distinguish between this kind of presupposition, which is encoded in the sentence or utterance, and a rather different kind of presupposition, which is to do with participants' mutual knowledge, and the cultural background assumptions they bring to bear on their interpretation of utterances.

Humour in dramatic texts can sometimes be explored by comparing the background assumptions of our own world, or culture, with those produced by the world of the text. Short says that 'some texts, particularly comic and absurd works, create special effects by assuming "facts" that are so at odds with our normal assumptions that we cannot "take them on" in the usual way' (1996: 234)

The following example is taken from a recording of a Radio 4 broadcast called *People Like Us*, a comedy programme based on media documentaries. In this extract, the conventional assumptions we hold about how people behave in television or radio interviews are deliberately parodied. The interview is between the 'journalist' (Roy Mallard) and a 'headmaster':

6   H: One of the first things I learnt in this job is that if you treat children like children they behave like children.
    RM: Yes (1.0) that's rather obvious innit.
    H: Yes very obvious yes that's why I learnt it first.
    RM   Do you think you're good at what you do?
    H: That's a very good question (1.0) I think it depends on what I'm doing really (0.5) I'm a reasonably good cook.
    RM: Um I was really thinking of you as a headmaster.
    H: I am a headmaster.

By taking the interviewer's questions literally and not relating them to the context, the headmaster is not only behaving in a way that clashes with our general background assumptions about headmasters, (e.g. that they are competent, professional members of society) but also in a way that clashes with our expectations about how people generally respond to questions in this particular form of speech event.

5.4.7 Status marked through language

Many of the properties of language discussed above can, as we have already said, be used to signal the relative status, and changes in status, of characters. In particular, language can be used to signal to what extent the relationship between a speaker and an addressee is based on a social power difference (or **asymmetry**), and to what extent it is based on solidarity. How people address one another usually signals where they perceive themselves to be socially in relation to their addressee: their equal, or their social inferior or superior (see Ervin-Tripp 1972, and Brown & Gilman 1972). A considerable amount of our language use is grounded in these perceptions.

The social 'rules' which make it acceptable for a head teacher to call a child by their first name: 'Simon' or 'Kate', while the child would respond with the teacher's last name and title: 'Mrs Griffiths', or with just a title such as 'Sir', are largely taken for granted by both parties. On the other hand, some relationships are negotiated moment to moment. A mother who calls her child 'Kate' when she is happy with her, may call her 'Katherine' in the next instant if she is angry with her and wants to assert her parental status. Playwrights can indicate to an audience this kind of information about the relationships between characters through the ways they address one another on stage.

The comedian Jo Brand was giving an account on a radio programme (R4, *Relatively Speaking* 8 April 1996) of the first time she took her first boyfriend home, and he and her father had a fight. She explained the fight started partly because her boyfriend kept calling her father 'old chap'. Presumably Brand's father took exception to the address term 'old chap' because he found it condescending, and also a signal of the class background of the boyfriend (Brand described her public school educated boyfriend as an act of rebellion against the socialist values of her parents). Thus the expression 'old chap' carried enough information about the boyfriend and his attitude towards Brand's father to provoke sufficient anger in Brand's father to start a fight.

The so-called *tu / vous* (*T/V*) distinction which existed in Elizabethan English, and which still exists in many languages, but which has been lost in modern English, is often used by Shakespeare to indicate relationships between characters. The form *thou* in Early Modern English, the second person singular pronoun (i.e. for addressing one person) equivalent to the French form *tu*, was used to signal either intimacy or that the speaker was of higher social status than the addressee. The form *you* in Early Modern English was equivalent to the Modern French form *vous*; it was used for the second person plural (i.e. for addressing two or more people), but was also used for the second person singular as a polite form used to mark social distance or coldness and/or respect. The *thou* form was already beginning to die out when Shakespeare was writing, but nevertheless, there are scenes in his plays where the characters switch between the use of *you* and *thou*, indicating the fluctuations in their relationships, from intimacy to distance, from respect to contempt. For example, in the extract below from Shakespeare's play *As You Like It*, analysed by Calvo (1994: 112), the cousins Celia and Rosalind differ in their use of pronouns to one another. Celia, who has been irritated by remarks Rosalind, madly in love with Orlando, has made about women, and by her general self-absorption, uses the distant and polite form *you*. Rosalind, completely wrapped up in her own emotions, apparently oblivious to Celia's annoyance and to the fact that Celia may feel rejected by Rosalind's obsession with Orlando, uses the intimate *thou* form in response.

7   Celia: You have simply misused our sex with your love-prate. We must have your doublet and hose plucked over your head, and show the world what the bird hath done to her own nest.

        Rosalind: O coz, coz, coz, my pretty little coz, that thou didst know how many fathoms deep I am in love! But it cannot be sounded. My affection hath an unknown bottom, like the Bay of Portugal.

        Celia: Or rather bottomless, that as fast as you pour affection in, it runs out.

        Rosalind: No. That same wicked bastard of Venus, that was begot of thought, conceived of spleen and born of madness, that blind rascally boy that abuses everyone's eyes because his own are out, let him be judge how deep I am in love. I'll tell the Aliena, I cannot be out of sight of Orlando. I'll go find a shadow and sigh till he come.

        Celia: And I'll sleep.

Without knowledge of the *T/V* distinction and what it can signal about social and personal relationships, we would lose some of the significance of this scene. Hamlet and his mother Gertrude in Act 3 scene 4 of *Hamlet* also use the *you / thou* forms in complex variations to indicate fluctuations in their relationship with one another.

5.4.8 Register

Register is the term used in linguistics to describe the relationship between a particular style of language and its context of use, discussed already in chapter 4. As language users, we can recognize a wide range of styles even though we might not be able to actively produce them. An example of a linguistic register is legal discourse – we recognize a legal document when we see one, but lawyers are generally the only people who are trained to produce them using appropriate linguistic choices.

In Shakespeare's *A Midsummer Night's Dream*, social order, and the importance of acting appropriately for your station in life are very important themes. Characters in the play include fairies, nobility and ordinary working people, and the different social status of each group is marked through their style of language. The 'ordinary' fairies talk in rhyming couplets of iambic pentameter (lines of ten syllables, with the stress on alternate syllables, as discussed in chapter 2):

8   Fairy: Either I mistake your shape and making quite
                 Or else you are that shrewd and knavish sprite
                 Call'd Robin Goodfellow. Are you not he
                 That frights the maidens of the villagery,
                 Skim milk and sometimes labour in the quern
                 And bootless make the breathless housewife churn . . .

The King and Queen of the Fairies, Oberon and Titania, use both rhyming couplets and blank verse, which is unrhymed lines in iambic pentametre. The mortals of higher social status – the Duke Theseus, Hippolyta, the Queen of the Amazons who is betrothed to Theseus, the young lovers and Hermia's father – all talk in blank verse:

9   Theseus: Now, fair Hippolyta, our nuptial hour
                    Draws on apace; four happy days bring in
                    Another moon; but, O, methinks how slow
                    This old moon wanes! She lingers my desires,
                    Like to a step-dame or a dowager,
                    Long withering out a young man's revenue

The 'mechanicals' (who work as a carpenter, a joiner, a weaver and other similar jobs) talk in unscanned speeches to indicate their lowly status:

10   Snug: Have you the lion's part written? Pray you, if it be, give it to me, for I am slow of study.
       Quince: You may do it extempore, for it is nothing but roaring.
       Bottom: Let me play the lion too. I will roar that I will do any man's heart good to hear me . . .

Thus every line spoken in the play reminds us of the status of that character in the scheme of things.

Modern drama uses devices such as rhyme and regular metrical patterning infrequently, but social status of a character can still be suggested by their dialect or accent, and by the register they use. Humour can also be produced through the incongruity between the choice of register for a particular context. Much of the humour in the films and television series of the British comedy team 'Monty Python' is derived from this mismatch between the language used and the situation it is used in, for example in their film *Monty Python and the Holy Grail*.

5.4.9 Speech and silence – female characters in plays

A considerable amount of work in linguistics has gone into looking at the distribution of talk between women and men, and there is some evidence that men tend to talk more than women in mixed sex conversations (see for example, Spender, 1990: 41–2 for an overview of this research). Spender has suggested that the reason why it is accepted that women are the talkative sex is that the amount they talk is not compared with the amount that men talk, but with silence, arguing that in fact silence is the preferred state for women in a patriarchal society. There is certainly some support for her hypothesis at least in our dramatic heritage: some of Shakespeare's characters notably regard silence in women as a virtue. Coriolanus, for example, greets his wife as 'My gracious silence, hail!' (*Coriolanus* Act 2 scene 1). King Lear grieves for his daughter Cordelia, and praises her quiet voice: 'Her voice was ever soft, / Gentle and low – an excellent thing in a woman' (*King Lear* Act 5 scene 3). In *The Taming of the Shrew*, as Katherina, the 'shrew' of the title, is reviled for being outspoken, her sister Bianca is praised for her silence:

11 Tranio: . . . That wench is stark mad or wonderful forward.
    Lucentio: But in the other's silence do I see
               Maid's mild behaviour and sobriety.

Anne Varty (1994) looks at how some contemporary women playwrights have handled the issue of women's rights to speak in drama. She suggests that women characters who appear strong in plays generally achieve their appearance of strength by manipulating the kinds of discourse they use, and adapting the stereotypes of masculine and feminine behaviour to serve their own ends:

The abilities to command many voices and to play many parts have emerged from this survey [of plays by Timberlake Wertenbaker, Liz Lochhead, Caryl Churchill, Pam Gems, Sarah Daniels, and Andrea Dunbar] as survival strategies for women. ... those who can switch linguistic codes according to context enjoy greater power whatever their status. Related to power generated by the switching of codes, is the ability to step in and out of both behavioural and linguistic stereotype. But, as Wertenbaker's plays seem to show, only so much female transgression will be tolerated by a male hegemony before there is a complete breakdown of the social order.

(Varty 94: 88)

In the representations of women she looks at however, she finds clear limits beyond which women trespass at their peril on men's authority.

5.5 Analysis of dramatic texts: checklist

Walter Nash (1989) suggests that dramatic texts can be analysed in a series of stages, starting with the most basic and least controversial, and working up to the most sophisticated and debatable. If you are required to analyse a dramatic text, you may find it useful to refer to these guidelines. The stages he outlines are as follows:

- *paraphrase the text* – i.e. put it into your own words
  This can be quite a crude approach, but it ensures that your basic understanding of the text is sound. It is a chance to check any unfamiliar words or grammatical constructions. It also allows you to check how each of the characters contributes to the plot of the play. Although your paraphrase should be as close to the content of the original as possible, there may be still some room for ambiguities or different interpretations. As far as possible you should note these, perhaps by indicating the various possible interpretations in different paraphrases.

- *write a commentary* on the text
  This is where you interpret what the significance of the extract you are analysing is in the context of the play as a whole: how does it contribute to the development of the plot and the

evolution of the characters? This is also a chance to check any literary allusions and ambiguities which give the text more than one possible reading.

- *select a theoretical approach*, perhaps from those discussed above

  This will be a narrower process, where you consider the text from a specific point of view, applying one theoretical model of the way language and communication work. This needs to be very thorough and detailed, and it is more likely to be debatable whether the approach you have selected is appropriate. Applying a theoretical model to the text may leave you feeling that you have learnt very little that is new, or that you have learnt a great deal – it is far more 'chancey' than either the paraphrase or the commentary in terms of what you get out of it.

ACTIVITY 5.2

Choose a scene from a play, one you have seen or read, one you have heard on the radio (there are published collections of radio plays available), or one you are studying;

(a) Write a *paraphrase* of it, as described in stage one above;
(b) Write a *commentary* on the same scene, as described above;
(c) Choose one of the discourse features discussed above, and *analyse* the same scene, for the use made of that feature in the scene, and the effect this has on your interpretation of it.

Discussion question:
Does your analysis change your attitude to anything you wrote in your paraphrase or commentary? If so, what, and how?

Suggestions for further reading

You may find the following texts useful in the applications of techniques from discourse analysis to dramatic texts.

Bennison, N. (1993) 'Discourse analysis, pragmatics and the dramatic "character": Tom Stoppard's *Professional Foul*', in *Language and Literature*, 2, 79–99.

Carter, Ron and Paul Simpson (1989) (eds) *Language, Discourse and Literature*, Unwin Hyman, London.

Coulthard, Malcolm (1985) *An Introduction to Discourse Analysis* (2nd edn), Longman, London.

Nash, Walter (1989) 'Changing the guard at Elsinore', in R. Carter and P. Simpson (eds) *Language, Discourse and Literature*, Unwin Hyman, London, 23–42.

Thomas, J. (1995) *Meaning in Interaction: An Introduction to Pragmatics*. London: Longman.

Chapter 6

From classic realism to modernism and postmodernism

6.1 Introduction

In this chapter we will be looking at the language used in another literary genre: fiction. Fiction is a generic term and includes short stories, novellas and novels. We will be attempting to define some of the characteristics of fiction writing by focusing mainly on novels written in the nineteenth and twentieth centuries.

Fiction is the kind of imaginative literature many people are most familiar with; it is the form that sells best, is publicized most widely, and is usually the most straightforward to read. We will be examining what makes reading novels seem 'straightforward' later in this chapter.

The reason for choosing novels written in the last two centuries is that the nineteenth century is the period when novel writing really flourished as a literary form, and when the style known as 'classic realism' dominated British fiction. George Eliot, Mrs Gaskell and Anthony Trollope are examples of some of the best known writers from this time. However, the label 'realism', as we will see later, can be applied to a wide range of texts and is a style of writing still popular today. Some writers in the twentieth century reacted against many of the assumptions made in novel-writing in the previous century, and by examining the contrast between nineteenth-century and twentieth-century forms, we hope to help you increase your understanding of the linguistic choices available to fiction writers.

We will be identifying the stylistic features which are typical of classic realism, and of modernism and postmodernism, two important twentieth-century literary movements. We think that being able to recognize the stylistic features associated with these movements can lead to a more thorough understanding of texts. We also believe that stylistic analysis helps to make labels such as 'postmodernism' or 'classic realism' more precise, and demystifies them by providing some concrete linguistic criteria as a basis for describing texts as either modernist or realist.

The stylistic features we focus on in this chapter are on a different, larger, scale from those we have been looking at up till now. Instead of looking at language choices made within sentences, we will be looking at any 'habits of language' which characterize different styles of fiction. These can include choices about how the narrative is structured, or even what themes are selected.

Finally, we want to point out that very few texts actually fit neatly into any category: the category labels are largely there for convenience. However, the process of evaluating whether a text fits into a certain category or not, and assembling evidence of why it does or does not, can be very useful for finding out more about the text and indeed, more about the category.

6.2 Literary perspectives on realist texts

In this section we will look at some accounts of what constitutes a realist text, particularly the views of literary theorists Roland Barthes, Colin MacCabe and David Lodge. In the following sections, we will look at what kinds of novel, and what features of the novel were distinct from previous literature. We will then look at some of the stylistic features and devices that enable us to classify and interpret a text as 'realist'. As we have noted above, the label 'realism' can be applied to a wide range of fiction, including contemporary texts, while 'classic realism' refers to a particular movement in the nineteenth century.

The social historian Raymond Williams (1972) has suggested that in the twentieth century, the realist tradition in the novel has subdivided into two separate categories of 'social' and 'personal' realism. Writers like George Orwell and William Golding are in the first category, Graham Greene and E. M. Forster in the second. As we will see, there are other kinds of novels which also use some of the stylistic features of realism to construct the textual world as real. Magic realist novels and science fiction do this, for example, although in other ways they contradict our expectations of the ordinary world.

One of the most influential accounts of the difference between realist and modernist writing is Roland Barthes' distinction between 'readerly' and 'writerly' texts. In the introduction to his analysis of a short story by Balzac, *S/Z*, Barthes defines a 'readerly' text as one which enables the reader to be a 'consumer' of the meanings, narratives and characters which are presented to them by the text, whereas a 'writerly' text is one which makes the reader actively engage in producing those meanings (1975: 4). Let's take a look at this idea in more detail to establish what these terms are actually referring to, and whether we can clarify them from a stylistic point of view.

We can start from Barthes' definition of an 'ideal' text, which he describes as 'plural', consisting of 'a galaxy of signifiers, not a structure of signifieds' (1975: 5). A signifier in linguistic terminology is the actual material of language, the written or spoken word or phrase that we use to represent a particular thing or a particular concept. So, for example, the combination of phonemes /k/, /æ/, and /t/ produces the item *cat*, which is the word we use to refer to the small four-legged domestic animal that purrs. The animal itself is the 'signified', the concept which the label *cat* refers to. But the word itself is unrelated to the animal in any way – there is no good reason why the group of phonemes /kæt/ should represent the animal described above, rather than any other group of phonemes. It is our knowledge of the English language that enables us to link this word, or linguistic signifier, to its 'signified' element: the animal itself.

Saussure (in Lodge, 1988) describes this relationship between signifiers and signifieds as *arbitrary*, that is to say, established through the systems and conventions of the language, and through an inherent relationship between the word and the thing it refers to. (A very few words do have this kind of 'inherent' relationship, as for example when the sound of the signifier imitates the sound made by the signified. This is the connection between the word 'cuckoo' and the call of that bird; this relationship of a word imitating the sound of what it refers to is known as 'onomatopoeia'.)

When Barthes uses these terms 'galaxy' and 'structure' in the quotation above to describe the difference between readerly and writerly texts, we can take 'a galaxy of signifiers' to mean groups or clusters of words which may have multiple meanings, which can be interpreted in different ways. This is in contrast to 'structures of signifieds', where the relationship between the things or concepts being referred to is fixed and stable, producing only one possible meaning. In postmodernist texts with overtly complex signifying systems, this relationship is much weaker. Readerly texts are those whose structures seem to be 'smooth' on the outside, the narration 'flows' and the language seems ordinary and natural. Writerly texts, on the other hand, challenge the reading process in some way, and make the reader work much harder to produce meanings from a range of different possibilities, undermining the 'naturalness' of the text.

We can illustrate this difference between readerly and writerly texts by using two contrasting examples: extract one is from *The Prodigal Daughter* by Jeffrey Archer and extract two from Russell Hoban's novel *Ridley Walker*.

1   It had not been an easy birth, but then for Abel and Zaphia Rosnovski nothing had ever been easy, and in their own ways they had both become philosophical about that. Abel had wanted a son, an heir who would one day be chairman of the Baron Group. By the time the boy was ready to take over, Abel was confident that his own name would stand alongside those of Ritz and Statler and by then the Baron would be the largest hotel group in the world. Abel had paced up and down the colourless corridor of St. Luke's Hospital waiting for the first cry, his slight limp becoming more pronounced as each hour passed. Occasionally he twisted the silver band that encircled his wrist and stared at the name so neatly engraved on it. He turned and retraced his steps once again, to see Doctor Dodek heading towards him.

2   There is the Hart of the Wud in the Eusa Story that wer a stage every 1 knows that. There is the hart of the wood meaning the veryes deap of it thats a nother thing. There is the hart of the wood where they bern the chard coal thats a nother thing agen innit. Thats a nother thing. Berning the chard coal in the hart of the wood. That's what they call the stack of wood you see. The stack of wood in the shape they do it for chard coal berning. Why do they call it the hart tho? That's what this here story tels of.

The first extract makes few demands on the reader. There is little difficulty or effort involved in interpreting this text. The characters and events are presented through third person narration, the hospital setting is familiar to the majority of readers, the action of a father pacing the corridor, waiting for the birth of his child is recognizable (even stereotypical), and the language does not draw attention to itself in any way.

The second extract, in contrast, not only foregrounds the use of language by using non-standard spellings and grammar, it also poses problems of interpretation for the reader. Meaning is not transparent in this text. The first person narrator points out that there are three possible meanings for the 'Hart of the Wud', and none of them is straightforward to understand.

ACTIVITY 6.1

We have pointed out that there are major differences between these two texts, and identified two of them:

1	2
narrated in the third person	narrated in the first person ('I')
standard English	non-standard English

What other differences can you identify and add to this list?

Reading writerly texts often involves a process of rereading, something that Barthes claims is 'contrary to the commercial and ideological habits of our society' (1975: 15). We tend to read stories in succession, not the same one again and again, and it is perhaps no accident that the popular novels we read as 'consumers' share many of the features of the realist texts from the latter part of the nineteenth century when this form of writing was at its height. Writerly texts are not 'consumable' in the same way, since they challenge our normal reading habits and interpretative practices, and often need to be read many times; each time a different interpretation may emerge.

Another related way of describing classic realist texts is to see them as containing a 'hierarchy' of levels of discourse: the discourse of the narrator, and the discourse of the characters (MacCabe, 1979). By 'discourse' in this context, we refer to the sets or types of sentences or utterances that can be attributed to one source (a character or a narrator) in the text. The narrative discourse provides a 'window on reality'. It presents the world of the text to the reader as if it were part of exterior reality, situating the events and the characters of the novel as if they were in the real world.

As we saw in the extract from *The Prodigal Daughter*, the narrator presents the character Abel Rosnovski in a hospital, waiting for news of the birth of his child, describing his thoughts and actions while he waits, as part of a world that is familiar to the reader. The discourse of the characters is then interpreted by the reader via the dominant discourse of the omnipresent narrator. Extract 3, from the same novel, illustrates this process:

3   'Congratulations, Mr Rosnovski,' he called.
    'Thank you,' said Abel eagerly.
    'You have a beautiful girl,' the doctor said as he reached him.
    'Thank you,' repeated Abel, quietly, trying not to show his disappointment.

Here we can clearly see this distinction between discourse, as we are given Abel's reaction to the news through the evaluative discourse of the narration ('. . . trying not to show his disappointment . . .') rather than the direct speech of the character ('"Thank you," repeated Abel . . .'). MacCabe labels these two levels of discourse as 'meta-discourse' (the discourse of the narrator) and 'object-discourse' (the discourse of the characters), and claims that the reader is guided in their interpretation of the text through the discourse of the narrator.

David Lodge (1990) disagrees with this idea of narrative discourse as 'transparent' prose, and suggests that there may be various discourses operating in a realist novel, not only in the form of the narration but also in the reported speech and thoughts of the characters. He argues that we cannot consider the voice of the narrator as being the controlling voice of the narrative, at the top of the hierarchy as it were, guiding the reader through the text. Instead, readers have to engage with a range of discourses and their interpretation will be influenced not only by the narrator but equally by the other voices present in the text. This is a topic we will return to later in the chapter. First let us look at what fiction was like before the development of realism.

6.3 The emergence of realism

Representing the textual world as 'real' was not always of paramount importance in fictional writing, particularly in very early fiction. Before the eighteenth century, literature was overwhelmingly concerned with mythical, romantic or heroic subjects, rather than the ordinary, domestic, everyday world typically represented in the later realist tradition. Poetry and drama were the genres writers used for imaginative literature, rather than prose.

Sir Philip Sidney's *Arcadia*, a mixture of prose and poetry, written in the latter half of the sixteenth century, is considered by many to be one of the earliest precursors of the English novel. In this text, the bardic tradition of oral narrative is very much in evidence. The story is situated at a time which is unspecified and a place which is very distant from the world of the reader. The pastoral setting of the country of Arcadia is a conventional literary landscape of the time, and nothing like the real Arcadia, a rather bleak mountainous area. The main characters are members of the nobility, and behave in a way that appears very stylized and lacking in psychological realism today.

The concern to produce fiction which could be accepted by the reader as if it were part of the real world began to appear in the late seventeenth and early eighteenth century. Stylistic devices for constructing an impression of reality in texts, through the supposed validity of documents like letters, or a written confession, started to be used and narratives began to look as if they were drawn from real life. One of these devices was to present a fictional story as if it were fact through a sequence of letters. In an epistolary novel, the letters create an impression of reality as it unfolds through time. As David Lodge (1992) points out, a real letter and a fictional letter look very similar, and the time-scale of the letters in Richardson's novels, *Pamela* (1741) and *Clarissa* (1747), represents the story as if it were unfolding in real time. Daniel Defoe, writing in the first quarter of the eighteenth century, used the device of the confessional novel for *Moll Flanders* (1722) and *Roxana* (1724), to convince readers of the 'truth' of the story. The following extract comes from the preface of *Roxana*, in which Defoe attempts to present the novel to his readers as based on fact:

4   He takes the Liberty to say, That this Story differs from most of the Modern Performances of this Kind, tho' some of them have

met with a very good Reception in the World; I say, It differs from them in this Great and Essential Article, Namely, That the Foundation of This is laid in Truth of Fact; and so the Work is not a Story, but a History.

The novel is written as a first person narrator telling the story of her life, and the reader is constantly reminded of the 'reality' of the story through devices such as 'disguising' the names of some of the characters:

5   At about Fifteen Years of Age, my Father gave me, as he call'd it in French, 25000 Livres, that is to say, two Thousand pounds Portion, and married me to an Eminent Brewer in the City; pardon me if I conceal his Name, for tho' he was the Foundation of my Ruin, I cannot take so severe a Revenge upon him.

The emergence of the 'classic realist' novel in the nineteenth century, of which George Eliot's writing is often regarded as the prototypical example, was an attempt to produce a 'whole' picture of life, community and characters as they could have existed in the real world, and that world was presented through the view of an exterior, 'omnipresent' narrator who was not part of it but who commented on it. As Raymond Williams observes, this method of representing a fictional reality is still the central organizing feature in most novels today: '. . . in the overwhelming majority of modern novels, including those novels we continue to regard as literature, the ordinary criteria of realism still hold' (1972: 583).

Realism is therefore a very significant development in the history of fiction. Let us now look at some of its defining stylistic features.

6.4 Stylistic characteristics of realist texts

If we are interested in analysing the stylistic features of realist texts, and exploring the similarities between classic realism and modern realist writing, we need to move from a general account of realism to a more detailed analysis of the level of linguistic choices in the text. Moreover, the term 'realism' has been applied to other literary and artistic genres including Hollywood films. A stylistic analysis of realism should therefore attempt to describe the devices used to construct the appearance of reality in very different kinds of texts.

Lodge (1990) suggests the following set of criteria for defining a 'realist' text, to contrast these more 'readerly' kinds of texts against the more 'writerly' texts of the modernist and postmodernist literary style:

- the language of the text is not foregrounded (i.e. it does not draw attention to itself);
- the narrator does not draw attention to his or her role in interpreting events, the events 'speak for themselves';
- there is an emphasis on detailed description of context (time, place, setting)
- there is a similarity with the conventions of non-fictional texts from the same culture which produces an impression of reality.

In the light of the above criteria, these are some areas that we could investigate as possible devices for constructing realism in texts. We will be focusing on the representation of time, place and dialogue, as well as discussing the role of the narrating voice and the device of narrative closure.

6.4.1 The omniscient narrator

The presence of an 'omniscient narrator' in realist texts allows the writer to build up a picture of the world of the text and the people in it as if they were real. The narrator not only tells the story, but also comments on and makes judgements about the events and the characters. However, as we suggested above, the distinction between the narrating 'voice' and the voices and thoughts of the other characters is not always clearly defined in a text. The passage below is taken from George Eliot's novel *Middlemarch*; Dorothea, a young woman with a provincial upbringing, is engaged to Mr Casaubon. She hopes he will teach her Latin and Greek, in part so that she can help him in his work:

6   She would not have asked Mr Casaubon at once to teach her the languages, dreading of all things to be tiresome instead of help-

ful; but it was not entirely out of devotion to her future husband that she wished to know Latin and Greek. Those provinces of masculine knowledge seemed to her a standing-ground from which all truth could be seen more truly. As it was, she constantly doubted her own conclusions, because she felt her own igno- rance: how could she be confident that one-roomed cottages were not for the glory of God, when men who knew the classics appeared to conciliate indifference to the cottages with zeal for the glory? Perhaps even Hebrew might be necessary – at least the alphabet and a few roots – in order to arrive at the core of things, and judge soundly on the social duties of the Christian. And she had not reached that point of renunciation at which she would have been satisfied with having a wise husband; she wished, poor child, to be wise herself. Miss Brooke was certainly very naive with all her alleged cleverness. Celia, whose mind had never been thought too powerful, saw the emptiness of other people's pretensions much more readily. To have in general but little feeling, seems to be the only security against feeling too much on any particular occasion.

The narrating voice here shifts through various levels or perspectives. In the first six lines, we could argue that the narrator is representing the situation from the perspective of Dorothea through a series of 'mental process' verbs. These are a group of verbs which refer to processes to do with thinking or feeling (see Halliday 1985: chapter 5). In the following examples, 'she' is the subject and agent of these mental process verbs: '*dreading* of all things to be tiresome', 'she *wished* to know', 'she constantly *doubted*', 'she *felt* her own igno- rance'. After the colon, the following two questions can be interpreted as Dorothea's own internal thought processes, since they occur without a descriptive, narrating frame such as 'she wondered' or 'she thought'.

> . . . how could she be confident that one-roomed cottages were not for the glory of God? Perhaps even Hebrew might be necessary.

This method of representing a character's thoughts or words is known as 'free indirect speech', where the discourse of a character and the narrator's discourse are blended, or indistinguishable as different voices in the text (see Wales, 1989, for a full definition). There is then a shift back from Dorothea's perspective to the narrator's external voice, commenting on the previous section with a description of Dorothea's mental state, but this time using a material process verb *reach*, followed by the very explicit *poor child*.

> . . . she had not reached that point of renunciation at which she would have been satisfied with having a wise husband; she wished, poor child, to be wise herself.

There is a further distancing of the narrator from the character in the use of her second name, *Miss Brooke* rather than *Dorothea*, and the paragraph ends with a general comment which is relevant not only to the situation at hand, but to the world at large. So in this paragraph there is movement from a shared narrator/character perspective, to a character perspective and then to a narrator-only perspective at the end, linking the specific situation with the 'real' world of the narrator and the reader.

The presence of an 'intrusive' narrator (i.e. one that comments and evaluates) is however not only a feature of realist texts. The difference between the intrusiveness of Eliot's narrator, and the narrators in texts which are much more likely to be categorized as postmodern, is that Eliot does not usually draw attention to her role as narrator, whereas postmodernist writers explicitly remind readers of the narrative process. Consider the following extract from the opening passage of *London Fields* by Martin Amis:

> 7   What a gift. This page is briefly stained by my tears of gratitude. Novelists don't usually have it so good, do they, when something real happens (something unified, dramatic and pretty saleable), and they just write it down?

Here Amis is foregrounding the process of telling the story, establishing his claim to representing 'reality', but at the same time undermining the whole enterprise by drawing attention to the formulaic nature of writing: a novel basically consists of finding 'something unified, dramatic and pretty saleable'. We will be looking more closely at postmodern forms of narration in the second half of this chapter.

6.4.2 Representation of place

Another device found in realist writing to create an impression of a real world is to describe places in great detail, which was taken to even further lengths in the 'naturalist' novels (Hardy, Zola and Flaubert in France) of the nineteenth century. In the following extract from Eliot's *Adam Bede* (1878), the narrator gives a detailed description of a place called 'the Hall Farm' which paints a very vivid picture of the building and surrounding land:

8   Evidently that gate is never opened; for the long grass and the great hemlocks grow against it; and if it were opened, it is so rusty that the force necessary to turn it on its hinges would be likely to pull down the square stone built pillars, to the detriment of the two stone lionesses which grin with a doubtful carnivorous affability above a coat of arms, surmounting each of the pillars. It would be easy enough, by the aid of the nicks in the stone pillars, to climb over the brick wall with its smooth stone coping; but by putting our eyes close to the rusty bars of the gate, we can see the house well enough, and all by the very corners of the grassy enclosure. It is a very fine old place, of red brick, softened by a pale powdery lichen, which has dispersed itself with happy irregularity, so as to bring the red brick into terms of friendly companionship with the limestone ornaments surrounding the three gables, the windows, and the door-place. But the windows are patched with wooden panes, and the door, I think, is like the gate – it is never opened: how it would groan and grate against the stone floor if it were!

The detail is made even more 'real' by the device of situating the narrator within view of the place being described, and using the present tense throughout the description. The narrator here acts as the 'eyes' (and potentially the legs and ears) of the reader. By using the word 'we', the first person plural pronoun, Eliot encourages the reader to see themself as if in a 'team' with the narrator:

... by putting our eyes close to the rusty bars of the gate, we can see the house well enough ...

The narrator's expression *I think* in the description of the door also creates an impression of shared reality – as if the reader and narrator were in the same space, from where only a partial view is possible. These devices in the text function to construct the experience of seeing this house as 'real'.

The level of description of the fictional world is also a feature of contemporary popular fiction, as this extract from Dick Francis's novel *Comeback* illustrates:

9 We sat round a small dark table in a corner of a room heavily raftered and furnished in oak. The level of light from the red-shaded wall lamps was scarcely bright enough for reading the menus and there was an overall warmth of atmosphere that one met nowhere else on earth but in a British pub.

Here we see the stylistic concern of realism to give lifelike and detailed representations of place can also be found in this 'readerly' novel of the twentieth century.

6.4.3 Representation of dialogue

The representation of speech in narratives can take various forms. In the extract below from Sir Philip Sidney's *Arcadia* which as noted above, still shows many of the features of oral narratives, there is no attempt to reproduce the characters' talk in the form of a recognizable dialogue:

10 It was in the time that the earth begins to put on her new apparel against the approach of her lover, and that the sun, running a most even course, becomes an indifferent arbiter between the night and the day, when the hopeless shepherd Strephon was come to the sands which lie against the island of Cithera; where viewing the place with a heavy kind of delight, and sometimes casting his eyes to the isleward, he called his friendly rival, the pastor Claius, unto him; and setting first down in his darkened countenance a doleful copy of what he would speak,

'O my Claius,' said he, 'hither we are now come to pay the rend for which we are so called unto by over-busy remembrance – remembrance, restless remembrance, which claims not only this duty of us but for it will have us forget ourselves. [. . .] Did remembrance grant us any holiday either for pastime or devotion – nay either for necessary food or natural rest – but that still it forced our thoughts to work upon this place where we last (alas, that the word last should so long last) did graze our eyes upon her ever-flourishing beauty?

The square brackets signal the omission of another six lines of declamatory prose in Strephon's speech to Claius. The register is highly poetic, the language contains many rhetorical structures, and it is monologic rather than dialogic, bearing very little resemblance to anything we would recognise as conversation.

We can compare this to the next example, taken from *David Copperfield*, when David meets Mr Creakle for the first time:

11 'Now,' said Mr Creakle. 'What's the report of this boy?'

'There's nothing against him yet,' returned the man with the wooden leg. 'There has been no opportunity.'

I thought Mr Creakle was disappointed. I thought Mrs and Miss Creakle (at whom I now glanced for the first time, and who were, both, thin and quiet) were not disappointed.

'Come here, sir!' said Mr Creakle, beckoning to me.

'Come here,' said the man with the wooden leg, repeating the gesture. 'I have the happiness of knowing your father-in-law,' whispered Mr Creakle, taking me by the ear; 'and a worthy man he is, and a man of a strong character. He knows me, and I know him. Do you know me? Hey?' said Mr Creakle, pinching my ear with ferocious playfulness.

'Not yet, sir,' I said, flinching with the pain.

In the extract above, the conversation is represented as if it were really taking place, through the conventional use of speech marks to indicate the words spoken, direct address between the characters, interactive question and answer sequences and reporting verbs like *said*, *whispered* and *returned*, discourse markers such as *now* and *hey*, as well as David Copperfield's commentary (as the first person narrator) on the conversation in 'real' time, as it occurs.

ACTIVITY 6.2 ▬▬▬▬▬▬▬▬▬▬▬▬▬▬▬▬▬▬▬▬▬▬

One of the three extracts below is taken from a nineteenth-century novel, the other two are twentieth-century texts.

(1) What stylistic conventions do they share, and what are the differences, in the way dialogue is represented?

(2) What kind of effect do the different representations have on you as a reader?

12 I had expected that the valet would be dismissed when I appeared, but nothing of the sort happened. There he stood, in front of his master's chair, trembling under the weight of the etchings, and there Mr Fairlie sat, serenely twirling the magnifying glass between his white fingers and thumbs.

'I have come to speak to you on a very important matter,' I said, 'and you will therefore excuse me, if I suggest that we had better be alone.'

The unfortunate valet looked at me gratefully. Mr Fairlie faintly repeated my last three words, 'better be alone,' with every appearance of the utmost possible astonishment.

I was in no humour for trifling, and I resolved to make him understand what I meant.

'Oblige me by giving that man permission to withdraw,' I said, pointing to the valet.

Mr Fairlie arched his eyebrows and pursed up his lips in sarcastic surprise.

'Man?' he repeated. 'You provoking old Gilmore, what can you possibly mean by calling him a man? He's nothing of the sort. He might have been a man half an hour ago, before I wanted my etchings, and he may be a man half an hour hence, when I don't want them any longer. At present he is simply a portfolio stand. Why object, Gilmore, to a portfolio stand?'

'I do object. For the third time, Mr Fairlie, I beg that we may be alone.'

13 She had settled down in the fireside chair, her hair thrown back against the headrest, both legs splayed wide. Dalgliesh pulled out one of the wheel-backed chairs and sat facing her.

'Did you know Father Baddley well?'

'We all know each other well here, that's half our trouble. Are you thinking of staying here?'

'In the district perhaps for a day or two. But it doesn't seem possible now to stay here . . . '

'I don't see why not if you want to. The place is empty, at least until Wilfred finds another victim – tenant, I should say. I shouldn't think that he'd object. Besides you'll have to sort out the books won't you? Wilfred will want them out of the way before the next incumbent moves in.'

'Wilfred Anstey owns this cottage then?'

'He owns Toynton Grange and all the cottages except Julius Court's. He's further out on the headland, the only one with a sea view. Wilfred owns all the rest of the property and he owns us.'

14   'Blue' the young priest said earnestly. 'All available evidence, my daughter, suggests that Our Lord Christ Jesus was the most beauteous, crystal shade of pale sky blue.'

The little woman behind the wooden latticed window of the confessional fell silent for a moment. An anxious, cogitating silence. Then: 'But how, Father? People are not *blue*. No people are blue in the whole big world!'

Bewilderment of the little woman, matched by perplexity of the priest . . . because this is not how she's supposed to react. The Bishop had said, 'Problems with recent converts . . . when they ask about colour they're almost always that . . . important to build bridges, my son. Remember,' thus spake the Bishop, 'God is love; and the Hindu love-god Krishna is always depicted with blue skin. Tell them blue; it will be a sort of bridge between the faiths; gently does it, you follow; and besides blue is a neutral sort of colour, avoids the usual colour problems, gets you away from black and white: yes, on the whole I'm sure it's the one to choose.'

6.4.4 Representation of time

There is also a concern in realist novels to situate the narrative in real, historical time, by referring to events that actually took place, ranging from the very specific to more general references to a given historical period:

> 15 Our tale begins in 1793; about seven years after the commencement of one of the earliest of those settlements, which have conduced to effect that magical change in the power and condition of the state, to which we have alluded.

Let's look at the different ways that time can be constructed, by considering the opening paragraphs of two nineteenth-century novels: extract 16 is from the classic realist text, *Middlemarch*; 17 is from Thomas Hardy's novel, *The Mayor of Casterbridge*.

> 16 Miss Brooke had that kind of beauty which seems to be thrown into relief by poor dress. Her hand and wrist were so finely formed that she could wear sleeves not less bare of style than those in which the Blessed Virgin appeared to Italian painters; and her profile as well as her stature and bearing seemed to gain the more dignity from her plain garments, which by the side of provincial fashion gave her the impressiveness of a fine quotation from the Bible, – or from one of our elder poets, – in a paragraph of to-day's newspaper. She was usually spoken of as being remarkably clever, but with the addition that her sister Celia had more common-sense.

> 17 One evening of late summer, before the nineteenth century had reached one third of its span, a young man and woman, the latter carrying a child, were approaching the large village of Weydon Priors, in Upper Wessex, on foot. They were plainly but not ill clad, though the thick hoar of dust which had accumulated on their shoes and garments from an obviously long journey lent a disadvantageous shabbiness to their appearance just now.

In both these extracts the characters are situated within a particular historical time – explicitly by Hardy: 'before the nineteenth century had reached one third of its span'; and by reference to contemporary time by Eliot: 'in a paragraph of to-day's newspapers'. The location is specified by Hardy; the existence of Miss Brooke within a social world is implied by Eliot in the phrase: 'she was usually spoken of as being remarkably clever' (i.e. by people who knew her). Eliot uses the first person possessive form 'our': 'from one of our elder poets', which not only foregrounds the 'voice' of the narration, but also implies a close relationship between reader and narrator by the suggestion of shared time. In Hardy's text, on the other hand, the description is given without foregrounding the voice of the narrator. However, the use of the phrase 'just now' in the Hardy extract brings the reader closely into the time of the narrated events, also creating the sense of a shared temporal perspective between the reader and the narration.

6.4.5 Realism in other fictional genres

To end this section, we want to look at other kinds of fiction which draw on the stylistic devices of realism to construct a 'real' textual world, even though they might not in other respects fit into our category of the 'realist' novel. Two of these genres are magic realism and science fiction, which share some of the characteristics of realist texts even though neither genre is in the business of representing the 'ordinary', everyday world. Science fiction is usually concerned with representing a world apart from ours, either separated by time or space; magic realism represents strange and inexplicable qualities in the world we know. Some writers of magic realism novels include Salman Rushdie, Jeanette Winterson, García Márquez and Angela Carter.

--- **ACTIVITY 6.3**

In extracts 18 and 19 – one taken from a novel by Jeanette Winterson, the other from a science fiction novel by David Eddings – how many of the stylistic conventions of realist writing described above can you identify? Do these texts contain any stylistic features which mark them out as *different* from realist writing?

ACTIVITY 6.4 ▬▬▬▬▬▬▬▬▬▬▬▬▬▬▬▬

Following Roland Barthes' distinction discussed in section 6.2 above, what are the features in these texts which would lead you classify them as being 'readerly' or 'writerly'?

18   In the middle of summer, when the dying sun bled the blue sky orange, the movement began. At first it was no more than a tremor, then an upheaval, and everyone ran to put their silver in boxes and tie up the dog.

During the night the shifting continued, and although no one was hurt the doctor of the place issued a written warning to the effect that anyone whose teeth were false should remove them in case of sudden choking. The prudent applied this to hair-pieces and false limbs and soon the vaults of the town hall were filled with spare human matter.

As the weeks went by, and it became clear that the under-ground activity had neither ceased nor worsened, a few brave citizens tried to make the best of it and strung ropes from one point to another, as supports to allow them to go about their business. In time all of the people started to adjust to their new rolling circumstances and it was discovered that the best way to overcome the problem was to balance above it. The ropes were no longer used as supports but as walkways and roads, and everyone, even those who had piled up their limbs in the town hall, learned to be acrobats. Carrying coloured umbrellas to help them balance, they walked in soft shoes from their homes to their usual haunts.

A few generations passed, and no one remembered that the city had ever been like any other, or that the ground was a more habitual residence. Houses were built in the treetops and the birds, disgusted by this invasion of their privacy, swept even higher, cawing and chirping from the banks of clouds.

19   Barak, Earl of Trellheim, was considered in some quarters to be an unreliable sort, and his companions in the vanishing were, if anything, even worse. The Alorn kings were disquieted by the potential for disaster represented by Barak and his cohorts roaming loose in the Gods only knew what ocean.

What concerned young King Kheva, however, was not so

much random disasters as it was the fact that his friend Unrak had been invited to participate while he had not. The injustice of that rankled. The fact that he was a king seemed to automatically exclude him from anything that could even remotely be considered hazardous. Everyone went out of his way to keep Kheva safe and secure, but Kheva did not *want* to be kept safe and secure. Safety and security were boring, and Kheva was at an age where he would go to any lengths to avoid boredom.

Clad all in red, he made his way through the marble halls of the palace in Boktor that winter morning. He stopped in front of a large tapestry and made some show of examining it. Then, at least relatively sure that no one was watching – this *was* Drasnia, after all – he slipped behind the tapestry and into the small closet previously mentioned.

6.5 After classic realism

Although we have been looking at forms of literary realism in twentieth-century fiction, classic realism, as we have discussed at length, was a form that developed in the nineteenth century. Fiction, just like other artistic forms of expression such as architecture, painting and clothing, has fashions, and sooner or later, new ideas will be developed which have different values and put emphasis on different aspects of the art form. In the area of fiction, the values and forms of classic realism were challenged in the early twentieth century by modernism. Later in the century, the ideas informing modernism were themselves challenged by postmodernism. The second part of this chapter is concerned with stylistic definitions of these two movements.

One of the clearest ways to illustrate the changes which occurred in fiction in the twentieth century is through another medium – that of painting. Consider the three paintings shown in figures 6.1, 6.2, and 6.3.

Figure 6.1, Constable's *The Hay-Wain*, was painted in the first quarter of the nineteenth century. It has an almost photographic quality; it appears to be objective. A photograph of the scene taken at the same moment would probably look very similar, and the personality of the painter does not conspicuously intrude into the painting.

FIGURE 6.1 *The Hay-Wain* by John Constable

It is a representation of an English scene so painstakingly accurate and detailed that you would easily be able to identify the place from the painting if you ever visited the spot. Attention has been paid to the exact spatial layout and proportions of all the objects in the scene, and great effort has been expended on making the light and colours precisely as they would be at a certain time of day, and in certain weather conditions. It is also an 'ordinary' scene, which anyone might have come across, i.e. it is a representation of 'ordinary life'.

All these features are similar to the defining features of classic realism, as we discussed above. For many people, the measure of whether or not they like a painting in this style is how closely it looks like what it represents (how 'accurate' it is) and whether they like the subject matter (although art critics might not share this perspective). These are also criteria many people use when they judge whether or not they like a classic realist novel.

The painting in figure 6.2, however, looks quite different, and it is probably apparent to you that it would need to be judged by different criteria. No longer are the questions 'How much does it look

FIGURE 6.2 *Les Demoiselles d'Avignon* by Pablo Picasso. Paris
(June–July 1907)
Oil on canvas, 8' × 7'8". The Museum of Modern Art, New York.
Acquired through the Lillie P. Bliss Bequest.
Photograph © 1998 The Museum of Modern Art, New York.

like real life?' or even 'Do I like what it represents?' important. This
painting by Picasso was first exhibited in 1907 and is titled *Les
Demoiselles d'Avignon* (Young women of Avignon). But your
reaction to it is unlikely to be 'that's just what five women from
Avignon would look like'. The painting is aiming for something
other than realistic representation. It is exploring the nature of space,
shape and colour, and the influence of non-European cultures on
European art, signified by the African masks over the faces of the
nude women.

Almost a century later, we are accustomed to seeing pictures such as this. Imagine however the effect of seeing *Les Demoiselles* for the first time if you were used to seeing pictures like *The Hay-Wain*, and you will understand why Robert Hughes named his book on twentieth-century art movements *The Shock of the New*. The differences between *The Hay-wain* and *Les Demoiselles d'Avignon* are the same kinds of differences found between classic realist fiction and modernist fiction. Similarly, the relationship between *Les Demoiselles d'Avignon* and James Rosenquist's *Marilyn Monroe* (1962) shown in figure 6.3 mirrors the relationship between modernist and postmodernist fiction. Postmodernism will be considered later in this chapter.

FIGURE 6.3 *Marilyn Monroe, I.* by James Rosenquist. (1962) Oil and spray enamel on canvas, 7'9" × 6'¼". The Museum of Modern Art, New York. The Sidney and Harriet Janis collection. Photograph © 1997 The Museum of Modern Art, New York.

6.6 The origins of modernism

The modernist movement was a period of great change, particularly for people involved in the arts. Music, architecture, painting, drama and poetry, were affected as well as fiction. It was perceived by some to be such a complete break with the past, that in 1924 Virginia Woolf wrote: 'On or about December 1910 human nature changed . . . All human relations shifted . . . and when human relations change, there is at the same time a change in religion, conduct, politics and literature.' (Woolf 1924: 321). When this period is written about, the term 'dislocation' is frequently used, to refer to a sense that cultural forms which had been popular in the past are no longer relevant, and that new ones must be developed to express a different world view. The term 'modernism' signals this break with the past. Because modernism erupted in so many forms and because it was so widespread, emerging in North America, Britain and mainland Europe, it must really have seemed to those involved with it to be a complete break with the world that had existed before.

There is little agreement on the exact dates of the modernist movement. Virginia Woolf, as quoted above, proposed 1910 as a key date. The year 1922 has also been identified as a key year, because so many significant modernist texts were published in it: *Ulysses* by James Joyce, *The Waste Land* by T. S. Eliot, Bertolt Brecht's first play, *Baal*, *Anna Christie* by Eugene O'Neill, and Virginia Woolf's first major experimental work, *Jacob's Room*. In art, Picasso's *Les Demoiselles d'Avignon* (1907) is often thought to be the first modernist painting. It is probably best to work with two sets of dates, placing the 'outer limits' of modernism between 1880 and 1950, and within that period, the height of modernism as being probably between 1914 and 1939, from the start of World War I to the start of World War II.

6.7 Stylistic characteristics of modernist texts

Modernist texts can be shown to differ stylistically from classic realist writing in some quite distinctive areas. In the following section, we will describe some of these differences, through analysing some examples of what are generally considered to be 'modernist' texts.

6.7.1 Language as a substance in its own right

If language in classic realist texts was 'transparent', and a 'mirror of reality', then in modernist texts, it was treated by writers as a substance in its own right. Modernism challenged the unquestioned relationship between the signifier (the sound or written form of a word) and the signified (the concept represented). The form of language became an object to be experimented with. In extract 20, from James Joyce's novel *A Portrait of the Artist as a Young Man*, the language does not simply record what Stephen, the protagonist, was like as a baby, it actually simulates the experience. The language is used to demonstrate a child's perception of the world.

20   Once upon a time and a very good time it was there was a moocow coming along the road and this moocow that was coming along the road met a nicens little boy named baby tuckoo. . . .

His father told him that story: his father looked at him through a glass: he had a hairy face.

He was baby tuckoo. The moocow came down the road where Betty Byrne lived: she sold lemon platt.

O, the wild rose blossoms
On the little green place.
He sang that song. That was his song.

The simple grammatical structures, the baby vocabulary, and the world view ('his father looked at him through a glass: he had a hairy face') are those of a child, not the adult who narrates most of the text. The language is not merely describing early memories and perceptions, it is being used to mimic them.

6.7.2 Departure from conventional literary structures

Classic realist novels are composed of two kinds of discourse usually, 'narrative' and 'dialogue'. Characters hold conversations with one another, and the narrator fills in any other information the reader receives, for example about what the room looks like or what the characters are thinking. The modernist novel, starting with the *Pilgrimage* novels by Dorothy Richardson, replaced some of the narrative and dialogue with 'stream of consciousness'.

The 'stream of consciousness' technique is used to provide direct access to a character's thoughts. The results can appear chaotic and difficult to read. The flow of language is meant to represent the movement of ideas through the brain, and all the memories, thoughts and impressions which can flash through someone's mind in a moment. Possibly the most famous example is the closing forty-five pages of James Joyce's novel *Ulysses*, in which the thoughts of the character of Molly Bloom are represented in an uninterrupted flow. Virginia Woolf is also famous for using this technique, demonstrated in extract 21, taken from *Mrs Dalloway*.

21 No, the words meant absolutely nothing to her now. She could not even get an echo of her old emotion. But she could remember going cold with excitement and doing her hair in a kind of ecstasy (now the old feeling began to come back to her, as she took out her hair pins, laid them on the dressing table, began to do her hair), with the rooks flaunting up and down in the pink evening light, and dressing, and going downstairs, and feeling as she crossed the hall 'if it were now to die 'twere now to be most happy'. That was her feeling – Othello's feeling, and she felt it, she was convinced, as strongly as Shakespeare meant Othello to feel it, all because she was coming down to dinner in a white frock to meet Sally Seton!

It was in this period too that poetry began to abandon the conventions of regular rhyme and metre, and to explore the less rigidly structured forms possible in free verse or *vers libre* (see chapter 2).

Modernism therefore involved experimentation with the possible forms literature could take, particularly with more flexible styles of expression.

6.7.3 Collage and allusion

Modernist texts often bring together fragments of other texts to create a kind of 'collage' of references. This was also happening in the paintings of the time. Braque, for example, incorporated strips of wallpaper into his work. T. S. Eliot's poem *The Waste Land* is constructed to quite a considerable extent from pieces of other texts, including works by Shakespeare, Webster, Goldsmith and Dante, extracts from the Bible and from Wagner's opera *Tristan and Isolde*. In Eliot's case, this was in part because he was identifying his poetry with the tradition of European literature, from medieval poets like Chaucer and Dante, to late nineteenth-century ones like Baudelaire. It was as if he were claiming that literature is like a relay race and that he was the appropriate person to take up the baton in the twentieth century.

For Eliot and others, the use of allusions to other works of literature was a way of exploring twentieth-century life and meanings in relation to the cultures which had gone before – the myths, religious and secular, on which Western culture is founded.

6.7.4 Register

Another feature typical of modernist writing is changes in register. An example would be a shift from a formal, rhetorical register, which sounds like writing from the Bible, for example, to the register of ordinary colloquial speech. The effect of this is to bring into juxtaposition a 'voice' from 'high culture' and a 'voice' from 'low culture', providing a contrast which is one of the key areas of interest in this period.

Another effect of different 'voices' is that the number of points of view offered by the text increases. The voice of the narrator carries less authority than in classic realism.

To summarize, some of the key features of modernism in fiction are:

- eclecticism (using lots of different sources)
- experimentation with form (using language in new ways, stream of consciousness)
- exploration of the relationship between 'high' and 'low' culture, and between European and non-European traditions.

6.8 The origins of postmodernism

Postmodernism emerged in Western literature, art and architecture, and other forms of thinking and expression, in the period 1945–50, and is still in progress. The name 'postmodernism' appears to be a strange contradiction. It suggests a time after the modern, perhaps 'the future'. It is important to emphasize the affixes: *post* and *ism*. The *ism* means we are dealing with a movement, rather than a chronological division; the *post* means *after*. Postmodernism is the movement which followed modernism, and the names emphasize the relationship between the two movements. Postmodernism did not simply follow modernism, it was a consequence of it. Modernism created the conditions necessary for postmodernism to happen.

Inevitably modernism, which had been so shocking when it first appeared, began to look less unconventional and more institutionalized. Its key writers appear on English literature syllabuses throughout the world; it has become the 'official culture'. To some extent modernism has been culturally 'defused'; it does not challenge the way people think as much as it did at first.

Postmodernism arose partly as a continuation of the ideas of modernism, in that it continues to challenge cultural forms and push back the limits of how we represent the world. But postmodernism pushes many of the questions and ideas further; it is more extreme and anarchic. Postmodernist texts often set themselves in radical opposition to authority, frequently by means of humour.

To return to the pictures discussed earlier in the chapter, figure 6.3 is the equivalent in art of some forms of postmodernism in writing. The image of Marilyn Monroe is drawn from popular culture, rather than 'high culture'. It looks rather frivolous next to the more austere *Les Demoiselles d'Avignon*. The face has been fragmented and turned upside down – a game is being played with the image; the picture is about the image and how it is used, rather than a portrait of the woman. Fragments of other material have also been included. A recognizable part of our culture has been repackaged and sold to us again, as a comment on the way our culture uses images. The comparative frivolity, the concern with popular culture, the recycling of images, the emphasis on the process of production, are some of the significant features of postmodernism. Let us now look at the stylistic features of postmodernist fiction.

6.9 Stylistic characteristics of postmodernist texts

6.9.1 Language as a free-floating entity

As we have said, classic realist texts treat language as if it could be used transparently to depict reality; modernism experimented with language as a substance in its own right, with a complex relationship to the world it is used to represent. Postmodernism, however, treats language as if instead of referring to a 'real world' independent of language, language in fact only referred to itself – as if it is the only reality. There is an emphasis on the material forms of language, and a loss of interest in the content.

Finnegans Wake, written by James Joyce and published in 1939, comes a little early in the time-scale suggested earlier for the beginnings of postmodernism. However, its use of language is very postmodern. Language as a material entity takes priority over the content, the story.

ACTIVITY 6.5 ————————————————————————

Try to retell as much of the extract from *Finnegans Wake* below in your own words as you can. You could look back to the analysis of an extract from *Finnegans Wake* in chapter 3 for some ideas, and you may need to make several attempts before it becomes intelligible at all!

22 Eins within a space and a wearywide space it was ere wohned a Mookse. The onesomeness wast alltolonely, archunsistlike, broady oval, and a Mookse he would a walking go (My hood! cries Antony Romeo), so one grandsumer evening, after a great morning and his good supper of gammon and spittish, having flabelled his eyes, pilleoled his nostrils, vacticanated his ears and palliumed his throats, he put on his impermeable, seized his impugnable, harped on his crown and steeped out of his immobile *De Rure Albo*. . . .

The extract seems to be about a 'Mookse' who lives alone and doesn't like it, so after his supper and getting himself ready, he goes out for a walk on a lovely summer's evening.

Within this extract, games are being played with language. Joyce has made up words, borrowed words from other languages (German and French), selected words that are ambiguous and can mean more than one thing. Part of the passage look like Old English or German, which could give the impression this story happened a long time ago, in a mythological past perhaps (*Eins* for example, is like *ein*, the German word for *one*; the *s* makes it more like *once*, the way traditional stories in English begin. The word *wohned* is like the German *wohnen*, which means *live* in the sense of *reside*, but with an English verb ending: *ed*. The conventional activity of story-telling is recognizable, but distorted. Instead of starting with 'Once upon a time', the story starts '[Once] within a space', a similar formula. Other words are reminiscent of English words. *Spittish* could mean *spinach*; *broady oval* sounds like *bloody awful*, and so on. With some effort, a story does begin to emerge.

However, it is clearly not the primary purpose of this text to communicate a story about the mookse. The text is much more about the process of telling a story, and how language works. Neither is it easy to read. To return to the distinction made earlier between 'readerly' and 'writerly' texts, this is clearly a 'writerly' text, not one that the reader can comprehend on a first brief reading, but one which must be laboured at to wring its meaning from it.

6.9.2 Loss of narrative closure

Closure is what happens when the problems which have arisen in a story are resolved at its end; death or marriage are ways in which closure is often achieved. All of Jane Austen's novels end with the heroines getting married, for example. In modernist novels, there is often some kind of closure; the action of *Ulysses* all takes place within a single day and ends with sleep, for example. In *To the Lighthouse* by Virginia Woolf, the novel ends when the journey to the lighthouse is made. Postmodernist novels have tended to abandon conventional narrative closure, however. In *The French Lieutenant's Woman* by John Fowles, instead of being presented with a neat conclusion, the reader is offered a choice of three endings. In one, the male protagonist, Charles, marries his fiancée, the dull and pious Ernestina; in another he marries Sarah, the French Lieutenant's woman of the title; in the third, he loses both women. When a film was made of the book, two possible endings were shown. The effect of these 'choices' is that the reader is left with a lack of resolution, a sense that the problems of the story cannot be tied up neatly, and also a sense that the novelist is playing a game by drawing attention to the process of writing.

6.9.3 Parody and pastiche

Postmodernism is characterized by parody and pastiche. Pastiche is the process of mixing styles or imitating the styles of other's work, sometimes to humorous effect; parody imitates other work in order to mock it. We have already said that modernist texts frequently allude to other texts, but the purpose differs from that of post-modernism. Writers like Eliot used intertextual references because they believed in the value of traditional literature, and in the impor-tance of the continuity of literary tradition. Postmodernism uses intertextual references often in order to mock the original texts, and for comic effect. The example below is from *Lolita*, a novel by Vladimir Nabokov first published in 1955.

23 To fill the pause, I proposed he read his own sentence – in the poetical form I had given it . . .
  'Just as you say. Shall I read it out loud?'
  'Yes'
  'Here goes. I see it's in verse.
    Because you took advantage of a sinner
    because you took advantage
    because you took
    because you took advantage of my disadvantage . . .
  That's good, you know. That's damned good.'

Nabokov has parodied lines from the poem 'Ash-Wednesday' by T. S. Eliot:

24 Because I do not hope to turn again
  Because I do not hope

Because I do not hope to turn
Desiring this man's gift and that man's scope . . .

Nabokov's version is parody, rather than merely allusion, for a number of reasons. The context in which the rewrite occurs is farcical – the reader of the 'poem' believes he is about to be shot by its writer (the first speaker) for kidnapping the first speaker's prepubescent lover. Second, although the poem is very clearly a plagiarism of the Eliot poem, neither character acknowledges it. Third, the poem become increasingly ridiculous, and is not at all deserving of the compliments its reader pays it. Thus the passage is a joke, partly at the expense of Eliot's poem. This also illustrates the next feature of postmodernism to be considered.

6.9.4 The end of cultural hierarchy

Postmodernism also differs from modernism in its anarchic disrespect for tradition and status. It juxtaposes 'popular culture' and 'high culture', without any sense that one has more value than the other, and has no hesitation in mocking or distorting high cultural forms (as in the example from Lolita above). Modernist texts also juxtapose high and low cultural forms, but frequently emphasize the difference in value between the culture of the elite, and the perceived sordidness and banality of everyday life. Postmodernism rejoices in erasing the divide between popular forms and traditional culture.

6.9.5 'All stories have been told before'

Postmodernist texts often include a sense that all stories have been told before and underline the 'usedness' of language – there is nothing new to say, only words already used by other people, and stories which have been told over and over. Modernist texts used allusions to link them with the greatness of past writing. Postmodernist texts recycle for parody and pastiche, as discussed above, and also because of a kind of weary and cynical belief that there is nothing new to say.

There is an apocryphal remark which sums this up; someone apparently commented that it is impossible to say in the late twentieth century 'I love you', because it has been said so often before that its meaning is tarnished. You have to say 'I love you, as Barbara Cartland would say' (Barbara Cartland being a very famous, and often parodied, romantic novelist). The implication of this anecdote is that you have to show an awareness of how the words have been used in other contexts.

Stories have always been retold; Chaucer and Shakespeare's writings are full of retold stories. Writers such as Umberto Eco and A. S. Byatt make very rich use of stories which have been told before. If all stories have been told before, however, this is a further reason for the *content* of fiction writing to become much less interesting that the *way* a story is told, and the forms of language which are used.

6.9.6 Self-referentiality

This is another version of a point that has been made several times already. While classic realism aimed to present the world as if language were a window to look through, and modernism explored the relationship between language and the world, postmodernist texts keep drawing attention to their own 'textuality'. They tend to dwell on the nature of texts and to a large extent ignore the world outside the text. Extract 25 is the opening paragraph of *If On a Winter's Night a Traveller* by Italo Calvino:

25 You are about to begin reading Italo Calvino's new novel, *If On a Winter's Night a Traveller*. Relax. Concentrate. Dispel every other thought. Let the world about you fade. Best close the door: the T.V. is always on in the next room. Tell the others right away, 'No, I don't want to watch TV!' Raise your voice – they won't hear you otherwise – 'I'm reading! I don't want to be disturbed!' Maybe they haven't heard you with all that racket; speak louder, yell: 'I'm beginning to read Italo Calvino's new novel'. Or if you prefer, don't say anything; just hope they'll leave you alone.

What are the features of this opening paragraph which are (a) different from the opening of a classic realist novel? (b) similar to it?

Our ideas are as follows:

Differences
- The use of deixis to refer to the reader's 'time' e.g. *new* in the first sentence (a number of years after publication, this is clearly not an accurate adjective);
- direct commands given to the reader e.g. '*Relax*', '*Concentrate*';
- direct reference to the existence of the novel itself;
- no reference to the 'novel action' – e.g. characters, setting, events – which most classic realist novels start with;
- references to the setting the reader is in – the rooms, the other people in the building, the TV.

Similarities
- This is clearly a beginning of a series of actions, although not clearly the beginning of a story!

You may have been able to add several points we have not thought of to both lists.

6.9.7 Irony and humour

If all texts can only be about other texts, as is assumed in post-modernism, then saying anything serious and with sincerity becomes a very difficult thing to do. Playfulness is central to postmodernism, since there is little else to do in this view of the world but play. Thus postmodernist texts are full of jokes about language, about other texts, and about themselves.

6.10 The function of style in fiction

This chapter has looked at some of the characteristics of fiction in the nineteenth and twentieth centuries. We have shown how ideas about language and social order are manifested in different writing styles. Classic realism is still very common in many novels (and films) and exists alongside the postmodernism that we encounter in advertisements and other forms of media all around us. As we have said, few novels actually fit 'tidily' into the categories of classic realism, modernism, or postmodernism, but we can still classify the general trends.

We have focused on stylistic characteristics of novels over the last century and a half, and the artistic reasons why a writer might choose one form over another. However, like any cultural form, fiction is not produced only for artistic reasons. Amongst other functions, fiction can have a didactic purpose, for example representing certain aspects of society or kinds of behaviour as more or less wholesome. An interesting area for debate or discussion is whether any of the styles discussed above is more suited than the others for challenging social conventions and the status quo.

Classic realist texts include novels such as Dickens's *Hard Times* and Mrs Gaskell's *North and South*, both concerned with the inhumanity which existed in industrialized Victorian England. Modernism incorporated ideas about the workings of the human mind, based on the ideas of psychoanalysis, and explored the relationship between high culture and popular culture, and between Western culture, and other civilizations. Postmodernism asserts the relativity of everything and challenges all claims to authority. All three therefore could be seen as defying aspects of the status quo.

Yet all three can equally be used to protect the status quo – classic realism, through its hierarchical discourse, modernism by the prestige it attaches to high cultural forms, and postmodernism because of its apoliticism and world-weariness, its resistance to taking anything at all seriously.

Style in fiction can be used to raise issues more or less independently of the content of the writing. However, style does not map onto one single function – indeed in the examples of these three ways of writing fiction, the styles can have quite different functions.

Below are extracts from three novels, one from the mid-nineteenth century, one from the early twentieth century, one from the latter end of the twentieth century. Identify any features in the texts which are associated with classic realism, modernism, or postmodernism. You might also comment on how the style of each extract makes you feel as a reader, and how that affects what you think of the content.

26   Miriam could not remember hearing Fräulein Pfaff go away when she awoke in the darkness feeling unendurably oppressed. She flung her sheet aside and turned her pillow over and pushed her frilled sleeves to her elbows. How energetic I am, she thought, and lay tranquil. There was not a sound. 'I shall never be able to sleep down here, it's too awful,' she murmured and puffed and shifted her head on the pillow.

       The win-ter may – pass. . . . The win-ter . . . may pass. The winter may . . . pass. The Academy . . . a picture in very bright colours . . . a woman sitting by the roadside with a shawl round her shoulders and a red skirt and red cheeks and bright green country behind her . . . people moving about on the shiny floor, someone just behind saying, 'that is the plein-air, these are the plein-airistes' – the woman in the picture was a house-keeper . . .

       A brilliant light flashed into the room . . . lightning – how strange the room looked – the screens had been moved – the walls and corners and little beds had looked like daylight. Someone was talking across the landing. Emma was awake. Another flash came and movements and cries. Emma screamed aloud, sitting up in bed. 'Ach Gott! Clara! *Clara!*' she screamed. Cries came from the next room. A match was struck across the landing, and voices sounded. Gertrude was in the room lighting the gas and Clara tugged down the blind. Emma was sitting with her hands pressed to her eyes, quickly gasping, 'Ach Clara! Mein Gott! Ach Gott!'

27   Lucy was lonely.

       Lucy dressed Praxis and Hypatia in white, and pattered them off to Sunday School, and slept apart from Ben, from time to time, to punish him. Punish herself more like. He fell into his drunken sleep and barely noticed.

It was all too much for him. No wonder he drank too much. Within a year [. . .] Ben had become enamoured of Ruth, the dark little waitress at the golf-club (where anti-semitic feeling ran high, but made an honourable exception for Ben, who was not only the only Jew they had ever encountered in person, but was universally liked), and presently ran off with her, and married her.

Ruth was free to marry; she was the daughter of a Jewish taxi-driver, made excellent beef sandwiches and her lowly social status was sufficient to keep Ben free from sexual anxiety and mental torment. He could love her, and make love to her, all at the same time. They were happy ever after.

Lucy was of course unhappy ever after, and so was Hypatia, and Praxis too [*the daughters of Ben and Lucy*].

Now what kind of memory is that to comfort anyone? The memory of the afflicted child one was: the knowledge of the wrongs unrighted and the wounds unhealed, the tearing pain of a past which cannot be altered? Unless of course I remember it wrongly, and it is my present painful and unfortunate state which casts such a black shadow back over what would otherwise be a perfectly acceptable landscape of experience? But I fear not.

I, Praxis Dudeen, being old and scarcely in my right mind, now bequeath you my memories. They may help you: they certainly do nothing to sustain me, let alone assist my old bones to clamber out of the bath.

Last night, doing just that, I slipped on the soap and cracked my elbow. This morning the pain was such that I took the bus to the hospital, instead of to the park.

My erstwhile sisters, my former friends: I did what you wanted, and look at me now!

28   At the present time there are few people at a public ball besides the dancers and their chaperones, or relations in some degree interested in them. But in the days when Molly and Cynthia were young – before the railroads were, and before their consequences, the excursion-trains, which take every one up to London now-a-days, there to see their fill of gay crowds and fine

dresses – to go to an annual charity ball, even though all thought of dancing had passed by years ago, and without any of the responsibilities of a chaperone, was a very allowable and favourite piece of dissipation to all the kindly old maids who thronged the country towns of England. They aired their old lace and their best dresses; they saw the aristocratic magnates of the countryside; they gossiped with their coevals, and speculated on the romances of the young around them in a curious yet friendly spirit. The Miss Brownings would have thought themselves sadly defrauded of the gayest event of the year, if anything had prevented their attending the charity ball, and Miss Browning would have been indignant, Miss Phoebe aggrieved, had they not been asked to Ashcombe and Coreham, by friends in each place, who had, like them, gone through the dancing-stage of life some five-and-twenty years before, but who liked still to haunt the scenes of their former enjoyment, and see a younger generation dance on 'regardless of their doom'.

6.11 Analysis of fiction: checklist

In this chapter we have suggested ways in which you can approach the analysis of works of fiction in relation to literary style. Some of these draw on more traditional 'literary' concerns with narrator, dialogue, character and plot, while others draw on more 'linguistic' analyses of voice, register and formal features of language use.

If you have to do a stylistic analysis of a fictional text, here are some of the questions you could deal with:

- Does the text appear to be 'readerly' or 'writerly'? What sort of demands does it make on the reader, and what are the features that help you categorize it as one or the other?
- What kind of narrating voice, or voices, are there in the text?
- What are the linguistic devices used to represent time, place and dialogue in the text?
- Is there any 'foregrounding' of specific linguistic forms – i.e. does the writer draw attention to the language of the text, for

example through changes in register, or the use of structural or lexical patterning?

- What is the structure of the plot, and narrative development? For example, is there a resolution, or 'ending', or no narrative closure? Is the story linear, or does the writer represent events in a non-linear way? Is the story portrayed as 'new', or does the writer make reference to other similar stories through inter-texuality and allusion?

This list is not exhaustive, and each text may generate different and original questions to do with stylistic form. However, many texts also share characteristics, which is what enables us to categorize them in the first instance (or at least try to categorize them) by identifying their similarities with other texts.

You may find some of the references below useful as sources of information concerning the analysis of literary styles, and about the theoretical approaches we have discussed in this chapter.

Suggestions for further reading

Appignanesi, Richard and Chris Garratt (1995) *Postmodernism for Beginners*, Cambridge: Icon Books (provides an entertaining overview of what postmodernism is – or is not – about!).

Barthes, Roland (1975) *S/Z*, London: Cape (the introduction contains Barthes' distinction between 'readerly' and 'writerly' texts).

Lodge, David (1990) *After Bakhtin: Essays on Fiction and Criticism*, London: Routledge.

Short, Mick (1996) *Exploring The Language of Poems, Plays and Prose*, London: Longman (this contains useful chapters on the discourse and style of fictional prose).

Williams, Raymond (1972) 'Realism and the contemporary novel', in David Lodge (ed.) *Twentieth Century Literary Criticism*, Longman: London (an essay which describes the origins and development of literary realism and its related sub-genres).

Chapter 7

Style in popular texts

7.1 Introduction

In the preceding chapters of this book we have been looking at how the forms and structures of language are used as resources for creating 'literary' texts. However, the potential that language offers us for creating those literary effects – its 'literariness' – is far from restricted to those texts that we may consider to be 'literary' in the classical sense of prose, poetry or drama. The literariness of language is exploited in many much more mundane contexts, from the headlines on your daily paper to an advertisement for shampoo, and the patterns that we have been exploring within the domain of 'literature' can be found pervasively in all manner of popular writing.

In addition to identifying what we term the 'literary potential' of language in popular texts, there are other stylistic features which tend to be more specific to the domains of media discourse – from magazine and advertising copy to the language of radio DJs and television presenters. In this chapter we will focus on some of these popular texts, and look at the language of newspapers, advertising and magazines to show how these media draw on the literary properties of language to produce certain effects. In the first section we will review the sound and meaning structures that were introduced in chapters 2 and 3, and look at some examples of their use in non-literary texts.

Media texts are not produced in a vacuum, for anyone who might be around to read them, but frequently target different groups of readers or audiences. Advertisements are produced with a 'typical' consumer in mind; magazines target particular groups of readers with different needs, from teenage girls to computer buffs. The way that radio and television presenters talk to their listeners and viewers usually gives us an indication of who their typical audience is. So in the second part of this chapter, we will look at how media texts construct and target their audiences through drawing on a range of linguistic resources such as address, deixis and presupposition.

7.2 Exploiting patterns in sound and meaning: headline texts

A brief glance along the shelves of any newsagents will provide a rich source of examples of the kind of patterning we tend to associate with poetic language. The use of sound patterns in the form of alliteration, consonance and assonance (see chapter 2) is a prominent feature of headline texts in newspapers and magazines. Here are some examples from a women's magazine *Options* and an equivalent men's magazine *GQ*.

> Will you be fat at 40?
> Steal from the stars
> High street fashion special: an insider guide
> Bruising for a cruising
> Ice Surrender

In these headlines the sound patterns created by alliteration are fairly common, as in '*Fat at 40*' (which works without the presence of the letter *f* itself) and *steal from the stars*, with the initial consonant cluster /st/. *Insider guide* contains examples of assonance created through repetition of the diphthong /aɪ/ as well as consonance, the presence of a final /d/, which combine to produce a strong rhyming link between these two words.

A similar strong rhyming pattern can be seen in the headline 'bruising for a cruising', where in the two rhyming words only the first phoneme differs. This is the headline text for an article about a round-Britain yacht race and the kind of qualities needed to take part in it, and, as well as the rhyme, we can also see another feature of headline texts, which is a tendency to play with meanings that are associated with the subject matter of the subsequent article in the headline. In this case, the article focuses on the tough physical challenge of sailing, while reversing the more usual word order of this colloquial expression 'cruising for a bruising'![1]

Another example of this tendency to exploit the semantic level of language in headline texts can be seen in the newspaper headline below:

> Cash Lesson for Schools: Clarke delivers a stern lecture on teachers' pay rises

Here the text relies heavily on the semantic field related to education (lesson, schools, deliver a lecture) for its message. There is also an alliterative relationship between the /k/ of *cash* and *Clarke*. A contrasting headline on the same story from a different tabloid newspaper which did use an alliterative pattern, combined with an alternative word for 'teacher', is the following:

Sir's pay plea turned down.

It is worth noting that in the search for short, striking headline text, the way groups of people get represented in the press can often be inaccurate or distorted. In Britain at the present time, the majority of teachers are women.

The final example is again taken from *GQ* and relates to a photo feature on fifty of the world's 'coolest women'. Here again the word play works on two levels. First, the semantic field of coldness links ice to cool, and there is also a strong collocation (see chapter 4) between these two words. Second, on the phonemic level, the word-final /s/ of *ice* is assimilated with the word-initial /s/ of *surrender*, which produces a secondary meaning *I surrender* – appropriate in this context of readers surrendering to the power of these cool women!

This manipulation of the rich potential of the sounds and levels of meaning in language is not limited to the tabloid press or glossy magazines. A recent headline in a broadsheet newspaper featured the following text:

Cereal killer shops prison.

The story concerned a man sentenced to life imprisonment who sued the prison shop for refusing to honour a voucher on a packet of cereal he had been sent. Once more the accuracy of representation (he had in fact only murdered one person) is secondary to the opportunity to produce a pun, and to tap into the resources of popular meanings through the association of breakfast cereals with porridge – a colloquial term for prison. There is also a pun in *shops* here: to shop can mean 'to purchase' as well as having the colloquial meaning 'to inform on' or 'tell on' someone.

We will return to the use of colloquialisms and cultural knowledge in more detail later in the chapter. To conclude this section on the use of sound and meaning in headline texts, how many different forms of sound patterning can you identify in the headline below? *Di* is of course Princess Diana, and the headline refers to the story of the photographs taken of her working out in a gym which were subsequently sold to the press.

Di wins six figure gym pics payout

There are five assonant occurrences of the phoneme /ɪ/, three of the phoneme /s/, two alliterative /p/ phonemes, and a close relationship between the voiced and unvoiced velar plosive /g/ and /k/ of *figure* and *pics*.

7.3 Lexical creativity

Seeing language as a source of material that can be played with, taken apart and put back together in different shapes, is not just a property of literary texts. One area in which this playfulness is evident is in the creation of new words, and as always media texts are fruitful areas for this kind of linguistic playfulness. However, this creativity cannot happen randomly, and the way new words are formed conforms to the morphological rules of the language (see chapter 3).

── **ACTIVITY 7.1**

In the poem by Edwin Morgan, *Verses for a Christmas Card*, he creates the following words:

harbourmoon
bejeweleavening
restorying
liftlike

Can you:

(a) decide to which part of speech each word belongs (e.g. noun, verb etc.);
(b) list other words they resemble;
(c) work out their morphological structure?

This kind of morphological creativity can also be found in popular texts, as the following words from an issue of the teenage girl's magazine *Just 17* illustrate:

swoonsome, groovesome, blushsome, hunkalicious, rawkfest

Again, think about how they are formed morphologically, and where you might find them in a sentence.

7.4 Targeting the reader

Most texts are written with a specific reader, or set of readers, in mind. If you write a shopping list for yourself, you will include only minimal information about what you have to buy. If you write one for someone else to do your shopping, you will probably include more information about the kinds of things you need, such as 'milk – semi-skimmed' or 'potatoes – red not white'. If you leave a note for the milkman saying 'three pints today please' – he/she will know that you mean three pints of milk (not beer) and that *today* refers to the day he/she reads the note. If however you leave a note on your office door saying 'gone out – back in two hours', then whoever reads that note has no way of knowing when the two hours might be up. So writers design texts, more or less successfully, for the people they intend to read them. Those people can be a specific, single reader (as in the case of the milkman or the person doing your shopping) or larger groups of readers. All the passengers waiting on a station platform would be the target group of readers for a notice saying 'Danger: do not cross the line'. Texts draw on various linguistic structures in order to address their readers. In the examples we have looked at above, 'three pints today please' has no direct imperative form of the verb, nor a direct addressee. The verb is left out, or 'elided' and the addressee is inferred from the content and context of the note. Nobody except the milkman would consider themselves to be addressed by it. 'Do not cross the line' however includes a direct imperative, and although there is no specified addressee, anyone who sees that notice while waiting for a train cannot escape being addressed by it. On the other hand, in public transport buses in

London, there is a notice above some seats which reads: 'Please give up this seat to elderly passengers or those with young children.' If you are not sitting in that seat, you are not the target reader of the notice. However, should you happen to sit down there, you would then become the addressee of that particular request. So, not all texts address all readers all the time, and readers, although they engage in a reading process, may not consider themselves to be addressed by all the texts they read. We move in and out of the position of 'targeted reader' depending on who we are, where we are, and what we might be doing at the time.

7.4.1 Direct address in media texts

Advertising in particular relies on targeting specific groups of readers, and one of the most frequent ways in which advertising language addresses a set of readers is by using the direct address term 'you'. The French political theorist Louis Althusser (1977) has described the way in which most people will tend to identify themselves as the addressee when they hear the call 'Hey, you!', even though they may not be the person it is addressed to. He calls this phenomenon **interpellation**, or 'hailing', as it is sometimes referred to, and it has been a useful way of accounting for the powerful device of direct address which 'positions' hearers in many forms of ideological discourse, including advertisements. (See Williamson, 1978, for a detailed study of the role of ideology in advertisements.)

In advertising, this use of the interpersonal dimension of language through direct address is one of the most prominent devices for targeting readers, although it is by no means the only one as we shall see later. Many advertising texts use some form of direct address in order to 'hail' or 'interpellate' the reader, to use Althusser's term. This can be in the form of a statement containing the second person pronoun 'you', such as in the Scottish Widows pensions advertisement below:

24 hours a day . . . 7 days a week . . . Now you can pick up the phone and get pensions information or advice and even set up a plan.

The use of questions in advertising discourse is also a powerful way of addressing readers, since questions do not usually occur without a potential answerer. In other words, the occurrence of a question usually presupposes that (a) someone is being addressed by that question and that (b) an answer will be forthcoming. In advertising text, questions tend to place the reader in the position of answerer, as in the following examples:

It's 100%. Are you?   (advert for multivitamin tablets)
Which Waterman are you?   (advert for Waterman pens)

If you answer 'no' to the first one, then you need to take the vitamins, while the second one presupposes that you are already a 'Waterman', and all you have to do is choose which one fits you best! The scope, or range of possible addressees, of the 'you' in these two adverts is arguably slightly different, as the 'you' in the vitamin advert is very general and could address any reader, while the use of the term 'Waterman' could restrict the scope of the 'you' to a category of people who are likely to buy and use this kind of pen. Often, in what appears to be a general address to any 'you', the reader, the scope of the 'you' is defined by the accompanying text (for further discussion of this, see Thornborrow, 1994). The function of an advertisement is not necessarily to sell a product to everyone, but to target the most likely groups of consumers for their products. Questions without a specific 'you' addressee, such as:

Were Pensions Designed for Women?

still position the reader as someone who may either be able to answer, or need an answer to, that question.

Adverts for products which have very few connotations of enhanced status or lifestyle tend to have the least restricted scope of 'you', as for example in the following advert for packet meats, where the only text is the statement:

When you want the best

A recent television advert for an Audi car actually parodied this tendency by featuring a young brash 'city-man' test-driving the car throughout the day, only to return it to the dealer's saying 'it's not my style', the implication being of course that the Audi image is for people who are *not* like him!

Collect a few magazine adverts and look for instances of direct address to the reader. Can you categorize these in any way – for example, according to whether they are questions or statements, or whether they restricted the scope of 'you'? Then think about what sort of products tend to feature direct address in their advertisements and how this is used to target readers as potential consumers.

One example is the text below advertising Midland Bank pension services (the pronoun 'she' in this advertisement refers to a baby pictured on the facing page):

> Before you know it she'll be grown up with dependants of her own. Don't be one of them.

You will have noticed the last sentence in the text above is the imperative *don't be one of them*. The use of this kind of utterance, which are called **directives**, is another way in which advertisements draw on the interpersonal dimension of language. Directives are a category of speech acts (see Austin 1962, Grice 1975) which involve the speaker requesting, instructing or ordering a designated hearer or group of hearers to do something. In advertising discourse, directives again create that interpersonal link between the text and the reader, as for example in the following:

Just do it	(Nike sports shoes)
Show your true autumn colours	(for men's brogue shoes)
Get wise, get *Which?*	(for *Which?* magazine).
Phone for your copy	(Next Directory)

These position the reader as the recipient of the commands, and as Greg Myers points out (1994: 48), in English culture we are taught to mitigate directives with politeness markers such as 'please' or by using question directives, like 'could you lend me your lecture notes?', unless the directive is going to benefit the hearer in some way, as in 'have a drink'. The lack of these politeness markers in advertising discourse is not to make the directives more direct, or forceful, but to make the actions they refer to appear beneficial to the consumer, not to the advertiser.

7.4.2 Addressing the listener

Direct address to readers is achieved in popular written texts in a range of different ways as we have discussed above. However, there is also a huge output of popular spoken media discourse which needs to target audiences in particular ways.

Contrary to what was once thought to be the case, radio and television presenters are constantly targeting specific groups of listeners, rather than addressing their listening audience as a single, amorphous mass. Martin Montgomery, in his research on DJ talk, found that radio hosts draw on a variety of devices to target listeners, ranging from the use of individual names, to regional identification (*anyone listening in Edinburgh*), occupation (*anyone who's a typist in a hospital*), star sign (*Hello Scorpio*) or other identifying categories such as age (*if you're over ten years old*). In this way, DJs continually engage in shifting the forms of address that they use to target different segments of the audience (Montgomery, 1986b).

7.4.3 Presupposition in advertising

Another way that texts address certain groups of readers is through the kind of background knowledge or assumptions that can be identified in them. Norman Fairclough (1989: 82) shows how a letter to a problem page headed 'Embarrassed by Boys' sets up a particular set of assumptions about what it is like to be a teenage girl and, more importantly, what constitutes a problem for teenage girls in general. The letter reads:

> Please help me. I'm 13 and whenever there's a boy on TV, and my Mum's in the room I get really embarrassed. I've never been out with anyone even though Mum says I'm quite pretty. How can I get over this problem?

Fairclough claims that there are several 'common sense' background assumptions that underlie this text: first, that problems can be solved by 'talking' to someone about them (and that this can be achieved in print); second, that pretty 13-year-old girls 'normally' go out with boys, and third, that being embarrassed by boys is actually recognized as a problem in the first place! In order to make sense of the text as a coherent whole, readers have to have particular forms of background knowledge available to them that are culturally specific.

Another illustration of how texts draw on readers' common-sense background assumptions can be found in the following advertisement for an electric oven by *Cookelectric*, which is headed:

'I've got a job and it isn't cleaning the oven.'

In order to make sense of this sentence, we have to draw on our knowledge of women's traditional role as suppliers of domestic labour – in other words, we have to identify the 'I' of the text, the textual voice, with someone whose job it might 'normally' be to clean the oven.

ACTIVITY 7.3

This text draws on a whole range of background assumptions about stereotypical gender roles. List as many examples as you can of sentences which rely on the reader making these kinds of assumptions in order to interpret the advert as a coherent text.

In this section we have been dealing with the various ways in which texts target their readers, both directly, through linguistic forms of address, and indirectly, through the background assumptions that need to be available to readers in order for them to make full sense of a text. In the next section we move on to another level in the construction of meaning, where we explore the linguistic concepts of reference and deixis which play a crucial role in our interpretation of texts.

Having a class of over thirty kids to cope with usually means I spend more time doing homework than housework. So I need all the help I can get.

In the kitchen that help comes in the shape of my built-in electric oven and hob.

With its stay-clean lining, the oven burns off any splashes as it cooks. While the

"I've got a job and it isn't cleaning the oven."

hob, having no crevices in which food can lurk, needs only a quick wipe with a damp cloth.

Of course, they shine in other ways, too. The fan oven is really a home economics lesson in itself. It not only heats up in seconds, it also cooks more quickly and at much lower temperatures, which saves both time and money.

And being electric, if I have a spare moment in the morning I can prepare a vegetable casserole and put it on autotimer.

That way, I arrive home to a beautifully cooked dinner, a happy husband and several gold stars of my own.

COOKELECTRIC

7.5 Reference and deixis

The way we interpret the meaning of texts also depends on two crucial properties of language: reference and deixis. We have already discussed this in chapter 4 and you may want to refer back for more information. Textual meaning is created on one level through our recognition of words in the text, and through our ability to relate them to objects or ideas in the world as speakers and readers of English. If we don't know what they mean, we can try to find out by using a dictionary. This is the 'referring' property of language. The other level of textual meaning is available to us through the context in which we encounter that text. Speakers and writers use deictic expressions to situate their words or their text within a particular context, and, unlike referring words, the meaning of these expressions cannot be fully recovered from the text itself, but from contexual elements outside the text. This is **deixis**, the linguistic property which forges the link between a sentence or utterance, and its context. Problems of interpretation may occur when the context in which a text is read differs from the context that was intended or assumed by its author.

In practice, written texts tend to contain many more explicitly referential terms and fewer deictic elements than spoken utterances, since writers cannot necessarily assume that readers will have access to the same contextual knowledge when they encounter the text. For many texts, the moment of writing and the moment of reading (interpretation) are usually separated in time and space. Can you think of any context where a text would be written and read within the same time frame? (Passing a note to someone instead of talking would be one example; the recent e-mail technology allows a message to be written then read almost immediately, although the sender is usually not in the same place as the receiver.)

The time of writing a fictional text may be years or centuries removed from when it is read, but other kinds of texts, such as instructions, guide books or news stories, also have to contain enough referential information for readers to be able to interpret them efficiently at the moment they are read. Compare the following three texts, taken from an instruction manual, a local newspaper and the opening page of a novel respectively. Which are the words and phrases that need contextual information in order to be fully interpretable? What kind of information is this, and how would a reader access it?

1   The illustration on the facing page shows all the equipment you will need to set up your computer and begin using it. Place your equipment on a sturdy, flat surface near a grounded wall outlet. Before following the setup instructions in this chapter, you may want to read 'Arranging your Office' in Appendix A for tips on adjusting your work furniture so that you're comfortable when using the computer.

2   A young Morden family struggling to pay their bills have scooped this week's Lottery Jackpot, winning nearly £3.3m. Fruit and veg seller SB and his wife C of Halesowen Road were facing spiralling debts and were about to have their gas disconnected when their number came up. Now S has given up work at New Covent Garden market and C has chucked in her cleaning work to enjoy a better life. . . . S, 26, said: At first I just could not believe it. I didn't check [the lottery numbers] until Sunday morning. C was doing the washing up when I realised.

3   It was to be the consultant physician's last visit and Dalgliesh suspected that neither of them regretted it, arrogance and patronage on one side and weakness, gratitude and dependence on the other being no foundation for a satisfactory adult relationship however transitory.

Your lists for 1 and 2 may consist of the following phrases:

1   *the illustration on the facing page, this chapter, your computer, your equipment*
2   *this week's lottery money, now, Sunday morning*

The phrases in example 1 situate the reader firmly within the specific time and context of reading the instruction manual – the reference to *the illustration on the facing page* directs the reader to look at a page of the manual they are reading, and *this chapter* refers to *the one you are reading now*. *Your computer* also refers to *the computer you have just bought* rather than any computer out there in the Mac world! Try rewriting this extract without the deictic words *the*, *this*, and *your*. What sort of words do you use to replace them, and what difference has this rewriting made to the way you would read this text?

In extract 2, the deictic expressions *this week* and *now* refer to a specific time when these events took place, as does *Sunday morning*. These time references are only meaningful if the moment of reading is very close to the moment of writing, and the writer of this story assumes that this will be the case – a fair assumption for a local newspaper. Reading this at a much later moment in time, we would only have access to when *this week* and *now* were if we were also able to see the date on the paper.

In extract 3 you probably have nothing written down! There are no deictic expressions in this opening sentence which link it to the context of reading. This is not to say that deictic expressions never occur in fictional texts, but their use is less common that in other types of writing. Some modernist and postmodernist writing may use deixis in order to draw attention to the assumption that fictional stories are context free, but in general the use of deixis tends to be a feature of more popular textual genres which adopt a more personal form of address to their readers.

7.5.1 Deixis in advertising

Deictic reference to a contextual element often occurs in advertising discourse where some part of the text takes its meaning from the visual structure of the advert. The following text is the heading of an advertisement for a computer game:

Fortunately, you won't have to face it alone

Here, the referent of *it* is recoverable from the rest of the advert, which features a picture of the game package beneath the heading text, and beneath that, a description of the game itself. Without this information, readers would be left with the question, 'face what?'. A similar example of this use of deixis is in an advert for a Filofax personal organizer:

You can find it all in Filofax

where the accompanying text provides the information about what *it all* is.

Another practice within advertising discourse is to draw on

deictic reference to things that form part of a reader's context in order to create a closer relationship between the textual 'voice' of the advert, and what is assumed to be the world of the reader. The following examples are again taken from a Filofax advert:

If you must ring *that* neighbour . . .
If your husband wants *that* suit cleaned by Friday . . .

where the deictic expressions *that neighbour* and *that suit* bring the entity being referred to closer to the reader's world by constructing them as familiar and specific. It is not just a neighbour or a suit, it is *that* particular neighbour, *that* particular suit, which are textually represented as belonging to the context of the reader (see Thornborrow, 1994). The same device can be found in the language of advice in teenage magazines. Look at the extract below and think about the effect of using deictic expressions *the class* and *that boy* in this context:

4   Practise visualising yourself achieving your goals – whether it's speaking in front of the class or asking that boy out.

7.5.2 Deixis in spoken media discourse

There are other occasions in media discourse where deictic expressions are used to create a closer relationship between a speaker and their listening audience by what has been called 'simulating co-presence' (Montgomery, 1986b: 429). In an analysis of radio talk, he found that hosts may pretend that the listeners have access to the same spatial environment as they do, and this is accomplished through the use of deictic expressions, as the extract below illustrates:

5   but here hang on
      let me just hold *this* up in front of the microphone
      so you can see my pumpkin
      can you see *that*
      a real Halloween pumpkin

If you listen regularly to popular radio stations, you can collect extracts of radio talk and look for other examples of deixis which create a similar effect of co-presence between the host and the listening audience.

We have only been able to introduce very briefly the concepts of reference and deixis in this chapter, and give you a few textual examples of how they function. If you want to find out more about this aspect of language you can find a more detailed discussion of referring expressions and deixis in Hurford and Heasley (1983), whilst Levinson (1983) provides a thorough analysis of the deictic function of language. In the final section of this chapter we will look at the use of metaphor in popular texts. Before reading this section however, you may want to refer back to chapter 4 to review the section which deals with the concept of metaphor and its significance in literary texts.

7.6 Transferring meaning: metaphors in advertising

In this section we explore the use of metaphor in advertising, focusing particularly on the features of car advertisements. The advertising of cars through their association with a certain lifestyle and social status has often relied on images of women to sustain it. One example of this is an advert for a Metro Rio which uses a picture of a seductive Asian woman with a car tattooed on her shoulder to draw attention to the 'exotic' colour range and 'eye-catching' features of this car (see Thornborrow, 1995). With the technical developments in sophisticated braking systems and air cushions, there has been a shift in the way cars are marketed, particularly the larger family saloon cars, which are now promoted for their safety features as well as for their engine power and physical appearance. The use of women's bodies to achieve this has however persisted. Let's look at how the meanings are constructed in the following advertisement for a Mitsubishi Space Wagon.

The picture of the pregnant woman adjacent to the car immediately creates a link between the two – the way the text is presented visually invites us as readers to relate the two images. We could possibly make this association by thinking of the woman needing a car that was large enough for her growing family, but the relationship between the car and the woman's pregnant body is made explicit by the text:

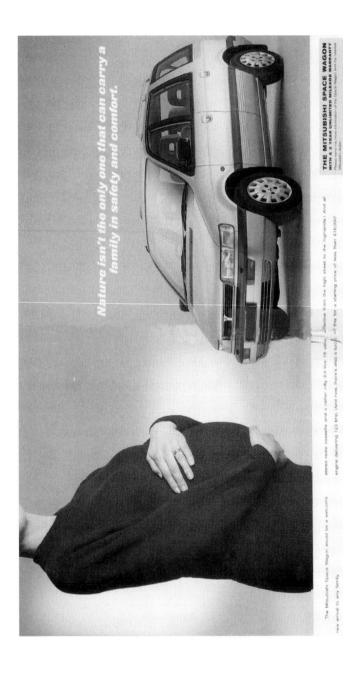

Nature isn't the only one that can carry a family in safety and comfort.

The Mitsubishi Space Wagon would be a welcome new arrival to any family.

It's large enough to carry 7 adults (or the equivalent in children), comes equipped with side impact bars and has a body incorporating high-tensile steel.

It has electric front and rear windows, child proof rear door locks, seat belts for everyone, central locking

stereo radio cassette and a rather nifty 2.0 litre 16 valve engine delivering 123 bhp. (And now, there's also a turbo off the line for a starting price of less than £16,000.)

diesel version available.)

It comes protected, of course, by one of the best warranty packages available. A 3 year unlimited mileage warranty, a 6 year anti-corrosion perforation warranty, plus a 3 year pan-European breakdown and recovery service

collective from the high street to the highlands. And all the while, is that you don't have to wait the one month for delivery.

Best of all however, is that you don't have to wait the one month for delivery.

For more information on the Space Wagon, and details of your nearest Mitsubishi dealer, complete the coupon or call free on **0800 123 263.**

THE MITSUBISHI SPACE WAGON
WITH A 3 YEAR UNLIMITED MILEAGE WARRANTY
Please send me more information on the Space Wagon and my nearest Mitsubishi dealer.

NAME

ADDRESS

POSTCODE   TEL.

MODEL   YEAR

To The Colt Car Company Ltd.   Watergate Road
Waterhouse, Cirencester, Gloucester GL7 1LF

DESIGNED TO BE DRIVEN

Nature isn't the only one that can *carry a family* in comfort

The metaphor created here is that the car is like the woman, both can 'carry' children safely inside them. The first sentence of the accompanying copy text however rather undermines this initial meaning by creating a second metaphor:

a welcome new arrival to any family

Now the car is being compared not to the pregnant woman, but to the expected child! The rest of the advertising text slips between these two metaphorical representations. On the one hand the car is the mother, emphasizing the high protection it offers to the family it carries, and on the other, the car is the child, the 'new arrival', reinforced by the sentence:

You won't have to wait nine months for delivery

The metaphorical relationship between the car and the unborn child is accomplished by the use of a pun on the word *delivery*, the moment when you actually possess the car, and the moment at the end of labour when the child is born. So by drawing on these two metaphorical representations of the mother and the child, the message that this advertisement seems to be constructing for its readers is that on the one hand, the car will carry their family safely, and on the other, it will also be a member of their family.

ACTIVITY 7.4

The following text is an advert for the Nissan 4-wheel-drive Terrano, published in the men's magazine *GQ* (September 1996). The car is pictured driving up a muscular male torso, which is coloured green like an oxidized bronze statue, and textured to give the surface an uneven, rugged look.

Can you identify the metaphorical structures at work in this text? How do they compare to the metaphors in the preceding advert for the Mitsubishi? Does this analysis enable you to say anything about the targeted addressee of the text?

6   More Pulling Power – The New Terrano II

Power, so they say, is an aphrodisiac. And you can't get much more powerful than the new Terrano II. Beneath that raunchy new exterior lies a 2.7 litre turbo diesel intercooler engine that delivers extra horsepower at lower revs, just when you need it. Switch to 4 wheel drive and you'll be down that rocky gorge (a doddle with the limited slip differential), through that stream (up to 450mm deep) and up that mountain (up to 39 degrees) with something close to wanton abandon. But perhaps you should begin with something more gentle. Like tarmac. For it's here that you'll appreciate the Terrano's more sensitive qualities. Its responsive handling. Its smooth as a satin sheet ride (thanks to anti-roll bars). The ease with which it will tow a trailer, pull a caravan, and more or less anything else you fancy. Add ABS and driver's airbag and you have a 4 × 4 that's too desirable for words. Which is exactly why it comes with engine immobiliser and an ultrasonic and perimetric alarm.

7.7 Analysis of popular texts: checklist

In this chapter we have given you some demonstrations of how the language of popular texts can be analysed in very similar ways to the language of literary texts, drawing on the linguistic concepts of address, reference, deixis and metaphor as well as analysing some of the phonological and morphological patterns which can be found in a diverse range of media contexts, from 'magazine speak' to radio talk. Just as texts acknowledged to be literary draw on the rich potential of language to create patterns in sound, rhythm, structure and meaning, so do the more popular forms of language use, particularly within the domain of the media. In our view, finding out about the stylistic features of non-literary texts can be equally as valid and enlightening an activity as analysing those texts which are normally deemed to be 'literary', and which are valued as part of the cultural capital. We may have different motives for analysing popular texts, but we can use our knowledge of the structures of language in just the same way in order to increase our understanding of how texts are

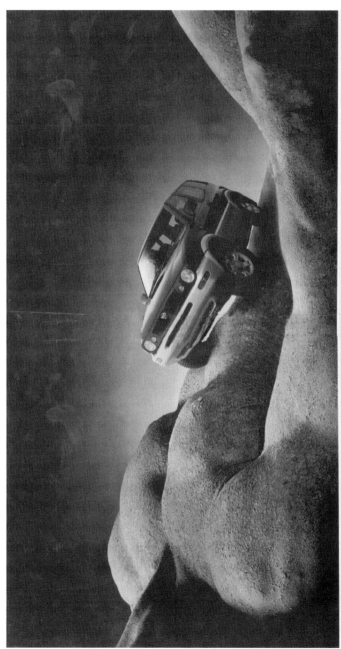

More pulling power.

THE NEW TERRANO II Power, so they say, is an aphrodisiac. And you can't get much more powerful than the new Terrano II. Beneath that raunchy new exterior lies a 2.7 litre turbo diesel intercooler engine* that delivers extra horsepower at lower revs, just when you need it. Switch to a wheel drive and you'll be down that rocky gorge (a doddle with the limited slip differential), through that stream (up to 450mm deep) and up that mountain (up to 39°) with something close to wanton abandon. But perhaps you should begin with something more gentle. Like tarmac. For it's here that you'll appreciate the Terrano's more sensitive qualities. Its responsive handling. Its smooth as a satin sheet ride (thanks to anti-roll bars). The ease with which it will tow a trailer, pull a caravan, and more or less anything else you fancy. Add ABS* and driver's airbag and you have a 4x4 that's too desirable for words. Which is exactly why it comes with engine immobiliser and an ultrasonic and perimetric alarm* For more information call 0345 66 99 66. **YOU CAN WITH A NISSAN**

situated with regard to their context and readership, our awareness of how meanings are created, and of how language provides an equally rich resource for playfulness and creativity in a whole range of different kinds of texts.

You should now be able to say something about the following aspects of popular texts:

- how newspaper headlines draw on sound patterning and semantic relations in headline texts
- how writers play with the morphological possibilities in the language to create new words
- how any text addresses, or targets, a particular group of readers
- how texts are situated in relation to time, space and context through the deictic function of language
- the use of metaphors in advertisements

Suggestions for further reading

For more examples of the application of stylistic analysis to non-literary texts, you may want to read:

Bhaya Mair, Rukmini (1992) 'Gender, genre and generative grammar', in Michael Toolan (ed.) *Language, Text and Context*, London: Routledge. 227–54.
Cook, Guy (1992) *The Discourse of Advertising*, London: Routledge.
Fairclough, Norman (1989) *Language and Power*, London: Longman.
Myers, Greg (1994) *Words in Ads*, London: Edward Arnold.
Thornborrow, Joanna (1994) 'The woman, the man and the Filofax' in Sara Mills (ed.) *Gendering the Reader*, Hemel Hempstead: Harvester Wheatsheaf, 128–52.

Note

1   For non-native speakers of English who may not be familiar with this expression, 'cruising for a bruising' means behaving in a way that is likely to get you into trouble of some sort, probably a fight!

Chapter 8

Theory and style: next steps

8.1 Overview

In this book our aim has been to introduce you to enough knowledge about the way language works, and to give you a range of ideas about how to apply that knowledge, for you to be able to approach the analysis of any text with a set of possible questions to ask about its structure. If you have completed the activities, you should be able to tackle most of the assignments you might be set if you are studying this area as part of a course dealing with a stylistic approach to written language.

Because this is only one introductory book, however, there are inevitably some gaps which it is as well to bear in mind. Firstly, phonetics and syntax are vast and complex areas, and our summaries are only a start on the road to understanding them. If you want a fuller understanding of either area, or indeed any other area of linguistic analysis we have touched on here, you will need to go else-where for the information. At the end of each chapter, we have listed a number of key texts which you can use as a first step in finding out more about the particular subject, and these in turn will lead you on to more specialist work in the field.

You will probably also find it helpful to look at other books that overlap with this one, because different authors will have different perspectives from the one that we adopt here. To make up your own mind about the value and usefulness of the information we have included, you should compare what we have said about language, and how we have structured it, with the way that other writers approach the subject. For example, we may well use different terms from ones you are accustomed to. This may or may not be significant, but you should be aware of these differences and be able to recognize them when you encounter a term that may not exactly 'fit'. The glossary at the end of the book gives you a summary of the way we have used linguistic terminology, but you may want to use other sources, such as David Crystal's *Dictionary of Linguistics and Phonetics*, (1991,

3rd edn) or Katie Wales's *Dictionary of Stylistics*, (1989) to check your understanding of the way a particular term can be used.

If you want to pursue the theoretical concepts behind stylistics, there is a growing collection of work in the field, and we recommend that you read further in this area. In the next section, we have provided a brief summary of some of the key work in stylistics and its areas of application to help direct your reading, but again, although we have covered what we believe to be the main areas of research, there will necessarily be gaps in our selection, and you will also need to look at other writers to build up a full picture of what stylistics is about. The summary below should help to indicate some useful starting points.

8.2 Linguistics and literary criticism

The development in theoretical linguistics during the 1950s and 1960s was mirrored by an increasing interest in what linguists could have to say about literary language. As we have mentioned at various points throughout this book, it was thought that the systematic and scientific study of literary texts would enable analysts to:

(a) differentiate between 'literary' and 'non-literary' forms of language;
(b) engage in objective descriptions of texts rather than in subjective evaluations.

Some of the earliest stylistic accounts of literary texts were those of the structuralist linguists in the 1960s (e.g. Jakobson, Mukařowský). They did not view meaning as something individual and unique to each text, but instead as the product of a system with various parts, which all fit together to make a structural whole. For these critics, the meaning of a word, or a line of a poem could only be interpreted in relation to the other words and lines in the poem, as part of a system of meaning.

Functional linguists like M. A. K. Halliday (see for example Halliday 1964, 1971) used detailed linguistic analysis as a powerful tool for explaining the meaning of texts. They related the formal properties of literary texts to the functions of language in a wider, social context. Halliday himself first published the type of analyses which depended on counting the frequency of particular linguistic structures in texts (see for instance his 1964 analysis of Yeats's *Leda and the Swan*). He later moved on to publish interpretative analyses which aimed to uncover social and ideological meanings in texts (Halliday 1973). This is the position still taken by many practising stylisticians today.

Mick Short, in his recent account of literary language (1996: 5), believes that stylistics plays a central role in helping us to decide what a text *means*:

> Stylistic analysis, which attempts to relate linguistic description to interpretation, is part of the essential core of good criticism, as it constitutes a large part of what is involved, say, in supporting a particular view of a poem or arguing for one interpretation over another.

One of the ways in which linguistic description can be used to this end is exemplified in Martin Montgomery's (1993) account of character in a Hemingway short story, *The Revolutionist*. Montgomery uses the linguistic concepts of transitivity and participant roles to analyse the textual cues which determine the interpretation of the character of the 'revolutionist' as someone who is essentially 'on the receiving end of actions done to him by others' (1993: 138), thus producing a contrast between the expectations set up by the title of the story, and the textual realization of the character.

This kind of analysis is something that you could use your knowledge of language to do if you are studying literature in English and are engaged in analysing literary texts. You may find that you can use linguistic evidence in the text to support an argument you are making about what the meaning of a particular episode may be, about the development of a character, or to contrast the construction of different characters in a text. This is one of the principal areas of application for stylistic analysis (see our discussion of Wareing 1994 later in this chapter).

A related area of application is the description and analysis of a text in order to talk about the aesthetic effects which are produced through the writer's choice of one linguistic form in preference to another. The aim of the analysis is to answer the question 'why was this way of writing selected rather than any other?' An example of this approach to stylistics can be found in the structural analyses presented in Wright and Hope (1996: 22), where they relate textual linguistic choices to the creation of a particular effect. For example, in an account of a passage from a novel by Graham Swift, they state that:

> Repetition of this syntactic structure [the noun phrase] serves to give a faintly cynical tone – not this time because the narrator wishes to mock, but in order to set up a certain distance between him and the case he is describing ... The narrator is a bureaucrat in the British civil service, and for some readers, this impersonal treatment will render the subject matter all the more disturbing.

Wright and Hope's concern here is to show how particular grammatical structures can contribute to an impression produced on the reader: in this case the 'distancing' and 'disturbing' effect of a series of noun phrases are examined.

8.3 Texts and the reader

Another view of stylistic analysis, put forward in the work of the American critic Stanley Fish (1980), is that we shouldn't be so much interested in what a text means, but rather what a text *does*. Fish claims that it is the reader who brings their own analytical processes to bear on what they read, and that texts can only have meaning in the context in which they are read. Terry Eagleton gives the following succinct description of Fish's position:

> For Fish, reading is not a process of discovering what the text means, but a process of experiencing what it *does* to you. [...T]he object of critical attention is the structure of the reader's experience, not any 'objective' structure to be found in the work itself.
>
> (Eagleton, 1983: 85)

This may lead to you think that there are as many interpretations as there are readers, and that texts can't be said to 'mean' anything at all in the usual sense of the word. Fish however gets round this problem by saying that readers do have shared 'interpretive strategies'. These interpretive strategies are acquired through common experiences, such as being members of an academic community, and it is these shared strategies which lead some readers to arrive at a consensus about the most appropriate way to interpret a text. But these interpretations, Fish claims, are to do with the institutional or cultural affiliation of the readers, rather than with anything which can be attributed to the linguistic structures of the text itself.

8.4 Text as discourse

Recently, work in stylistics has benefitted from developments in pragmatic theory, which is primarily concerned with the relationship of language to its context of use. This has broadened the range and scope of stylistic analysis, and resulted in some rather different avenues of investigation.

Some analysts have drawn on the work of Austin (1962) and Searle (1975) on speech act theory, and also on Grice's (1975) theory of inferential meaning. These have generated an approach to texts (particularly dramatic texts) which focuses on interactional features, dealing with the language as contextualized utterances rather than isolated sentences. Examples of this kind of analysis are William Downes's article on 'Lear's question to his daughters' (1988), and Leech's (1992) account of Shaw's play *You Never Can Tell*, which approach the dramatic text as discourse (i.e. as language governed by the principles of spoken interaction). This approach opens up a new level of textual analysis, which explores the interaction between characters within a fictional or dramatic text.

Another consequence of the appeal to pragmatics is that it enables analysts to approach texts as objects situated in the real world rather than as independent aesthetic artefacts, and to account for the interactive relationship between texts and their readers. In other words, it becomes possible to unravel that part of the meaning of a text which comes from the context in which we read it: the time, the culture and the social conditions under which we encounter it. We all approach texts with different sets of assumptions and experiences which will inevitably have an effect on how we interpret them. This brings us back to Stanley Fish's view, as discussed earlier, that meaning is essentially produced by the reader, and does not reside within the text itself.

However, rather than seeing the reader as 'usurping' the role of the author as principal producer of textual meaning, we would argue that meaning is derived from a combination of factors, including the formal structure of the text, and the contextual circumstances in which it is read. We also believe that meaning is not always absolutely fixed, but is something fluid that cannot always be pinned down once and for all through a process of analysis. It is rather the case that those analytic procedures can often help to account for and explain how particular interpretations of a text may arise. As David Birch (1989: 42) points out:

> We don't need linguistics to help us interpret a text – people have been doing that for years without linguistics. What linguistics can do is to give a vocabulary for understanding and explaining how the text means.

Access to knowledge about language can therefore help you to construct stronger arguments about the meanings a text may have for particular kinds of readers. Sara Mills, arguing from a feminist perspective, clearly emphasizes the importance of the reader's role in the interpretation of a text when she states that:

> [I]t is clear that the reader is addressed by the text, and that s/he is affected by and can make an effect on the interpretation of the text. S/he is an active participant negotiating with the meanings which are being foisted onto her/him, and resisting or questioning some of those meanings.
>
> (Mills, 1995: 35)

There is now an established field of 'Discourse Stylistics' which aims to further both these avenues of intra-textual analysis and text/reader interaction, and you will find some examples of this approach in Carter and Simpson (1989): *Language, Discourse and Literature: An Introductory Reader in Discourse Stylistics*.

8.5 Critical text analysis

A further development in the field has been in the use of stylistics in the critical analysis of texts. The range of texts which have been the target of such analyses has also broadened, and now includes not only so-called 'literary' texts but also texts from the media and popular fiction. In fact, nowadays any written text can be considered a valid object of critical attention.

The term 'critical' in this context means something rather

different from its more general meaning within the context of literary criticism. It was initially associated with the work of linguists such as Roger Fowler, Gunther Kress, Robert Hodge and Tony Trew (1979) and Hodge and Kress (1993) who were interested in the relationship between linguistic structures and processes of representation. In other words, they constructed theories about how particular selections in grammatical and semantic structures affected the way in which people, events and processes were talked about and written about, particularly within the context of the news media, but also in other genres of popular texts. These linguists argued that the structures of representation were ideologically based, and that particular social and cultural groups, and their associated activities, tended to be represented in ways which reinforced the dominant, 'common sense' ways of viewing those groups. This research into language and representation focuses particularly on the role of agency and transitivity patterns – put simply, 'who does what to whom [and how and when]'.

Examples of this kind of research can be found in Trew's (1978) analysis of newspaper reports of civil unrest in South Africa in 1975, and Montgomery's (1986a) account of the press coverage of the 1984–5 miners' strike in Britain. A good summary of the relationship between language, representation and ideological structures can be found in Paul Simpson's *Language, Ideology and Point of View* (1993), and also in David Lee's *Competing Discourses* (1992).

One area where the development of a critical approach to language has been particularly important is in the feminist critique of texts. Examples of stylistic analyses which draw on linguistics to build an argument about how texts can be seen to have particular contextual interpretations can be found in the work of Burton (1982), Mills (1995), Thornborrow (1994) and Wareing (1994).

In her wide-ranging book *Feminist Stylistics* (1995) Sara Mills draws on the theoretical position developed by Norman Fairclough (1989, 1995) in order to analyse texts in their social and cultural contexts. Mills argues that representations of women, on every level of language from word to discourse, can be shown to be grounded in the ideological systems and structures of patriarchy, and suggests that a critical linguistic analysis of both literary and non-literary texts can demonstrate how these representations are constructed, as well as creating a space for alternative systems of representation.

Through an analysis of the transitivity patterns in an extract from *The Bell Jar*, a novel by Sylvia Plath, Deirdre Burton (1982) argues that the writer's choice of agency and verb forms contributes to the creation of a sense of powerlessness in the central character. Burton also asked her students to experiment in rewriting the scene using different transitivity structures, and found that this considerably changed the readers' impression of the character's control over what was happening to her.

Wareing (1994) also focuses on the grammatical transitivity structures in recent popular fiction where the traditional gender roles are reversed, and the central characters are portrayed as women who have struggled to become strong and successful in their own right. However, despite this reversal, in scenes which describe sexual encounters the woman is still represented as passive and it is the male character who remains in control of the sexual action. Wareing argues that although romantic fiction is undergoing changes in the way its heroines are represented, reflecting social and cultural changes in the position of women in modern Western societies, there is still a deeply rooted tendency to represent female characters as fragmented objects of sexual desire rather than active originators of it. This tendency can be identified and described through an analysis of the linguistic processes at work in the construction of such scenes.

The central concern of this work is to show, through systematic linguistic analysis, how women get to be represented in specific and consistent ways which reproduce, to a greater or lesser extent, the social and ideological structures in which the text is written and is read.

8.6 Theory and practice: some further questions

One way of using this book is to see it as providing one part of a set of questions that you might need to draw on in approaching the study of literary texts. There are of course many questions which arise from different areas of interest within the study of literature; for example, developments in the study of psychoanalysis, in social and historical theory, and in cultural identity have all had their effect on the kind of questions that get asked about the meaning of texts in general, and literary texts in particular.

If you are studying a course which introduces you to literary theory, and contains information about historical, social and psychoanalytical perspectives on texts, you may find that asking questions which are linked to issues of language and discourse will play an important part in your understanding of those perspectives. In this book we have dealt essentially with knowledge about language; if you want to fit this knowledge into the broader area of literary theory, some useful places to start are Durant and Fabb (1990) *Literary Studies in Action*, and Green and LeBihan (1996) *Critical Theory and Practice*. Both these texts refer to the place of language and style in relation to the study of literature, and both are designed to be used for self-study as well as in class with a tutor.

8.7 Conclusions

We hope that you have found this book practical and accessible, and that it will help you to become aware of the richness and diversity of the material that writers are working with. You may also find it enables you to become more reflective about your own writing practices. We are *all* producers of texts of one sort or another, whether they are written coursework and assignments, letters to friends, or explorations in creative writing of our own. The relationship between reading and writing is a constant exchange between recognizing the conventions people use when they write, and being able to reproduce them when you write. Once you know about these conventions, you can begin to stretch their boundaries by breaking some of the rules and experimenting with new forms and styles, particularly in the process of creative writing. Most of all, we hope that in knowing more about the formal structures of the language, your enjoyment of reading anything, from an advertisement on the 72 bus, to the latest prizewinning, postmodernist novel, will be enhanced.

Suggested answers to activities

Chapter 2

Activity 2.2

(1) pet (2) paperclip (3) fingertip (4) haircut (5) book (6) salt and pepper (7) views (8) film (9) chocolate (10) petrol station

Activity 2.3

(1) spʌn	(2) kaɪt	(3) sɛl	(4) pɒt
(5) kɑ	(6) taɪɡə	(7) tæŋk	(8) lɛŋɡθ
(9) sɪnəmə	(10) træfɪk	(11) teɪbl̩	(12) eɪmləs
(13) ðæt, ðət	(14) prəʊtɛst, prətɛst	(15) sʌdʒɛstʃən	
(16) bəlif	(17) pəsweʃn̩	(18) rəlɪdʒən (19) θæŋkju	

The pronunciation of many of these words will differ with your accent, and also in what context you actually say them. If the vowels you have transcribed are not the same as our answers, it does not necessarily mean that you are wrong.

Activity 2.4

a b a b b c b c d e d e f f

Activity 2.5

cupboard – 2   mirror – 2   cat – 1   walls – 1   table – 2   strewn – 1
admirable – 4   elevator – 4   persuasive – 3   honeysuckle – 4
inadvisable – 5   gladiator – 4   oregano – 4   blushed – 1

Activity 2.6

alliteration	**assonance**	**consonance**
store / same	Lord / store / fall	man / in
Lord / lost	Though / most	
this / thy / then / the	same / decaying	
fall / further / flight		
more / me		

rhyme	**half-rhyme**	**repetition**
more / poore / store	rise / victories	more / more
became / same		me / me
thee / me / harmoniously		

Activity 2.7

perfórm   mírror   wálls   unkínd   stréwn
admírable   persuásive   cúpboard   hóneysúckle   inadvísable
gládiator   orégano   blúshed   élevator

You may place the stress differently on some of these words, particularly if you are from the USA. Except for *honeysuckle* and *admirable*, we have only marked the main stress on each word. Stress in English words however tends to fall on alternate syllables, so once you have found the main stress in a polysyllabic word, you can be fairly sure that any secondary stress will fall either two syllables before or after it (e.g. *inadvisable* has a secondary stress on the first syllable).

Activity 2.8

27   Wild Nights – Wild Nights!   2 stresses: 2 iambs

      Were I with thee   2 stresses: 2 iambs

      Wild Nights should be   2 stresses: 2 iambs

      Our luxury!   2 stresses: 2 iambs

This stanza is entirely in iambic dimetre.

28   He is not here; but far away   4 stresses: 4 iambs

      The noise of life begins again,   4 stresses: 4 iambs

      And ghastly through the drizzling rain   4 stresses: 4 iambs

      On the bald street breaks the blank day   4 stresses: 2 pyrrhics,
                                            2 spondees

The first three lines are in iambic tetrametre. The fourth line consists of two spondees alternated with two pyrrhic feet (although you might read the word 'break' in the final line as stressed as well, giving you an additional stress).

29   Nobody heard him, the dead man,   2 dactyls, 1 trochee

      But still he lay moaning: 1 dactyl, 1 trochee

      I was much further out than you thought 3 anapests

      And not waving but drowning.   2 anapests

In a poem like this, where the metre varies, it can be very difficult to determine where the feet begin and end; it is not an exact science. Unstressed syllables are much less significant than stressed ones, and poems can sometimes contain quite a lot of 'stray' unstressed syllables which can actually be ignored when you try to work out the metre. The first two lines could be classified as free verse (or *vers libre*) because there is not a regular metre. However, the last two lines, the dead man's 'refrain', switch into anapestic metre, helping them to stand out against the rest of the poem.

Chapter 3

Activity 3.1

To find out the word class for *brillig*, you need to test what other words could fit in the slot after *twas*. Some examples are:

[I]t was – twilight / dusk / evening / Tuesday

These are all words to do with *time*, most of them are *nouns* of some sort, (i.e. you can put 'the' in front of them – *the twilight, the evening.* Tuesday is a name, or *proper noun.*

[I]t was – cold / dark / misty / bright

These are all words which fit into the class of *adjective*, as they can modify a noun, coming in between the determiner and the noun, as in the *cold* evening, the *misty* evening.

A further set of words that could come after *twas* belong to a set of expressions to do with time:

[I]t was – late / teatime / five o'clock

These are more difficult to assign to a particular word class, but you could argue that they behave in the same kind of way as nouns and adjectives in this particular case.

Activity 3.2

nouns:	November, months, London, bridge, pelicans, necks, bundles, wings, beaks, lake, water, fists, jacket, accent, St James's Park
verbs:	pause, watch, float, arching, burying, clench, test
adjectives:	low, white, awkward, cold
adverbs:	swanlike, slightly, secretly.

Some of the words you have left over will be determiners, like *the, their, my* and prepositions, like *in, on, over* and *of. Eight* is a numeral, modifying *months* in this example. *Marks and Spencer's* functions like an adjective here, because it modifies *jacket*, although in other cases it would probably be a noun (e.g. 'I shop at Marks and Spencer's'). You may have had a problem with *ruffled*. It occurs here in a long rather complex noun phrase: 'only slightly ruffled bundles of wings'. The main noun in this phrase is *bundles*, combined here with *wings* to form a larger noun phrase similar to *bunches of flowers* or *packets of crisps*. This in turn is modified by the word *ruffled*, which is behaving like an adjective here (although it derives from the verb *ruffle*), and the words *only slightly* further modify this adjective, so they are adverbs.

You may want to read section 3.6.1 'The noun phrase' for more details.

Activity 3.3

The noun phrases are listed below. The 'head' noun is italicized in each one:

> A *succession* of hands; *Grace Willison*, the middle aged *spinster*; a *study* in grey; *skin*; *hair*; *dress*; *stockings*; all of *them*; *she*; an old-fashioned stiffly jointed *doll*; a dusty *cupboard*.

You will notice that these noun phrases vary from a single pronoun (*she*) to the much longer *an old-fashioned, stiffly jointed doll*, which has two premodifying adjective phrases (*old-fashioned* and *stiffly jointed*), preceding the head noun *doll*. A noun phrase can therefore consist of just one word, like *skin*, a name, *Grace Willison*, or a combination of different types of phrases, as in the last example.

Activity 3.4

The verb phrases in this extract are:

> stood; turning; travelled; scattered; glassed-in; pursed; might have been going to whistle; did not whistle, turned the ring; freshly washed.

The *finite*, or *main* verbs are those which are marked for tense, person and mood. These are:

He *stood*	(third person, past tense)
His glance *travelled* coolly	(third person, past tense)
He *pursed* his lips	(third person, past tense)

He *might have been going to whistle*	(third person, modality *might have been going to*, past tense)
He *did not whistle*	(third person, past tense)
[He] only *turned* the ring	(third person, past tense)

The other verbs are *non-finite*, and are used in non-finite phrases like the gerundive *-ing* form *turning*; or the past participle form *scattered*, (giving more information about the tables and chairs), *glassed-in*, (giving more information about the veranda) and *washed*, (giving more information about his hands). These last three function as adjectives in this case.

Activity 3.5

The finite verb phrases in extract 10 are:

> began to lead; was; were; was assailed; squashed,
> entered; had taken to; was; had called; meant

which are all marked for tense and person. In the case of *was assailed* and *squashed*, the verb phrase is in the passive voice (*she was assailed*, *she was squashed*) where the entity *doing* the assailing and squashing is *the talking washing chests of her past* rather than the subject of the sentence, *she* (see section 3.6 for more on subjects).

The non-finite verb phrases are:

> living, studying, cultivating; including; talking; descending.

The non-finite verb forms are used to build up the description of what sort of things Mumtaz Aziz did in her life: *living* chastely, *studying* mediocrely, *cultivating* gifts, *descending* through a trap door. *Including*, although it looks like a verb (it has the *-ing* gerundive ending) behaves more like a preposition in the phrase *up to and including*. *Talking* is also a non-finite verb form used as an adjective here to describe the *washing chests*.

There are nine sentences in extract 11.

Subject	Predicate
The king	was working in the garden.
He	seemed very glad to see me.
We	walked through the garden.
This	is the queen.
He	said.
She	was clipping a rose bush.
She	said.
We	sat down at a table under a big tree.
The king	ordered whisky and soda.

The clauses in extract 14 are:

1   Miss Brooke had that kind of beauty

2   which seemed to be thrown into relief by poor dress.

1 is the main clause, 2 is the subordinate clause beginning with the relative pronoun *which*. This kind of relative, subordinate clause gives more information about an element in the preceding clause, in this case *that kind of beauty*.

The clauses in extract 15 are:

1   In Devonshire [. . .] leaves were still thick on the trees

2   where the round red hills and steep valleys hoarded the sea air

This complex sentence follows the same pattern as (14) – the two clauses are linked by a relative pronoun, this time *where* – and provides more information about *Devonshire*.

This project is based on the language used by first generation Jamaicans who have been living in the UK since the 1950s.

Given that they are first generation Jamaican, as opposed to their children, who may have been born in England, their speech will be explored to see whether there is a constant use of Jamaican Creole or whether there are any other influences, such as London Jamaican. This is a term used by Mark Sebba to describe a linguistic variety used by young people, some of whom may not be of Jamaican descent, which is in part similar to Jamaican Creole, as well as being the English which is spoken by White London contemporaries.

Chapter 4

Activity 4.1

emasculate	perhaps *defeminized* – but this does not really have the dual meaning of being physically without genitals as well behaving in a way appropriate to the other gender. The term *unsex me* is used by Shakespeare's character Lady Macbeth, but this term is not gender specific.
virile	perhaps *fecund* or *fertile* but these do not really have the same sense of sexual activity. They are also gender-free terms that can be applied to males or females.
nymphomaniac	*pervert* is usually used to mean someone with an interest in strange sexual practices and can probably be used about women as well as men, so it's not gender-specific in the way *nymphomaniac* is. Neither *sex fiend* nor *sex addict* is gender-specific.
old woman	there does not seem to be a direct equivalent of this insult that we know of. 'He's a bit of an old woman' usually means someone is fussy and prim. Old men do not seem to be characterized in the same way.

tomboy   Although there are terms like *sissy* or *girly*, they have strongly negative connotations, whereas *tomboy* is not a particularly negative term (for most people).

These are our interpretations of the words – as we said, there is some 'slippage' around terms like these, so your answers may be slightly different.

Activity 4.2

Possible hyponyms

For the media: newspapers, television, radio, the Internet
For jewellery: necklaces, earrings, bracelets, brooches
For soup: broth, consommé, stew
For fastenings for clothes: zip, buttons, laces, ties
For stationery: envelopes, writing paper, postcards, notebooks

Possible superordinates

jazz: music
wheat: cereals
fountain pen: writing implements
central heating: heating systems
igloo: houses or buildings
dictionary: reference books
suitcase: containers

Activity 4.3

discommode is more formal than *inconvenience*, and unlikely to be used in exactly the same contexts.

sorrow is more formal than *sadness*.

intelligent and *clever* are probably synonyms in most contexts – although *clever* is probably slightly lower in register. You can also use *clever* in contexts to do with skills – 'She was clever with her hands', 'he's clever at getting things out of you', where *intelligent* is inappropriate.

apprehensively is more formal than *nervously*.

journalist is more specific in terms of job than *newspaperman*, which might refer to editors and perhaps owners of newspapers, as well as those who write for them; *journalist* is also gender-neutral, in that it can refer to either women or men.

inquire is more formal than *question*.

recollect is more formal than *remember*.

admonish is more formal than *scold*, and also less severe.

Activity 4.4

We have identified the metaphors and similes in the Plath poem, and the tenors and vehicles. We have made suggestions as to what the grounds of the comparisons are, but these are rather more individual so there is some room for variation in the answers.

you're *clownlike*	i.e. you are like a clown = simile; tenor = baby, vehicle = clown, ground = the baby's movements including turning upside down
you're *moon-skulled*	metaphor; tenor = baby's skull, vehicle = moon, ground = pale, hairless curve of the baby's skull looks like the moon
you're *gilled like a fish*	simile; tenor = baby, vehicle = fish, ground = both have gills (embryos have gills during their development)
you're *a common-sense thumbs-down on the dodo's mode*	metaphor; tenor = baby, vehicle = thumbs down sign, ground = the baby is shaped like a thumbs-down sign, and also represents a positive affirmation of existence over extinction (the dodo's mode)

you're *wrapped up in yourself like a spool*

> simile; tenor = baby, vehicle = spool of thread, ground = the way the baby is tightly curled up on itself

you're *trawling your dark as owls do*

> metaphor; tenor = baby, vehicle = owls, ground = both explore in the dark

you're *mute as a turnip* simile; tenor = baby, vehicle = turnip, ground = neither makes a noise

O high-riser metaphor; tenor = baby, vehicle = a metonymic reference to bread (i.e. because bread rises – see below), and / or a reference to a high-rise block of flats, ground = in either case, the capacity to grow tall

my little loaf metaphor; tenor = baby, vehicle = bread, ground = both grow or rise (in the oven – a perhaps pun on 'bun in the oven', a colloquial term for pregnancy)

you're *vague as a fog* simile; tenor = baby , vehicle = fog, ground = indeterminacy

you're *looked for like mail*

> simile; tenor = baby, vehicle = mail, ground = eagerly anticipated

you're *farther off than Australia*

> simile; tenor = baby, vehicle = Australia, ground = both a great distance away (metaphorically in the baby's case)

you're *bent-backed Atlas* metaphor; tenor = baby, vehicle = Atlas, the mythological giant who supports the world on his shoulders, ground = the curved shape of their backs

you're *our travelled prawn* metaphor; tenor = baby, vehicle = (travelled) prawn, ground = the physical similarities between a prawn and the baby: both are pink, naked, small, curved. The baby has travelled inside its mother you're *snug as a bug*   simile; tenor = baby, vehicle = a bug, ground = physical similarities between the baby and a bug, as for prawn above, and the baby is 'snug' in the womb in the way the bug is allegedly snug in its rug (from the expression: 'snug as a bug in a rug')

you're *at home like a sprat in a pickle jug*

simile; tenor = baby, vehicle = a sprat, ground = again, as above, perhaps physical similarities between the baby and a sprat, and also the appropriateness of their respective environments.

you're *a creel of eels all ripples*

metaphor; tenor = baby, vehicle = a creel of eels, ground = perhaps physical similarities again, as for the prawn, bug and sprat, and also the gills of the baby and the fish, and also the wriggling movements of the baby are like the movements of eels

you're *jumpy as a Mexican Bean*

simile; tenor = baby, vehicle = Mexican Bean, ground = the jumpy movements of both (see eels above)

you're *right, like a well-done sum*

simile; tenor = baby, vehicle = a well-done sum, ground = the completeness / perfection / appropriateness of both a correct sum and the baby

you're *a clean slate, with your own face on*

metaphor; tenor = baby, vehicle =a clean slate, with your own face on, ground = the baby has unsullied potential in common with an unmarked slate, but not so unmarked that it is not its unique self.

Activity 4.5

Announced by all the trumpets of the sky

The snowstorm is not literally announced by trumpets (which might normally herald the arrival of an important figure like a king, thus making a comparison between the snowstorm and a powerful person). Trumpets of the sky (vehicle) might refer to thunder or wind (possible tenors), and the ground for the comparison would be the noise and magnitude of the thunder or wind, and that they precede the storm, thus warning of its approach.

masonry

The forms made from snow (the tenor) are not literally masonry (i.e. stonework – the vehicle); what they have in common (the ground) is presumably the appearance of being grand, solid constructions. By association, the north wind is a 'mason', someone who builds in stone (personification).

the fierce artificer

The north wind (the tenor) is compared to a fierce artificer (the vehicle) presumably because it seems to build edifices (like a person – this is also personification) which imitate solid buildings but which are in fact snow.

white bastions

Bastions (the vehicle) are architectural features, projections which contribute to fortification, again describing the forms made by the snow (the tenor) which appears to be solid (the ground).

he hangs Parian wreaths

'he' is a further example of personification: the wind (tenor) is compared to a person who hangs up white wreaths (vehicle), on the ground that the snow falls and collects in forms that resemble wreaths.

Activity 4.6

1   The use of 'axed' is a metaphor, since the train will not literally be chopped up like wood. However, there a two choices for the tenor / vehicle / ground. Tenor = train, vehicle = tree, ground = they can both be cut ('axed') or tenor = rail network authorities, vehicle = woodcutter, ground = they both 'axe' things.

2   England and India = metonymic reference to the cricket teams which represent England and India. 'A right old spin' = metaphor; tenor = the cricket team, vehicle = a cricket ball, ground = they both 'spin' (i.e. the cricket ball because of the way it is thrown; the team because they are confused and in turmoil).

3   Red tape = metonym; red tape is used in bureaucracies to prevent access. By association it is used to refer to bureaucratic regulations which prevent access.

Chapter 5

Activity 5.1

A suggested rewrite:

Mary and Susan's Conversation – part 2

20   M: do you think it's worth having something written up about them for people to read or do you think (.) no one's really going to be interested and they'll just eat the food and go?

21   S: yes, that's the problem – well I think if it's something very

short and it's not as if we're making them wade through a whole lot of (.) information – that'll be cool

22   M: Ok fine (.) so can you think of anything else we should take?

23   S: not really (.)

24   M: you know, it really seems quite criminal (.) to have an African theme and not to have African food

26   S: Yeah, I know. We'll just have to try and make it up with the surroundings.

We have made the utterances longer, cutting out some of the back channel support and occasionally changing who said what to make the conversation seem more 'whole'. We have also tried to make it more explicit, so that it would be easier to understand for an audience. We have left in words like *yeah* and *cool* because they tell us something about the age of the speakers and the context of the exchange (i.e. that they are young and talking informally), but we have altered some of the words that might make the exchange ambiguous.

Chapter 6

Activity 6.1

Text 2 has non-standard spelling and punctuation, uses forms more usual in registers of spoken language than written like the tag *innit* (an informal pronunciation of *isn't it*), and the marker *you see*; the semantic referents are not immediately available because of the deviant spelling (see chapter 3 for more on deviation) – for example, do we know what chard coal is? Does *a stage* refer to a stage in a theatre, or a stage in a process (for instance a stage in the sequence of events in a story)? Do the words *Wud* and *wood* refer to the same thing? The different semantic fields in the extract are not easily related to one another.

In contrast, Text 1 has none of this ambiguity; the spelling and

231

punctuation are conventional, the register fits our expectations of narration using past tense forms, the semantic fields are clearly the themes of birth, hospitals and doctors, and the world of finance. The semantic referents are easily recoverable, either from the context or from background knowledge the reader is likely to have about the world.

Activity 6.2

Dialogue: extracts 12 and 13 both represent dialogue as direct speech, in speech marks. However, extract 12 contains explicit verbal process items (*said, faintly repeated*), and gives some indication as to how the utterance was spoken (*Mr Fairlie arched his eyebrows and pursed up his lips in sarcastic surprise*) but extract 13 does not.

Extract 14 uses a mixture of both direct speech and verbal process items, but also brings an episode of previous speech (*The Bishop had said . . .*) into the scene.

Activity 6.7

Extract 26 has predominantly modernist characteristics. You might have identified the following:

1 Within this extract, language is used to imitate Miriam's actual experience of beginning to dream as she drifts into sleep, and her thoughts become confused: 'The win-ter may – pass. . . . The win-ter . . . may pass. The winter may . . . pass. The Academy . . . a picture in very bright colours . . . '

2 There are examples of the modernist form, 'stream of consciousness', in this extract: 'brilliant light flashed into the room . . . lightning – how strange the room looked – the screens had been moved – the walls and corners and little beds had looked like daylight. '

3 You might have included the words from German as examples of collage: '"Ach Clara! Mein Gott! Ach Gott!"'.

The text comes from *Pointed Roofs*, a novel by Dorothy Richardson, first published in 1915 (p. 145).

You probably identified extract 27 as the example of postmodernism.

1   There are many examples of postmodern parody and pastiche in this passage. Familiar registers and styles are exploited and played with. For example, the traditional fairy story conclusion is presented, but then subverted: 'They were happy ever after. / Lucy was of course unhappy ever after'. The wording of a will, a legal document, is borrowed, but also adapted (by the inclusion of 'old and scarcely in my right mind') to mock and amuse: 'I, Praxis Duveen, being old and scarcely in my right mind, bequeath you . . .'

   The contrast and conflict between the different discourses is also used as a source of humour, and to subvert their usual authority. Apart from the examples given above, you might also have included the contrasts between the amusing superficial summary of the separation of Lucy from Ben (for example, the sentence beginning 'Within a year [. . .] Ben had become enamoured . . . ') and the greater psychological depth of the section that follows ('The memory of the afflicted child one was . . . '). The clash between the styles (and there are other instances you may have identified) is a good example of the postmodern tendency to regard all discourses as equal and none having a closer relationship with 'the truth' than any other. Even the names of the girls themselves suggest that the text invites the reader not to take it too seriously: 'Praxis' and 'Hypatia'.

2   There is also evidence of the postmodern belief that 'all stories have been told before'. The repetition of elements from fairy stories is one example of this: 'They were happy ever after'.

3   If you were looking for examples of humour, you might have focused on the last two paragraphs – the contrast between the relatively elevated register of 'I, Praxis Duveen, . . . bequeath you my memories . . . ' and the much more mundane: 'Last night, doing just that, I slipped on the soap . . . '. There are many other examples of humour in the text. For an example of irony, you might have noted ' . . . the golf-club (where anti-Semitic feeling ran high, but made an honourable exception for Ben, who was the only Jew they had ever encountered in person, but was universally liked)'.

This comes from the novel *Praxis*, by Fay Weldon, first published in 1978 (pp. 11–12).

You probably identified extract 28 as an extract from a classic realist text. You might have noted the following features as typical of such a text:

1   The narrator knows the behaviour and the likely feelings of all the characters mentioned, and resents them as if viewing it all from a position of greater knowledge and impartial under-standing, i.e. the text has an omniscient narrator. For example: 'The Miss Brownings would have thought themselves sadly defrauded of the gayest event of the year, if anything had prevented their attending the charity ball, and Miss Browning would have been indignant, Miss Phoebe aggrieved . . . '. The other two passages are on the whole presented from a specific, explicitly limited, point of view.

2   The incorporation of place names which sound as if they might really exist, and places which do exist outside the novel, contributes to a concrete presentation of place: for example, references to 'the country towns of England', 'Ashcombe and Coreham' and 'London'.

3   The extract certainly attempts to convince the reader the actions described occurred in 'real time', by including time references linked to real events. Examples of this include refer-ences to 'At the present time . . . ', ' . . . in the days when Molly and Cynthia were young – before the railroads were, and before their consequences, the excursion-trains, which take every one up to London now-a-days . . . '.

This extract is taken from *Wives and Daughters*, a novel written by Elizabeth Gaskell and published between 1864 and 1866 (p. 322).

Chapter 7

Activity 7.1

harbourmoon	probably a noun, formed from the free mor-phemes *harbour* and *moon*
bejeweleavening	looks like a gerundive form of the invented verb *bejeweleaven*, formed from the bound morpheme *be*, the noun *jewel*, which combine to form a verb

	bejewel (e.g. you could say someone was *bejewelled* in the same pattern as *bedecked*, or *befriended*). The free morpheme *leaven* is then built on, (e.g. to *leaven* bread). Finally, the inflectional morpheme *-ing* is added at the end, indicating that the whole word can function as a verb.
restorying	similarly, this looks like a gerundive form built out of a combination of the verb *restore*, and an invented verb *restory* (perhaps meaning something like, *to tell a story again*) formed by combining the morpheme *-re* with the noun *story*, and the inflectional morpheme *-ing*.
liftlike	this term appears to be made up of the combination of the free morpheme *lift* and the adjectival morpheme *like* (as in *lifelike*, or *swanlike*).

Activity 7.3

You can start your analysis by listing the expressions which are used to describe the car: it is *powerful*, it has a *raunchy exterior*, it has *sensitive qualities*, *responsive handling*, it is a *smooth* (as a satin sheet) *ride*, *desirable*.

These descriptions seem to fall into two categories: *powerful* and *raunchy* on the one hand versus *sensitive*, *smooth*, *responsive* and *desirable* on the other. Both categories of adjective can also be used to describe people, so there is a personification metaphor at work here: the car is described in terms of a set of sensuous qualities that could also be applied to humans.

You could also list the expressions which fit with the semantic field of sexual attraction found in one of the meanings of the opening phrase: *more pulling power*. There is a pun on the word *pull* here, which can mean the act of towing a caravan or trailer, or colloquially, the act of successfully attracting a member of the opposite sex.

Power [....] is an aphrodisiac.

you'll be up that mountain with something close to wanton abandon,

it will pull [....] anything else you fancy.

Our view of this advert is that it draws on two aspects of human experience: the concept of physical power and conquest, linked to the power of sexual attraction. This advert quite cleverly subsumes both these aspects, again by 'slipping' between two metaphorical representations: the linguistic choices made in the text on the one hand connote qualities of strength, power and control, on the other, qualities of sensuous eroticism. The Terrano is represented both as physically (and sexually) powerful, and as sensitive, responsive and desirable. This metaphoric duality was also present in the advert for the Mitsubishi Space Wagon discussed earlier.

We will leave the second part of this question open for discussion – depending on your own background assumptions and cultural knowledge, you may have different opinions as to who are the targeted consumers/drivers of the Terrano II.

Glossary

accent a speaker's pronunciation system. All speakers have an accent, which carries information about their social, regional and national background. Accent is one aspect of **dialect**, which includes a speaker's **syntax** and **lexis** as well as their accent.

adjacency pair a **turn** sequence (a conversational exchange) which has two parts: the occurrence of the first part predicts the occurrence of the second; for example, a greeting adjacency pair:

> Speaker A: 'Hi!'
> Speaker B: 'Hi!'

adjective a **class** of word which is generally used to describe or **modify** a **noun**, such as *cat*; e.g. a *sleepy small furry brown cat*.

adverb a **class** of word which is used to describe or **modify** a **verb**; for example, the verb *purr* can be modified by the **adverb** *loudly*: *the cat purred loudly*. Adverbs can also modify **adjectives**; the adverb *absolutely* can modify the adjective *fabulous*, in the phrase *Absolutely Fabulous*.

allusion a reference in a text to another text.

anapest a unit of metre; see page 36.

anthropomorphism a term to describe the attribution

of human qualities to non-human beings or things. See page 104.

antonym   a term to describe lexical opposites, such as *alive* and *dead*. See page 85.

aspect   grammatical information contained in the **verb phrase** about the duration of an action; for example *I was walking* in contrast to *I walked*.

asymmetry   non-equality; often used to describe non-equality in lexical representation; for example the title *Mr* for men is asymmetrical compared to the titles *Miss*, *Mrs* and *Ms* for women. The term is also used in **discourse** analysis to refer to the distribution of speaker rights in a conversation, or their access to different kinds of turns (i.e. who gets to talk, and who gets to say what kind of things). For example, in a law court, the defendant does not have the same rights to ask questions as the examining lawyer.

auxiliary verb   a part of the verb phrase, separate from the lexical verb, which carries information about **tense**, **mood** and **aspect**. See page 67.

back channel   back channel support is the feedback participants give to each other in a conversation. It can include nodding, listening noises like 'uhuh', 'mmm' or words like 'yeah'.

bound morpheme   a type of **morpheme** (such as *-ed* or *-tion*) which cannot stand on its own but must be attached to a **free morpheme** (such as *pollute*, to produce *polluted*, or *pollution*). See also **derivational morpheme** and **inflectional morpheme**.

class   a term which can be used generally to mean a group of similar things. See **word class** for a specific linguistic use of this term.

clause   a grammatical unit containing a **main verb**. A sentence has to contain at least one clause. There are various kinds of clauses. A **main clause** is one which contains a main **finite verb**, and can stand on its own as a sentence. A **subordinate clause** needs to be attached to a main clause to be grammatically complete. One kind of subordinate clause, the **relative clause**, usually starts with a relative pronoun such as *who, which, that, where*. See page 71.

closed class words   sometimes called function words or grammatical items. These carry grammatical rather than **lexical** information, and are used to indicate the structure of a sentence. Examples include: *the, a, on, at, because, who, where, very*, and *not*. They are known as closed class words because new ones are seldom created; therefore there is a finite number of them.

collocation a term used to describe the relationship between words which often occur near each other, such as *big*, *bad* and *wolf*, or in the same context, such as *tree*, *grass* and *picnic*.

consonant a sound (**phoneme**) that is made by blocking the flow of air leaving the lungs, in contrast to a **vowel** sound, where the air is not blocked. See page 20.

consonant cluster a group of **consonants** with no intermediate **vowel**, for example the consonant cluster *str* in the word *stream*. See page 26.

conversation analysis an approach to analysing the organization of talk which originated in the work of Harvey Sacks. See page 130.

cooperative principle this is a concept developed by the philosopher H. P. Grice to describe the underlying principle that governs the expectations of speakers and allows us to make sense of superficially non-coherent, or indirect, utterances. See page 133.

dactyl a unit of metre. See page 37.

deixis (deictic) some words require part of their meaning to be retrieved from the context; this is the process of deixis. Examples include elements to do with time (*now*, *then*, *last week*), place (*here*, *there*), and **person** (*I*, *you*, *he* and *she*). See page 65, 197.

derivational morpheme a type of **bound morpheme** which is used to build words; for example, in the words *confront*, *confrontation*, *confrontational* and *confrontationally*, -*ation*, -*al*, and -*ly* are derivational morphemes. See page 54.

determiner one of a set of words found before a noun, like *a* or *the*, which gives information about specificity (i.e. a sun vs. the sun) and about number (i.e. *one* biscuit, *some* biscuits).

deviation a stylistic concept used originally by the linguist Jan Mukařowský to describe language use which departs in some way from everyday usage. It is sometimes used as a test for whether language usage is 'literary' or not. See page 51.

dialect the grammatical, lexical and phonological system which constitutes a variety of a language. For instance, speakers of a Cumbrian dialect will have some different sounds, words, and grammatical rules from speakers of a Devon dialect; both are dialects of English.

directive a **speech act** which is intended by the speaker to bring about some action (which may not have been specified directly in the directive itself). For example: *could you sit down please*, *take* *a seat*, *sit down* and *aren't your legs tired* are all directives which aim to produce the same response from the hearer.

discourse this is a term used frequently in linguistics, which confusingly has a range of meanings. It is used to refer to any piece of connected language, written or spoken, which contains more than one sentence; this is the meaning it has in the phrase 'linguistic analysis at the level of phonetics, syntax and discourse'. It is also used to refer specifically to spoken language; this is the meaning it has in the branch of linguistics called *discourse analysis*. It is also the term used in sociology to refer to a person's or a society's belief system and values; this is the meaning it has in a phrase like 'the discourse of socialism'. Generally, you can tell from the context which meaning is intended.

felicity conditions a set of contextual and social conditions necessary for a **speech act** to be legitimate; for example, only the starter can say 'ready, steady, go' for a race to be officially started. If a spectator said it, it would not have the same effect (hopefully)!

finite verb this is a verb which can be grammatically marked for **tense**, **mood** and **person**, and is found in a **main clause**. For example, in the sentence *she rides her bike to work*, the *s* **morpheme** in *rides* indicates present tense and third person singular, in contrast to *she rode her bike to work*, (past tense) or *they ride their bikes to work* (third person plural).

foregrounding a stylistic concept originally developed by the linguist Jan Mukařowský to describe the process by which language forms are drawn to the attention of the reader/hearer. See page 75.

free morpheme a **morpheme** which can exist as a word in its own right, such as *eye*, *pollute*, or *butter*. See also **bound morpheme**.

homonyms words which have the same form (i.e. spelling and pronunciation) but different meanings, for example the word *bank* in *river bank* has the same form but a different meaning from *bank* in *bank manager*.

hyponym a word which refers to something which forms part of a larger set; for example, *cat* is a hyponym of *animal* (the **superordinate** term); *dog* is also a hyponym of *animal*, so *cat* and *dog* are co-hyponyms of the larger category *animal*. Similarly, *Persian*, *Siamese*, and *tabby* are all co-hyponyms of the superordinate term *cat*.

iamb a unit of metre, consisting of an unstressed syllable followed by a stressed syllable. See pages 35–6.

iambic pentametre a term referring to the metre of lines of verse, which are ten syllables in length, the syllables arranged as five **iambs**. See page 35.

inflectional morpheme a type of (**bound**) **morpheme** which carries grammatical information about **tense**, **person**, **possession** and **number**. See page 55.

internal rhyme a rhyme (two or more syllables ending in the same vowel and consonant) which occurs within a line of verse rather than across the ends of lines.

interpellation the process of identifying with a subject position created by a text (see page 191), or with the addressee of an utterance. The philosopher Louis Althusser uses a now famous example of a policeman shouting 'hey, you!', at which everyone within hearing turns round.

intertextuality intertextuality occurs when one **text** makes reference to another. Also referred to as **allusion**.

lexical gap a concept for which there is no word in the **lexicon** of your language.

lexical item linguists' term for a word!

lexicon all the words in a particular language; or the total number of words an individual speaker has access to. For example, the lexicon of a three-year-old will not normally be as extensive as the lexicon of a ten-year-old.

lexis basically a term that means vocabulary. Used by linguists to contrast with other levels of language: **phonetics**, **morphology**, **syntax** and **discourse**.

main clause (see **clause**)

marked / unmarked Unmarked linguistic forms are 'neutral', in so far as they represent the '**norm**', and carry no additional information. Marked terms refer to anything which deviates from the 'norm' and this deviation is signalled by additional information. For example, the unmarked form 'nurse', is often assumed to refer to a female nurse. To refer to a nurse who is a man, the additional term 'male' is often added: 'male nurse' (the marked form). The same often happens in reverse for doctors: a 'woman doctor' or a 'lady doctor' (the marked form) versus 'doctor', the unmarked form.

metaphor a type of figurative language use. See page 96.

metonymy a type of figurative language use. See page 109.

metre rhythmical patterning of syllables in verse. See page 16.

minimal response the linguistic forms used to give **back channel support**. For example: *mmm, right, uhuh, oh yeah*.

modification the process of giving additional information about a **noun**, **verb**, **adverb** or **adjective**. A single word, such as an adverb or adjective, can be used, as in *green grass*, where *green* is an adjective which modifies *grass*. Sometimes a phrase is used, such as *freshly baked bread*, where *freshly baked* consists of an adverb and an adjective.

monosyllabic a word consisting of one **syllable**, for example *tree, leaf* and *grass*.

mood (modals) information about a speaker's stance in relation to their utterance. Speakers can indicate the extent to which they feel something to be a possibility, a certainty, or an obligation, amongst other things. This information can be contained grammatically in an auxiliary verb, such as *might* or *could*, or in lexical items such as *possibly* or *definitely*. For example, 'I *will definitely* go to the pub tonight' (high certainty), 'I *might* go to the pub tonight' (low certainty), and 'I *have* to go to the pub tonight' (obligation).

morpheme the smallest unit of meaning, both grammatically and semantically. A word must consist of at least one morpheme. Examples of one-morpheme words are: *butter*, and *eye*. These are both **free morphemes**, which can stand alone (but cannot be split into smaller meaningful units) or can be combined with other morphemes to make words such as *buttercup* and *eyeliner*. Other types of morpheme are **inflectional morphemes** and **derivational morphemes**.

morphology the study of the form and structure of words.

narrator a term used to describe the 'voice' in poems or novels that tells the story. If the narrator is a character within the text who uses the pronoun *I*, the text is described as having first person narration. If the narrator is not a character in the text, but tells the story from outside, and with an overview of what happens, the text is described as having an external omniscient narrator. See page 154.

non-finite verb a **verb** which is not marked for **tense** or **mood**. Usually occurring as a participle i.e. an *-ing* form (*skipping*) or an *-ed* form (*skipped*), or as an infinitive (*to skip*). Non-finite verbs can only occur in dependent **clauses**, in contrast to finite verbs, which can occur in both dependent and independent clauses. See page 67.

norm a term used in social science to refer to standard forms of behaviour and expectations.

noun nouns are hard to define. You may have heard them described as 'names' (e.g. *Shân*, *Joanna*, *language*, or *cat*), but they can also refer to abstract concepts such as *emptiness*, *joy*, and *age*. However, many words more usually thought of as verbs, or even as adverbs or adjectives, can be used as nouns, and it is its **syntactic** behaviour which makes a word a noun rather than anything else. Nouns can usually be singular or plural, they can be **modified** by **adjectives** and they can be preceded by **determiners**.

   For example, in the sentence 'Have you read a good *book?*', *a* is a determiner, *good* is an adjective, and *book* is a noun. Similarly, in the sentence 'Did you have a good *swim?*', *swim* is a noun, although in a different sentence it could be used as a verb ('I *swim* every Monday').

noun phrase a grammatical unit built around a **noun**. For example, *car*, *the car*, and *the red car* are all noun phrases. See page 64.

number used in linguistics to refer to whether a **verb** or a **noun** is marked as singular or plural. For example, in standard English, in the sentence *Jane goes shopping*, the verb *goes* is marked with an *s* to indicate that only one person is shopping. If Jane goes with a friend called Jim, producing a sentence: *Jane and Jim go shopping*, the verb ending changes accordingly. Nouns generally indicate plurality by an *s* morpheme, for example, cat*s*. See page 55.

object a constituent of a **clause**, which is part of the **predicate** and follows the **main verb**. In the sentence *I ate the chocolate bar*, *I* is the **subject**, *ate* is the **main verb**, and *the chocolate bar* is the object.

onomatopoeia a term used to describe the phenomenon of language sounding like the thing it refers to, e.g. the name of the *cuckoo* imitates its song. See page 45.

open class words items in the **lexicon** which are **nouns**, **verbs**, **adjectives** or **adverbs**. They are called open class words because different ones are constantly being added to the lexicon, such as *Internet*, or *lycra*; thus the class is open, rather than finite. See also **closed class words**.

oxymoron a phrase which unites two opposing meanings, e.g. *bittersweet*. See page 86.

person the grammatical category that indicates the number of participants in a situation, and gives some information about who they are. In English, person is marked in verb endings, in noun endings and in pronouns. For example, in standard English there is first person singular, *I*, first person plural, *we*; second person singular and plural, *you*; third person singular, *he she* and *it* and third person plural, *they*.

personification the treatment of a non-human concept or entity as if it were human (see **anthropomorphism**).

phoneme the smallest significant unit of sound in a language. See page 20.

phonemic / phonetic notation the representation of the sounds of speech by the use of symbols. This is in contrast to the way words are spelt, which often bears no relation to the way we say them. A phonetic notation is more detailed than a phonemic one. See page 20.

polysyllabic words consisting of more than one **syllable** are polysyllabic, for example *strenuous* (three syllables), in contrast to *hard*, a **monosyllabic** word.

pragmatics a term used broadly to refer to the study of language in use, dealing with interactional and contextual aspects of linguistic behaviour, including **speech act** theory, Grice's **co-operative principle**, and more recently, **conversation analysis**.

predicate a term which refers to that part of a clause which comes after the **subject**. See page 70.

prepositions a **class** of words which include items such as *in, on, over, through, out,* etc.

pronouns pronouns are a **word class** which can replace **nouns** in a sentence. Examples include *she, I, you, them, him, its, theirs*.

pyrrhic a unit of metre. See page 37.

RP (Received Pronunciation) The accent which is typically used by presenters of national news programmes, leaders of the Church and members of Parliament (but more by right-wing than left-wing MPs). It is not marked for region; an RP speaker can come from anywhere in Britain. However, it is marked highest for social class amongst speakers of British English: only about 3 per cent of the population are thought to use RP.

reference this term is used in a variety of ways in academic discourse. It can be used at the level of **semantics** to talk about the way language can refer to things and concepts in the world (the objects/concepts referred to are called *referents*); e.g. the word *book* is a *reference* which has a corresponding *referent*, the referent in this case being an object made of pages of typescript bound together designed to be read.

Reference is also used on a grammatical level to talk about the relationship between words in **sentences** or **utterances**. **Pronouns** can refer to **nouns**, and **deictic items** can refer to other elements in the **text** or to **information** outside the text. For example, in the sentence 'On the first day of her holiday, Jane soaked up the sun', the word *her* is a reference to the word *Jane*.

Reference can also be used to refer to the bibliographical details of source materials (i.e. information about a book or journal article for inclusion at the end of an essay or other assignment).

register a term that refers to the level of formality (or informality) of spoken or written language. The more formal the language, the higher the register. Formal language is usually less personal than language of a lower register, has longer, more complex, sentences, and a higher frequency of **polysyllabic** words.

relative clause (see **clause**)

semantics semantics is the study of the meanings of words. Sometimes in a debate, you will hear one opponent say to another something like 'you're splitting hairs; it's only semantics'. This is not a convincing retort to linguists, who usually believe semantics are very important, and essential to communication taking place at all!

sentence a grammatical unit consisting of at least one main **clause**, with a **subject** and **predicate**. For example, *I hate eating bananas* is a sentence: *I* is the subject, *hate eating bananas* is the predicate, and *hate* is the main verb. In contrast, *eating bananas* is not a sentence because it does not contain a main, **finite** verb.

simile a figurative use of language, in which one thing is compared to another. See page 95.

speech act refers to types of utterances which are used to 'do' things with language: for example, *promising*, *apologising*, *threatening* and *complimenting* are all types of speech acts. One particular set of speech acts are known as 'performatives'. These are used in specific contexts, such as *I name this ship 'The Fairy Queen'*, or *I declare this building open*, and can only be used by a restricted set of speakers (see **directives**, **felicity conditions**).

spondee a unit of metre. See page 37.

stress when talking in the context of literary language, this term usually refers to the way a **syllable** is said. Some syllables in words and utterances are produced with more force (stress) than others. Patterns can be created with stressed and unstressed syllables which is the foundation of **metre**, i.e. stress patterning in verse, and sometimes in prose. See page 33.

subject refers to that element of a **clause** preceding the **predicate**, usually a **noun phrase**, but which can be other types of phrases. See page 69.

subordinate clause (see **clause**)

superordinate a superordinate is a general **reference** which can be applied to a number of more specific references. For example, *animal* is the superordinate term for *cat, dog, gorilla, rabbit* and *crocodile* (which are all **hyponyms** of *animal*). See page 87.

SVO refers to **subject**, **verb**, and **object**; the usual order, or arrangement, of grammatical elements in English.

syllable syllables are the smallest unit of a sequence of sounds which can act as a unit of rhythm. They consist of a single **vowel** sound, which may have a **consonant** or **consonant cluster** before it, after it, or both before and after. A word consists of at least one syllable. See page 25.

syllabic consonant the consonants /n/ and /l/ can sometimes stand alone as syllables without the need for a vowel in the pronunciation, as they do in the final syllables of the words *flatten, trouble* and *table*.

synecdoche a type of figurative language use. See page 110.

synonym a word with the same meaning as another word.

syntax a term which refers to the system of grammatical rules for combining words into phrases and clauses. See page 52, 57.

tense refers to the way grammatical information about time is represented within the verb phrase. English has two tenses, present and past, in contrast to French, for example, which has three: past, present and future. To talk about events in the future in English, we can use various forms, including *will* (an **auxiliary modal verb**) or *going to* (*I'm going to have tea with the Queen tomorrow*).

text the term *text* is used in several slightly different ways in literary studies and linguistics. It can refer to any written material which is the subject of analysis: *the text of the advertisement*. It can refer specifically to works of literature: *this is a reference by Hardy to another text*. Less frequently, it is used to refer to any stretch of language, whether written or spoken.

transcript is a written representation of spoken interaction. See page 122.

trochee a unit of metre. See page 36.

trope the use of figurative language, usually to make an idea more persuasive.

turn-taking the interactive system through which participants in a conversation organise their turns at talk, including selecting the next speaker, avoiding interruption, and avoiding long gaps in conversation.

unmarked (see **marked**)

utterance a unit of speech (in contrast to **sentence**, which is a unit of grammar). Utterances may consist of one word, e.g. *now!*, or a phrase, e.g. *over there!*, and are not necessarily always grammatically complete.

verb phrase a grammatical unit containing either a **finite** or **non-finite** verb. See page 64.

vowel a sound (**phoneme**) which is made without fully blocking the air as it leaves the lungs. There are more vowels in the pronunciation system than there are in the spelling system. See page 20.

word class refers to the category to which a word belongs. Words in the same class share certain characteristics, which distinguish them from other categories. For instance, **adjectives** can be used to **modify nouns**; verbs can be inflected for **tense**, **mood** and **person**.

References

Original dates of publications are followed throughout by the date of the edition used in the text.

Chapter 2

1 Anonymous.
2 Anonymous.
3 William Shakespeare. *Macbeth*. (1606). Act I, scene i. *The Complete Oxford Shakespeare* (1989) Oxford: Oxford University Press. This edition is used for all quotations from Shakespeare in the book.
4 Emily Dickinson. 'Exultation is the going'. (*c.*1859, 1890, 1975). *The Complete Poems of Emily Dickinson* edited by Thomas H. Johnson. London: Faber & Faber.
5 Tune by F. Mendelssohn (1840) and lyrics by Charles Wesley (1739). 'Hark! the herald angels sing'.
6 Marge Piercy. 'Northern lights of the skull'. (1988). *Available Light*. London: Pandora Press.
7 William Barnes. 'My Orcha'd in Linden Lea'. (1856; 1987). *The New Oxford Book of Victorian Verse*, edited by Christopher Ricks. Oxford: Oxford University Press.
8 Christopher Marlowe. 'The Passionate Shepherd to His Love'. (1599; 1983). *The Norton Anthology of Poetry* edited by A. W. Allison *et al.* London: Norton.
9 William Shakespeare. *Macbeth*. (1606). Act I, scene i.
10 Edmund Spenser. 'Of this world's theatre in which we stay'. (1595; 1983). *The Norton Anthology of Poetry*.
11 Louis MacNeice. 'Sunlight on the garden'. (1937; 1988). *Selected Poems* edited by Michael Longley. London: Faber & Faber.

12 Rupert Brooks. 'Peace'. (1914; 1970). *The Poetical Works of Rupert Brooke* edited by Geoffrey Keynes. London: Faber & Faber.
13 Edwin Morgan. 'Glasgow Sonnets'. (1985). *Selected Poems*. Manchester: Carcanet Press.
14 Gerard Manley Hopkins. 'Goldengrove'. (1876–89; 1953). *Poems and Prose* edited by W. H. Gardner. Harmondsworth: Penguin.
15 Ogden Nash. 'The Rhinoceros'. (1933; 1985). *The Best of Ogden Nash*. London: Methuen.
16 Anonymous.
17 Gerard Manley Hopkins. 'God's Grandeur'. (1876–89; 1953).
18 Christopher Marlowe. 'The Passionate Shepherd to His Love'. (1600).
19 George Herbert. 'Easter Wings'. (1633; 1986). *George Herbert and Henry Vaughan* edited by Louis L. Martz. Oxford: Oxford University Press.
20 William Shakespeare. *Romeo and Juliet*. (*c.*1597). Act I, scene iv.
21 William Shakespeare. *Romeo and Juliet*. (*c.*1597). Act I, scene iv.
22 Alfred, Lord Tennyson. 'The Lady of Shalott'. (1833; 1971). *Tennyson's Poetry*. London: Norton.
23 David Garrick. 'Jupiter and Mercury: a Fable'. (Eighteenth century; 1973). *The Penguin Book of Eighteenth-Century English Verse*. Edited by Dennis Davison. Harmondsworth: Penguin.
24 Anonymous.
25 Ted Hughes. 'Wind'. (1957). *The Hawk in the Rain*. London: Faber & Faber.
26 S. T. Coleridge. 'Metrical feet'. Reproduced in *A Dictionary of Literary Terms*. (1977). Edited by J. A. Cuddon. Harmondsworth: Penguin.
27 Emily Dickinson. 'Wild Nights – Wild Nights!'. (*c.*1861; 1975). *The Complete Poems of Emily Dickinson* edited by Thomas H. Johnson. London: Faber & Faber.
28 Alfred, Lord Tennyson. (1850). From *In Memoriam A. H. H.*, 7. *Poetical Works of Alfred Lord Tennyson*. London: Macmillan.
29 Stevie Smith. 'Not Waving but Drowning'. (1957; 1985). *The Collected Poems of Stevie Smith* edited by James MacGibb. Harmondsworth: Penguin.
30 Lady Mary Wortley Montagu. ' The Lover: A Ballad'. (1747; 1983). *The Norton Anthology of Poetry*.
31 William Wordsworth. 'The Mad Mother'. (1798; 1963). *Lyrical Ballads* edited by R. L. Brett and A. R. Jones. London: Methuen.
32 William Goldsmith. 'When lovely woman stoops to folly'. (1766; 1983). *The Norton Anthology of Poetry*.
33 Robert Browning. 'Andrea del Sarto'. (1855; 1983). *The Norton Anthology of Poetry*.
34 Michael Drayton. 'Since there's no help'. (1619; 1983). *The Norton Anthology of Poetry*.
35 Valerie Sinason. 'Pin Money'. (1985). *No Holds Barred* edited by the Raving Beauties (Sue Jones-Davies, Anna Carteret and Fanny Viner). London: The Women's Press.
36 Anonymous.
37 Anonymous.
38 Anonymous. 'Perle'. (*c.* Fourteenth century; 1976). *Pearl, Cleanness, Patience, Sir Gawain and the Green Knight* edited by A. C. Cawley and J. J. Anderson. London: J. M. Dent.

39 Wilfred Owen. 'Anthem for Doomed Youth'. (1917; 1983). *The Norton Anthology of Poetry.*
40 John Keats. 'Ode to a nightingale'. (1820; 1983). *The Norton Anthology of Poetry.*

Chapter 3

1   Angela Carter. *Wise Children.* (1991). London: Vintage. Page 19.
2   E. E. Cummings. 'Love is more thicker than forget' (1958). *Selected Poems.* London: Faber & Faber.
3   James Joyce. *Finnegans Wake.* (1939; 1975). London: Faber & Faber. Page 415.
4   E. E. Cummings, 'Love is more thicker than forget'.
5   Lewis Carroll. 'The Jabberwocky' (1865; 1962). *Alice Through The Looking Glass.* Harmondsworth: Penguin Books. Page 202.
6   Fleur Adcock. 'Immigrant' (1983). *Selected Poems.* Oxford: Oxford University Press.
7   P. D. James. *The Black Tower.* (1977). London: Sphere Books Ltd. Page 48.
8   Katherine Mansfield. 'The Man without a Temperament' (1920; 1962). *Bliss and Other Stories.* Harmondsworth: Penguin Books. Page 139.
9   Angela Carter. *Wise Children.* (1981). Page 19.
10 Salman Rushdie. *Midnight's Children.* (1981). London: Pan Books. Page 58.
11 Ernest Hemingway. 'In Our Time: L'Envoi'. (1926; 1977). *The Essential Hemingway.* London: Granada, Panther Books. Page 358.
12 Kate Chopin. 'Desiree's Baby' (1894; 1979). In *Portraits.* London: The Women's Press. Page 49.
13 George Eliot. *Middlemarch.* (1872; 1994). Harmondsworth: Penguin Books. Page 7.
14 Virginia Woolf. *The Years.* (1937; 1968). Harmondsworth: Penguin Books. Page 73.
15 Edwin Morgan. 'Glasgow Sonnets' (1972; 1983). *Noise and Smoky Breath: An Illustrated Anthology of Glasgow Poems 1900–1983.* Glasgow: Third Eye Centre (Ltd) & Glasgow District Libraries Publications Board. Page 91.
16 Angela Carter. *Wise Children.* Page 19.
17 William Shakespeare. 'Richard II' Act 2 scene ii. (1595).

Chapter 4

1   William Shakespeare. *Romeo and Juliet.* (*c.* 1597). Act I, scene i.
2   Gerard Manley Hopkins. 'Pied Beauty'. (1876–89; 1953). *Poems and Prose* edited by W. H. Gardner. Harmondsworth: Penguin.
3   George Herbert. 'Virtue'. (1633; 1986). *George Herbert and Henry Vaughan* edited by Louis L. Martz. Oxford: Oxford University Press.
4   Anonymous.

5   David Lodge. *Small World*. (1985). Harmondsworth: Penguin. Page 3.
6   Robert Burns. 'O, my love's like a red, red rose'. (1759–96; 1983). *The Norton Anthology of Poetry*.
7   Emily Dickinson. 'The Clouds their Backs together laid'. (*c*.1870; 1975). *The Complete Poems of Emily Dickinson* edited by Thomas H. Johnson. London: Faber & Faber.
8   Sylvia Plath. 'You're'. (1960; 1981). *Collected Poems* edited by Ted Hughes. London: Faber & Faber.
9   Ralph Waldo Emerson. 'The Snowstorm'. (1841; 1983). *The Norton Anthology of Poetry*.
10   T. S. Eliot. 'The Love Song of J. Alfred Prufrock'. (1917; 1969). *The Complete Poems and Plays of T. S. Eliot* edited by Valerie Eliot. London: Faber & Faber.
11   Alice Walker. 'I'm Really Very Fond'. (1985). *Horses Make the Landscape Look More Beautiful*. London: The Women's Press.
12   Sir Philip Sidney. 'With how sad steps'. (1582; 1983). *The Norton Anthology of Poetry*.
13   W. B. Yeats. 'When you are old'. (1893; 1983). *The Norton Anthology of Poetry*.
14   George Eliot. *Middlemarch*. (1871–2; 1965). Harmondsworth: Penguin. Pages 867–8.
15   Liz Lochhead. 'The Furies: III – Bawd'. *Dreaming Frankenstein and Collected Poems*. Edinburgh: Polygon Books.
16   Liz Lochhead. 'The Furies: III – Bawd'.

Chapter 5

1   G. B. Shaw. *Arms and the Man*. (1894; 1946). Published in *Plays Pleasant*. Harmondsworth: Penguin. Act I scene i.
2   Caryl Churchill. *Top Girls*. (1982; 1984). Methuen: London.
3   Harold Pinter. *A Night Out*. (1961). Published in *A Slight Ache and Other Plays*. London: Methuen. Act I scene iii.
4   Tom Stoppard. *Professional Foul*. (1978). Published in *Every Good Boy Deserves Favour*. London: Faber & Faber. Act I scene iv.
5   Harold Pinter. *A Night Out*. (1961). Published in *A Slight Ache and Other Plays*. Act III scene ii.
6   *People Like Us*. Radio 4 broadcast.
7   William Shakespeare. *As You Like It*. (*c*.1599). Act IV scene i.
8   William Shakespeare. *A Midsummer Night's Dream*. (*c*.1596). Act II scene i.
9   William Shakespeare. *A Midsummer Night's Dream*. (*c*.1596). Act I scene i.
10   William Shakespeare. *A Midsummer Night's Dream*. (*c*.1596). Act I scene ii.
11   William Shakespeare. *The Taming of the Shrew*. (*c*.1592). Act I scene i.

Chapter 6

1 Jeffrey Archer. *The Prodigal Daughter*. (1983). London: Coronet, Hodder & Stoughton. Page 7.
2 Russell Hoban. *Ridley Walker*. (1982). London: Picador, Pan Books. Page 2.
3 Jeffrey Archer. *The Prodigal Daughter*.
4 Daniel Defoe. 'The Preface'. *Roxana*. (1724; 1982). Harmondsworth: Penguin Books. Page 1.
5 Daniel Defoe. *Roxana*. (1724; 1982). Page 7.
6 George Eliot. *Middlemarch*. (1872; 1994). Harmondsworth: Penguin Books. Page 64.
7 Martin Amis. *London Fields*. (1989). London: Cape. Page 1.
8 George Eliot. *Adam Bede*. (1858; 1960). London: Dent. Page 70.
9 Dick Francis. *Comeback*. (1992). London: Pan Books Ltd. Page 34.
10 Sir Philip Sidney. *Arcadia*. (1593; 1973). Oxford: Clarendon Press. Page 61.
11 Charles Dickens. *David Copperfield*. (1850; 1907). London: J. M. Dent & Sons. Page 76–7.
12 Wilkie Collins. *The Moonstone*. (1868; 1994). Harmondsworth: Penguin Popular Classics. Page 137–8.
13 P. D. James. *The Black Tower*. (1977). London: Sphere Books Ltd. Page 26.
14 Salman Rushdie. *Midnight's Children*. (1981). London: Pan Books. Page 103.
15 James Fenimore Cooper. *The Pioneers*. (1959). London, New York: Holt, Rinehart & Winston. Page 4.
16 George Eliot. *Middlemarch*. Page 7.
17 Thomas Hardy. *The Mayor of Casterbridge*. (1886; 1974). London: Macmillan. Page 37.
18 Jeanette Winterson. *Sexing the Cherry*. (1990). London: Vintage. Page 96.
19 Eddings, David. *Enchanters' End Game*. (1985). London: Corgi. Page 56–7.
20 James Joyce. *A Portrait of the Artist as a Young Man*. (1916; 1977). London: Triad Grafton. Page 1.
21 Virginia Woolf. *Mrs. Dalloway*. (1925; 1976). London: Triad Grafton. Page 39.
22 James Joyce. *Finnegans Wake*. (1939). London: Faber & Faber. Page 152.
23 Vladimir Nabokov. *Lolita*. (1955; 1980). Harmondsworth: Penguin. Page 298.
24 T. S. Eliot. 'Ash Wednesday'. (1930; 1969). *The Complete Poems and Plays of T. S. Eliot* edited by Valerie Eliot. London: Faber & Faber.
25 Italo Calvino. *If On a Winter's Night a Traveller*. (1979; 1982). London: Picador. Page 9.
26 Dorothy Richardson. *Pointed Roofs*. (1915; 1979). Published in *Pilgrimage I*. London: Virago. Page 145.
27 Fay Weldon. *Praxis*. (1978). London: Hodder and Stoughton. Pages 11–12.
28 Mrs. Gaskell. *Wives and Daughters*. (1864–6; 1969). Harmondsworth: Penguin. Page 322.

Chapter 7

1 Macintosh User's Guide. (1995). Cupertino, CA: Apple Computer, Inc.
2 *The Wimbledon Guardian*. Thursday 14 November 1996.
3 P. D James. *The Black Tower*. (1977). Page 1 and on: Sphere Books Ltd.
4 *Just 17*. 26 January 1994. Page 16
5 Martin Montgomery. 'DJ Talk'. *Media, Culture and Society*, 8 (4). Page 421–40.
6 Terrano II Advertisement, 'More Pulling Power'. Nissan. September 1996.

Bibliography

Althusser, Louis (1977) (2nd edn) *Lenin and Philosophy and Other Essays*, London: New Left Books.

Appignanesi, Richard and Chris Garratt (1995) *Postmodernism for Beginners*, Cambridge: Icon Books.

Austin, John L. (1962) *How To Do Things With Words*, Oxford: Clarendon Press.

Barthes, Roland (1975) *S/Z*, London: Cape.

Bennison, Neil (1993) 'Discourse Analysis, pragmatics and the dramatic "character": Tom Stoppard's *Professional Foul*', *Language and Literature*, 2 (2) 79–99.

Bhaya Mair, Rukmini (1992) 'Gender, genre and generative grammar', in Michael Toolan (ed.) *Language, Text and Context*, London: Routledge. 227–54.

Birch, David (1989) *Language, Literature and Critical Practice*. London: Routledge.

Bradley, Andrew (1905) *Shakespearean Tragedy*, New York: St Martin's Press.

Brown, Gillian and George Yule (1983) *Discourse Analysis*, Cambridge: Cambridge University Press.

Brown, Penelope and Stephen Levinson (1987) *Politeness*, Cambridge: Cambridge University Press.

Brown, R. and A. Gilman (1972) 'Pronouns of power and solidarity', in Pier Paolo Giglioli (ed.) *Language and Social Context*, Harmondsworth: Penguin.

Bullock, Allan and Oliver Stallybrass (eds) (1988) (2nd edn) *Fontana Dictionary of Modern Thought*, London: Fontana.

Burton, Deirdre (1982) 'Through dark glasses, through glass darkly', in Ron Carter (ed.) *Language and Literature*, London: Allen & Unwin, 195–214.

Calvo, Clara (1994) 'In defence of Celia: discourse analysis and women's discourse', in Katie Wales (ed.) *Feminist Linguistics in Literary Criticism*, Cambridge: D. S. Brewer. 91–116.

Carter, Ron and Paul Simpson (eds) (1989) *Language, Discourse and Literature: An Introductory Reader in Discourse Stylistics*, London: Unwin Hyman.

Chomsky, Noam (1957) *Syntactic Structures*, The Hague: Mouton.

Coates, Jennifer (1983) *The Semantics of the Modal Auxiliaries*, London: Croom Helm.

—— (1994) 'No gap, lots of overlap: turn taking patterns in the talk of women friends', in David Graddol, Janet Maybin and Barry Stiever (eds) *Analysing Language and Literacy in Social Context*, Clevedon: Multilingual Matters.

Cook, Guy (1992) *The Discourse of Advertising*, London: Routledge.

Coulthard, Malcolm (1985) (2nd edn) *An Introduction to Discourse Analysis*, London: Longman.

Crystal, David (1991) (3rd edn) *A Dictionary of Linguistics and Phonetics*, Oxford: Blackwell.

Downes, William (1988) 'Discourse and drama: King Lear's "question" to his daughters', in Willie van Peer (ed.) *The Taming of the Text: Explorations in Language, Literature and Culture*, London: Routledge, 225–57.

Durant, Alan and Nigel Fabb (1990) *Literary Studies in Action*, London: Routledge.

Eagleton, Terry (1983) *Literary Theory*, Oxford: Blackwell.

Elgin, Suzette Haden (1985) *Native Tongue*, London: The Women's Press.

Ervin-Tripp, Susan (1972) 'Sociolinguistic rules of address', in J. Pride and J. Holmes (eds) *Sociolinguistics*, Harmondsworth: Penguin,

Fairclough, Norman (1989, 1995) *Language and Power*, London: Longman.

Fish, Stanley (1980) *Is There a Text in this Class?*, Cambridge MA: Harvard University Press.

Fowler, Roger, Gunter Kress, Robert Hodge and Tony Trew (1979) *Language and Control*, London: Routledge.

Graddol, David, Jenny Cheshire and Joan Swann (1994) (2nd edn) *Describing Language*, Buckingham: Oxford University Press.

Green, Keith and Jill LeBihan (1996) *Critical Theory and Practice: A Coursebook*, London: Routledge.

Grice, H. P. (1975) 'Logic and conversation', in Peter Cole and Jerry L. Morgan (eds) *Syntax and Semantics 3: Speech Acts*, London: Academic Press, 41–58.

Halliday, M. A. K. (1964) 'Descriptive Linguistics in Literary Studies', in Donald Freeman (ed.) (1970) *Linguistics and Literary Style*, New York: Holt, Rinehart & Winston, 57–72.

—— (1967) 'Notes on Transitivity and Theme in English', *Journal of Linguistics*, (3) 37–81.

—— (1971) 'Linguistic function and Literary Style: An Inquiry into the Language of William Golding's *the Inheritors*' in Halliday (1973), 103–43.

—— (1973) *Explorations in the Functions of Language*, London: Edward Arnold.

—— (1985) *An Introduction to Functional Grammar*, London: Edward Arnold.

Hodge, Robert and Gunther Kress (1993) (2nd edn) *Language as Ideology*, London: Routledge

Hurford, James and Brendan Heasley (1983) *Semantics: A Coursebook*, Cambridge: Cambridge University Press.

Hutchby, Ian and Wooffitt (forthcoming) *Conversation Analysis*, Cambridge: Polity.

Kuiper, Koenran and W. Scott Allan (1996) *An Introduction to English Language*, London: Macmillan Press.

Lakoff, George (1989) *Women, Fire and Dangerous Things: What Categories Reveal About the Mind*, Chicago: University of Chicago Press.

Lakoff, George and Mark Johnson (1980) *Metaphors We Live By*, Chicago: University of Chicago Press.

Lakoff, George and Mark Turner (1989) *More Than Cool Reason: A Field Guide to Poetic Metaphor*, Chicago, London: University of Chicago Press.

Lee, David (1992) *Competing Discourses*, London: Longman.

Leech, Geoffrey (1969) *A Linguistic Guide to English Poetry*, London: Longman.

—— (1992) 'Pragmatic principles in Shaw's *You Never Can Tell*', in Michael Toolan (ed.) *Language, Text and Context: Essays in Stylistics*, London: Routledge, 259–80.

Levinson, Stephen (1983) *Pragmatics*, Cambridge: Cambridge University Press.

Lodge, David (ed.) (1988) *Modern Criticism and Theory*, London: Longman.

—— (1990) *After Bakhtin: Essays on Fiction and Criticism*, London: Routledge.

—— (1992) *The Art of Fiction: Illustrated From Classic and Modern Texts*, London: Secker & Warburg.

MacCabe, Colin (1979) *James Joyce and the Revolution of the Word*, London: Macmillan.

Mills, Sara (1995) *Feminist Stylistics*, London: Routledge.

—— (1996) 'Knowing your place: a marxist feminist stylistic analysis', in Jean-Jacques Weber (ed.) *The Stylistics Reader*, London: Arnold. 241–59.

Milroy, James and Lesley Milroy (eds) (1993) *Real English*, London: Longman.

Montgomery, Martin (1986a) *An Introduction to Language and Society*, London: Methuen.

—— (1986b) 'DJ Talk', *Media, Culture and Society*, 8 (4), 421–40.

—— (1993) 'Language, character and action: a linguistic approach to the analysis of character in a Hemingway short story', in John Sinclair, Michael Hoey and Gwyneth Fox (eds) *Techniques of Description*, London: Routledge, 127–42.

Montgomery, Martin, Alan Durant, Nigel Fabb, Tom Furniss and Sara Mills (1992) *Ways of Reading*, London: Routledge.

Mukařowský, Jan (1970) 'Standard Language and Poetic Language', in Donald Freeman (ed.) *Linguistics and Literary Style*, New York: Holt, Rinehart & Winston, 40–56.

Myers, Greg (1994) *Words in Ads*, London: Edward Arnold.

Nash, Walter (1989) 'Changing the guard at Elsinore', in Ron Carter and Paul Simpson (eds) *Language, Discourse and Literature: An Introductory Reader in Discourse Stylistics*, London: Unwin Hyman, 23–42.

Palmer, Frank (1979) *Modality and the English Verb*, London: Longman.

Quirk, Randolph and Sidney Greenbaum (1973) *A University Grammar of English*, Harlow: Longman.

Quirk, Randolph, Sidney Greenbaum, Geoffrey Leech and Jan Svartvik (1985) *A Comprehensive Grammar of the English Language*, London: Longman.

Richards, Ivor. A. (1929) *Practical Criticism: A Study in Literary Judgement*, London: Routledge & Kegan Paul.

Sacks, Harvey (ed. Gail Jefferson) (1995) *Lectures on Conversation*, Oxford: Blackwell.

Sacks, Harvey, Emanuel Schegloff and Gail Jefferson (1974) 'A simplest systematics for the organization of turntaking in conversation', *Language* 50 (4) 696–735.

Saussure, Ferdinand de (1988) 'The Object of Study', in David Lodge (ed) *Modern Criticism and Theory: A Reader*, Harlow: Longman, 2–14.

Schegloff, Emanuel and Harvey Sacks (1973) 'Opening up closings', *Semiotica* 7 (4), 289–327.

Searle, John (1975) 'Indirect speech acts', in Peter Cole and Jerry L. Morgan (eds) *Syntax and Semantics 3: Speech Acts*, London: Academic Press, 59–82.

Sebeok, T. (ed) (1960) *Style in Language*, Cambridge, Mass: MIT Press.

Short, Mick (1996) 'Discourse analysis and the analysis of drama', in Jean-Jacques Weber (ed.) *The Stylistics Reader*, London: Arnold.

—— (1996) *Exploring The Language of Poems, Plays and Prose*, London: Longman.

Simpson, Paul (1989) 'Politeness phenomena in Ionesco's *The Lesson*', in Ron Carter and Paul Simpson (eds) *Language, Discourse and Literature: An Introductory Reader in Discourse Stylistics*, London: Unwin Hyman, 171–93.

—— (1993) *Language, Ideology and Point of View*, London: Routledge.

Sinclair, John and Malcolm Coulthard (1975) *Towards an Analysis of Discourse*, London: Oxford University Press.

Spender, Dale (1990) (2nd edn) *Manmade Language*, London: Pandora.

Stallworthy, Jon (1983) 'Versification', in *The Norton Anthology of Poetry*, New York: Norton, 1403–22.

Steen, Gerard (1994) *Understanding Metaphor in Literature*, London: Longman.

Thomas, Jenny (1995) *Meaning in Interaction: An Introduction to Pragmatics*, Oxford: Blackwell.

Thornborrow, Joanna (1994) 'The woman, the man and the Filofax', in Sara Mills (ed.) *Gendering the Reader*, Hemel Hempstead: Harvester Wheatsheaf, 128–52.

—— (1995) 'Women in the arts and the media', in Jennifer Coates and Beryl Madoc-Jones (eds) *An Introduction to Women's Studies*, Oxford: Blackwell, 206–27.

—— (1997) 'Playing power: gendered discourses in a computer games magazine', *Language and Literature*, 6 (1), 43–55.

Trew, Tony (1978) 'Theory at Work', *UEA Papers in Linguistics*, 6, 39–60.

Varty, Anne (1994) 'Status, sex and language in women's drama', in Katie Wales (ed.) *Feminist Linguistics in Literary Criticism*, Cambridge: D. S. Brewer. 65–90.

Verdonk, Peter (ed.) (1993) *Twentieth Century Poetry: From Text to Context*, London: Routledge.

Wales, Katie (1989) *A Dictionary of Stylistics*, London: Longman.

Wardaugh, Ronald (1995) *Understanding English Grammar: A Linguistic Approach*, Oxford: Blackwell.

Wareing, Shân (1994) 'And then he kissed her: the reclamation of female characters to submissive roles in contemporary fiction', in Katie Wales (ed.) *Feminist Linguistics in Literary Criticism*, Cambridge: D. S. Brewer. 117–36.

—— (forthcoming) 'Classroom discussions and gender: do girls and boys have different styles?'

Waugh, Patricia (1989) *Feminine Fiction: Revisiting the postmodern*, London: Routledge.

Wells, John C. and Greta Colson (1971) *Practical Phonetics*, London: Pitman.

Williams, Raymond (1972) 'Realism and the contemporary novel', in David Lodge (ed.) *Twentieth Century Literary Criticism*, Longman: London.

Williamson, Judith (1978) *Decoding Advertisements: Ideology and Meaning in Advertising*, London: Marion Boyars.

Woolf, Virginia (1924; 1966) 'Mr and Mrs Brown' in *Collected Essays Vol. 1*, London: Hogarth Press.

Wright, Laura and Jonathon Hope (1996) *Stylistics: A Practical Coursebook*, London: Routledge.

Index